SOLVING AMERICA'S
SEXUAL
CRISES

IRA L. REISS WITH HARRIET M. REISS

This is a substantially revised and updated
edition of a book previously published as
Ira L. Reiss, *An End to Shame: Shaping Our
Next Sexual Revolution* (1990)

Prometheus Books

59 John Glenn Drive
Amherst, New York 14228-2197

Published November 1997 by Prometheus Books

01 00 99 98 97   5 4 3 2 1

Library of Congress Cataloging-in-Publication Data

Reiss, Ira L.
    Solving America's sexual crises / Ira L. Reiss with Harriet M. Reiss.
        p.   cm.
    Includes bibliographical references and index.
    ISBN 1–57392–172–6 (pbk. : alk. paper)
    1. Sex customs—United States. 2. Sexual ethics—United States. I. Reiss, Harriet M. II. Title.
HQ18.U5R433   1997
306.7'0973—dc21   97–37334
                                                                            CIP

Printed in the United States of America on acid-free paper

To Bert Aronson and Arny Fragin,
friends of my youth whose promise
was never allowed to blossom.
This book is for you.

Contents

Acknowledgments

By far my greatest debt is to my wife, Harriet, who is listed on the cover of this book with special acknowledgment. Harriet took time out from her own professional work, first as a corporate researcher and later as an artist, to read and discuss every draft of the book. She suggested and clarified important issues and ideas and edited and polished the style and grammar. We talked at great length about every major idea in the book and she directly challenged my thinking whenever she did not agree. There is no better critic, no better advisor than someone who loves you and yet speaks her mind. For all that and more, Harriet, I thank you.

Another family member, my nephew Spence Porter, a playwright from New York City, graciously consented to help me develop a more popular style for this book. Developing a style of writing for the public to replace my more academic style was like learning a new language. Over and over Spence and I discussed passages and phrasings to make sure they clearly communicated the urgency and the dramatic quality that they deserved. It was a personal course in writing. With deep appreciation, thank you, Spence.

My former chairman at the College of William and Mary, Professor Wayne Kernodle, always believed in what I was doing, even way back in the late 1950s when I taught at William and Mary shortly after receiving my Ph.D. So it was natural that I would ask him to read my manuscript and see if I had done justice to my training as a sociologist. His comments were insightful and immensely helpful and his encouragement very important. Wayne is a rare human being—a person who encourages and fully enjoys the successes of others. Thank you, Wayne, for your abundant help.

Bill and Jill Bensch, two of my oldest friends, also helped me on this book. Bill and I took our M.A. degrees in sociology together at the Pennsylvania State University and we have kept in touch ever since. Bill and Jill long ago went into the travel business in California, and so they read from a broader perspective than the academic. They read the entire first draft of the book and gave me the benefit of their insights. Thanks, Bill and Jill.

Another old friend of mine, Morty Friedman, dates back to my high school days. Morty is a businessman who has always promised to read my books but never really did. I sent him the first draft of two chapters and he responded to them in his direct, critical way and helped me to improve the manuscript significantly. I think he will read this book. Thank you, Mort.

There were others who also helped significantly. I learned in graduate school to always call the specialists whose opinions I respected and ask for their advice. I did that with many people. I will note below only those I spent considerable time talking to.

Sandy Hofferth, now at the University of Michigan, spent several hours with me on the phone explaining the fine details of her brilliant analysis and interpretation of teenage pregnancy. No one knows the research in this area better than she. I wish her well in her new research focus on child care in America.

William Darrow of the Centers for Disease Control was always ready to clarify the research findings on AIDS and to offer his interpretations. He is a fellow sociologist who has done much to help us understand the sexual world of today. Margaret Fischl of the University of Miami Medical School explained to me some of the intricacies of her research on couples with AIDS. It was particularly helpful to learn how poor her couples were at condom usage despite the fact that one partner had been diagnosed with AIDS.

One of the premier researchers on AIDS is Warren Winkelstein at the University of California, Berkeley. I served with Warren on a subcommittee of the National Academy of Sciences and met him for a very long lunch when I was in California. In addition, I consulted with him many times on the phone. His longitudinal study on the spread of HIV in San Francisco is one of the finest in existence. He was always helpful and available when I needed to discuss some key findings. One of his recent Ph.D.s was Nancy Padian, who had her own sample of couples where, at the start, only one person was infected. She was very knowledgeable concerning the heterosexual spread of HIV and graciously shared her understanding with me.

Dulcie Hagedorn of my own Hennepin County in Minnesota asked me to be on the task force on AIDS she was administering. I learned much from her insight into the politics of AIDS as well as her in-depth understanding of our local studies on AIDS. Another local person, Professor Robert Leik of my sociology department, developed the computer model that we used to test our ideas concerning how to minimize the risk of HIV infection. He worked long and hard with me on that project and I am grateful.

Professor David Finkelhor of the University of New Hampshire, with whom I communicated several times concerning the explanation of child sexual abuse, was always gracious with his time and helpful with his comments. He helped put me in touch with the latest work and thinking in this area.

My thanks also to Professor James Hunter of the University of Virginia, whom I have never met but with whom I spoke at length on the phone discussing the nature of Evangelicalism in America and how that bears on sexual and family issues. Professor Rodney Stark of the University of Washington, whom I have also never met, took it upon himself to analyze national data on religion and sexuality for me in order to further clarify the relationship that existed. This was quite useful in my discussion of sex and religion.

My children, David, Pamela, and Joel, and their partners were inexhaustible in their willingness to discuss my ideas. They read chapters of my manuscript and responded with excellent suggestions. Pamela and her husband, Brian Russ, both have extensive social-work training and experience, and I benefited much from their insights into teenage sexuality.

There are other specialists in sexual problems to whom I spoke when my ideas for the book were just forming during a stay in San Francisco in the winter of 1987: Linda Alperstein, Lonnie Barbach, Jules Bernstein, E. J. Bonner, James Chin, Eve Gendel, Peter Goldblum, Charles Moser, Diana Russell, Merv Silverman, Bob Staples, and Paul Walker.

To all of these wonderfully helpful people and to others that I contacted more briefly or whom I may have inadvertently omitted, I give you my deepest thanks. I hope I have the chance to return the favor. You have been essential to my work on this book.

Finally, I want to express my gratitude to the staff at Prometheus who worked on this book. Vern Bullough as series editor was very supportive. Bob Basil, senior trade editor, managed the project of producing my book in record time. He knew its timeliness and accomplished its publication in the most efficient fashion. Mark Hall was an excellent copyeditor who understood my thesis and who made many improvements in the manuscript. My appreciation to Eugene O'Connor, who so effectively supervised the final work on this book. To Steven Mitchell and the others at Prometheus Books, I congratulate you on creating a true family of professionals who work closely and cooperatively with one another. Judging from my experience in publishing, this is indeed a rare accomplishment.

Introduction

This book is about America's rendezvous with sexual reality. We are the nation in the Western world with the highest rate of virtually every sexual problem: rape, AIDS, teenage pregnancy, child sexual abuse, and many more. These are problems that nobody wants to have, and so it is apparent that we must be unknowingly thinking and behaving in ways that produce these tragic outcomes.

As a sociologist who has studied American sexual life for over forty years, I felt I understood how we were unwittingly producing these sexual problems and I felt obligated to share that knowledge with the public. I do not see social science as existing in an ivory tower where you just "state the facts." Rather, I see science as the handmaiden of those who wish to build a better society. It is to that aim that this book is dedicated.

My conclusion is that our sexual crises all have the same root cause. These multiple crises are produced by the lack of a sexual ethic and a supportive institutional structure that is integrated with the new type of society in which we live. But there is such a new sexual ethic developing and it is what I call Sexual Pluralism. This is the ethic that is sweeping over Western Europe and in the 1990s it has increasingly taken root in America. I describe the meaning of this ethic in the opening chapter and show its relevance for resolving our sexual crisis throughout the book. I compare it to our traditional "one size fits all" sexual ethic and indicate how, while that old ethic may have worked for an agricultural society, it will not work for the knowledge-based society that is evolving as we enter the twenty-first century. Thus, this book is a statement of the new sexual ethic that I believe is required to help America and the rest of the Western world resolve its sexual problems.

In the first edition of this book* I predicted that in the 1990s our society would move increasingly toward this new sexual ethic and that we would increase our level of control over our sexual crisis. Among other things, I predicted increased condom use, lower teenage pregnancy rates, decreased HIV/AIDS rates, lower rape rates, and greater tolerance for gays and lesbians. In the years since 1990 all of these things have begun to happen. Whether we know it or not, we are in the midst of the third sexual revolution of the twentieth century. I document that in this book and I indicate how our new emerging sexual ethic of pluralism is a key force behind these changes. However, as a sociologist I know that society changes only if its basic institutions also change. There, too, my predictions of increased gender equality in the areas of family, religion, education, the politics, and the economics of our lives have begun to come true in the 1990s. But our sexual crisis is still a very serious problem and we have a long way still to travel. To accelerate this process we need to see more clearly how our sexual choices are part of an overall lifestyle choice that Americans are making now in all our basic institutions.

Despite all the social changes just since the 1990 edition of this book, I believe many Americans do not have a clear grasp of the emerging new sexual ethic, which is a major reason for my revising and updating this book. I believe we in America are in a new sexual and social revolution. But to continue to increase our control over our sexual crises, we must become more conscious of how and why this revolutionary change is happening. If we understand what promotes and what constrains our sexual problems we can consciously strive to reduce them with much greater effectiveness. The solution to our sexual problems lies within each of us. The book is my statement of how we can avoid the sexual tragedies of the past decades and how we can achieve more joys and rewards from our sexual lives. It is vital that each of us, private citizen and public leader alike, become better acquainted with our sexual crises. We owe this to ourselves, as well as to our children and grandchildren.

Ira L. Reiss
Minneapolis, Minnesota
September 1997

---

*Published under the title *An End to Shame: Shaping Our Next Sexual Revolution* (Amherst, N.Y.: Prometheus Books, 1990).

1

America's Rendezvous with Sexual Reality

On opening day of the fifth International AIDS Conference in Montreal, my wife and I were at the Queen Elizabeth Hotel attending a luncheon hosted by a large pharmaceutical firm. I struck up a conversation with an interesting looking, middle-aged physician who was sitting across from me. We spoke about sex in America, and I told him that I thought the American approach to sexuality was unrealistic and conflicted. I mentioned the great difficulty we have in getting our major television networks to broadcast messages about how condom use can help prevent AIDS and unwanted pregnancies. He agreed that America's approach to sexuality was unrealistic and conflicted and needed to be changed. I felt pleased at his response, thinking to myself that he very likely shared many of my own ideas about what was wrong with our sexual customs. But then he added: "You know the main reason our country is so messed up about sex? It's that we talk too much and too soon with our children about it. This gives them ideas and encourages them to try sex and that's the cause of our sexual problems."

I thought to myself: Oh no! Here we go again! I leaned forward and, trying to sound calm, replied: "How in the world can you prepare young people for sexual relationships if you don't talk openly to them about sex when they are children? Aren't our television networks just reflecting that same fearful view of sex when they refuse to help promote condom use? Isn't it a bit absurd to think that our kids need us to give them ideas about sex and that if we didn't talk to them about it, we'd have a safer sexual world?"

My critical response shook him up a bit. He apparently wasn't used to being told he might be wrong, so my comments pretty well ended our

15

luncheon discussion of sex in America. But his remarks were a perfect example of the buzzing confusion of ideas that makes up the American sexual philosophy. As he turned to strike up a conversation with someone else, I thought to myself: He thinks he has the solution, but he's really part of the problem and he doesn't even know it.

America is long overdue for a rendezvous with sexual reality. Much of what we believe about sexuality is just not true. Our future depends on our facing up to the sexual realities of today's world and developing a sexual philosophy that will enable us to live safely and happily in that world. Our unrealistic and ambivalent approach to sex has perpetuated the many serious sexual crises that confront us today. It's time to do something about it.

Let's start by looking at the unbelievable dimensions of these crises. Acquired Immune Deficiency Syndrome (AIDS) is but one of them. It has been estimated that there are almost 1,000,000 HIV-infected Americans, most of whom don't even know they carry in their bodies the virus that will almost certainly develop into AIDS. The United States has one of the highest numbers of reported cases of AIDS of any country in the world—581,000 cases by the end of June 1996. More than 360,000 people diagnosed with AIDS have already died.[1]

Our rate of teenage pregnancy for those under fifteen years of age is *five times* that of other developed countries in the world, even though our rate of sexual activity is no higher. Every year more than 30,000 girls under age fifteen and more than a million teenage women from fifteen to nineteen years old become pregnant. In any one year a sexually active teenage woman has a better than 20 percent chance of becoming pregnant.[2] Contraceptive protection is poorest at the youngest ages, and even today a quarter of our teenagers start having intercourse without using any contraceptive method at all.[3] Contrary to popular belief, teenage pregnancy is not just a problem for poor blacks—our white teenage pregnancy rates are also higher than those in any Western European country.

In regard to rape, even conservative estimates indicate that a woman in the United States has *at least* a 25 percent chance of being raped at some time in her life. There are almost 100,000 rapes reported every year, but it is likely that more than a million rapes actually occur each year. The rape rate in the United States is several times that in England, West Germany, and France. Date rape among college students is seldom reported, but studies show that about 15 percent of college women have been raped—most often by men they know. Only recently has there been any indication of a decline in rape. The frequency of reported rapes continued to rise throughout the 1980s.[4]

We also have evidence that the United States has one of the highest rates of child sexual abuse in the industrialized world. A summary of national studies found that 20 percent of women and 7 percent of men said they had been sexually abused as children.[5] It is estimated that more than 1 percent of all female children have been sexually abused by their fathers. This would amount to more than one million women living today with this memory.

Growing up sexually in America is like walking through a mine field, and few escape unscathed. It is not just that we are a complex modern country. As mentioned, other developed countries do not have these high rates. The signs of a catastrophic sexual crisis are all around us. But many Americans are unaware of its dimensions and underestimate the very grave threat to our futures that it carries. None of us want this crisis and yet in many ways we help to create it. Throughout this book I will be discussing why this occurs.

One of the most important points I can make here is that AIDS, teenage pregnancy, rape, and sexual abuse of children are *not* separate problems, each with a different, specific social cause. Common causes underlie all these sexual problems, but most Americans are unaware of what those causes are. If we understood them and saw how we ourselves are implicated, I believe we would change our way of looking at sexuality. We need new, realistic attitudes that will change our traditional way of thinking about sex. I will offer just such a perspective that, instead of perpetuating our sexual problems, will enable us to resolve them.

I am a sociologist who has devoted his career to the study of how society shapes our sexual lives. In my first book, *Premarital Sexual Standards in America,* I signaled the approach of a new sexual revolution and accurately predicted what would happen in the late 1960s.[6] There were many people who said that I was surely wrong. After all, we were just finishing eight peaceful years with Dwight Eisenhower as president, and we were in the midst of a baby boom and a renewed emphasis upon religion and the family. Nevertheless, we did have a sexual revolution. Today, once again, I see the unmistakable signs of dramatic changes in our sexual customs. Americans are now increasingly recognizing the difficulties of our present way of dealing with sexuality, and they are searching for a way out of the sexual maze in which we are wandering.

In 1960, I was simply a predictor and observer of the changes that were happening; but this time the stakes are far too high to play such a passive role. In a crisis, you don't just watch and analyze. You feel compelled to help as best you can. Accordingly, I feel I must offer the insights and understanding I have gained from my years of studying our sexual customs. My major goal is to increase our awareness of how we have produced our own sexual crisis and to suggest a way of looking at sexuality that will enable us to resolve this crisis before its destructive effects are beyond our control.

Let's be clear about what our sexual crisis is not about. It is not only about AIDS, teenage pregnancy, rape, child sexual abuse, or any other specific problem area. Without a doubt, these are very serious problems which we will discuss, but they are all promoted by our basic attitude toward sexuality. The fundamental causes of our sexual crisis are the underlying unrealistic and self-defeating ideas about sexuality that have crippled our society's ability to cope with any sexual problem. If we could press a magic button and wipe out all of today's sexual problems, by tomorrow morning we would have a whole set of new ones to cope with. Ask yourself: How can we have such overwhelming sexual problems unless there is something fundamentally wrong with our whole societal approach to sexuality?

The Sound of Sexual Dogma Is Heard in the Land

Even in this relatively liberated era, the national political scene offers abundant evidence of the fear and anxiety in our traditional views of sexuality. Let's take a brief look at some of the key events of the last ten years. Republican Senator Jesse Helms of North Carolina and many others on Capitol Hill frequently suggest that the cure for our sexual problems is to become more sexually restrictive. You may remember that back in the summer of 1989, Helms spoke out against what he called "obscene and indecent" artistic works supported by federal money in the Mapplethorpe and Serrano art exhibits in Washington, D.C.

Jesse Helms's wife, Dorothy, had seen some of the homosexual scenes in the show catalogue of the Mapplethorpe exhibit and declared to her husband: "Lord have mercy, Jesse, I'm not believing this." Helms, too, was shocked by what he called "sacrilegious and offensive" photo art, and he proposed legislation to prohibit using federal funds to support any artwork that Congress felt was "obscene and indecent."

Many other senators and representatives were afraid to oppose Helms for fear their constituents would think they were favoring "obscene and indecent" materials. But the real issue was not whether you liked Mapplethorpe and Serrano's art; rather, it was how willing you were to impose your personal standards on all artwork the government supports. We should not forget that libraries, too, are supported by state funds. Should we censor the books politicians find objectionable? When President Lyndon Johnson signed the legislation creating the National Endowment for the Arts, he stressed that: "Freedom is an essential condition for the artist, and in proportion if freedom is diminished so is the prospect of artistic achievement."[8]

The House did vote to remove $45,000 from the National Endowment for the Arts (NEA) budget—the amount of money NEA had granted for the Mapplethorpe and Serrano exhibits. A modified version of Jesse Helms's bill, which opposed only "obscene" art, passed both the House and the Senate. The passage of even such a modified bill is evidence of the political clout of Victorian prudery in Congress. And the battle over NEA continues: several conservative Republicans in 1997 were moving to eliminate it altogether.

Two years before attacking the Mapplethorpe and Serrano exhibit, Senator Helms introduced a bill to ban all federally financed educational materials that do not both explicitly stress abstinence and oppose homosexuality. President Reagan expressed his strong support for this legislation, and our senators displayed their usual unwillingness to question the wisdom of such a "virtuous" approach by passing the bill by a 94 to 2 vote. Politicians like to stay in office, so even though many of them may not think this narrow moralistic approach will help control the spread of AIDS, they must believe that their most vocal constituents would favor Helms's restrictive approach and would want their congressional representatives to vote for it. It is the silence of the ambivalent majority that encourages this type of unprincipled political action.

Other restrictive sexual views among our political leaders are not hard to find. In 1987, with the AIDS crisis becoming ever more urgent, President Reagan was asked what to do about AIDS. He promptly replied that premarital abstinence was the solution:

> When it comes to preventing AIDS, don't medicine and morality teach the same lessons? . . . Abstinence has been lacking in much of the education. No kind of values of right and wrong are being taught in the educational process.[9]

And when the government prepared educational guidelines on AIDS, President Reagan, in line with these views, approved the following directive for all materials to be used for teaching children in high schools and elsewhere:

> Any health information developed by the Federal Government that will be used for education should encourage . . . placing sexuality within the context of marriage . . . [and teach] that children should not engage in sex.[10]

Keep in mind that the "children" referred to here include eighteen-
and nineteen-year-old high school students, the great majority of whom
have already experienced premarital intercourse.[11] Such conservative recommendations appeal to the emotional needs of those who are already
sexually restrictive and to the many millions who are perplexed and pan-
icked by the scope of the sexual crisis that confronts us. But, as I shall
show, such tactics are useless in controlling AIDS or any of our other
sexual problems.

In October 1987, at the height of the AIDS crisis, William Bennett,
then Secretary of Education under President Reagan, distributed three
hundred thousand copies of a brochure expressing his views on how
schools should handle the AIDS crisis. His advice was that public schools
should tell all young people in high school and below not to engage in
sex. Accordingly, Bennett informed teachers that "materials should . . .
emphasize that young people can avoid premarital sex and drug use."[12]
Note how sex is linked to drug use, implying that sex, like drugs, once
started is addictive and uncontrollable. This panicky, negative view of sex
is straight out of the sexual dogma of nineteenth-century Victorianism.

Further evidence of our residual Victorianism is found in the 1981
Adolescent Family Life Act, known as the "Chastity Bill," which was
proposed by Senators Denton of Alabama and Hatch of Utah—two well-
known political conservatives. The bill set up an Office of Adolescent
Pregnancy, which to the present day spends millions of tax dollars each
year on programs to encourage chastity for high school students. In 1986,
the government put out a chastity workbook called Sex Respect with slo-
gans like: "Score on the field, not on your date," "Control your urgin'—
be a virgin," and "Don't be a louse, wait for your spouse." The chastity
program, like Bennett, identified teenage sex with drug use and alcoholism as can be seen in the following advice:

> You can stop if you want to. If Bill could stop taking drugs and my dad
> could stop drinking, why can't you stop having sex?[13]

The 1990s witnessed government aggression against scientific
research concerning sexuality even when it was aimed at helping us
understand how to contain the spread of HIV/AIDS. Two government
surveys were canceled despite their high ratings as scientific work
because they were in the area of sexuality. One of them was the well-
known national survey conducted by Edward Laumann and his colleagues. Laumann had to eventually get private support and had to reduce
his project to one much smaller in order to accomplish anything.[14]

The dogmatic, sexually restrictive approach in all these attempts has not worked to stem the tide of sexual activity by teenagers, and more important, it has not reduced any of our sexual problems. On the contrary, it has probably made millions of teenagers give up on any hope of ever getting sensible advice from adults.

Victorianism is a key part of our sexual heritage and so a very brief comment on it may be useful. Victorianism gets its name from Queen Victoria, who ruled Great Britain from 1837 to 1901. The period was known for its moral severity and self-righteous conservatism. Sexuality was viewed as a threat that needed to be severely contained. To get the flavor of this Victorian sexual philosophy in America, we need only recall Anthony Comstock (1844–1915), who in 1873 convinced the United States Congress to suppress what he, as Inspector for the Post Office, felt was "obscene literature." Here is what Comstock said about such "obscene" literature:

> It breeds lust. Lust defiles the body, debauches the imagination, corrupts the mind, deadens the will, destroys the memory, sears the conscience, hardens the heart, and damns the soul. . . . Like a panorama, the imagination seems to keep this hated thing before the mind, until it wears its way deeper and deeper, plunging the victim into practices he loathes.[15]

In 1906 Anthony Comstock as part of his campaign against "obscene" materials had the bookkeeper of the New York Art Students' League arrested for distributing the League's catalogue, because it contained reproductions of nude female life-class drawings. Jesse Helms would have surely had a vocal supporter if Anthony Comstock was around to see the Mapplethorpe and Serrano exhibits!

Comstock's views were shared by many others in the late nineteenth century. John Harvey Kellogg (1852–1943), a medical doctor, endorsed the same ideas. In the late 1890s, he invented a breakfast food that was supposed to help inhibit masturbation and extinguish sexual desire. This product became Kellogg's Corn Flakes.[16] (If that's your breakfast food, don't be frightened—the claims are not true!) Kellogg was a follower of the health food system invented earlier by Sylvester Graham, who thought of Graham crackers and Granola as health foods that could help control sexual desires. All these efforts simply reflected the great fear that many Victorians had of the "evil" of masturbation, particularly in children, and the efforts to control sexual desire in everyone.

When we hear the words of Helms, Bennett, and, more recently, Senator Mitch McConnell, we are hearing the echoes of the restrictive attitudes of Comstock, Kellogg, and Graham. The remnants of Victorianism are still with us today, and they create a great deal of conflict and confusion in the American approach to sexuality.

Not many of our young people today would listen to Victorian advice about sexual restraint. That advice has been given, to no avail, throughout this century, in an attempt to prevent pregnancy and sexually transmitted diseases. Young people typically view themselves as indestructible and are generally much more likely to take risks than are older people. The young people of today have learned to value their freedom even more than prior generations have; so there is little likelihood they will deprive themselves of sex because of views like Secretary Bennett's on chastity. I think Senator Paul Simon put it rather well when he said: "It has been too long since [Bennett] has been a teenager."[17]

In my opinion, we have no realistic possibility of stopping the sexual activity of our youth, but we do have a realistic possibility of making their sexual experiences safer and of increasing the ability of young people to responsibly decide for themselves when they are ready. Unfortunately, the clamor of those who want to impose restraints has drowned out the efforts of those who would like to prepare young people to make responsible sexual choices. The "Just say no" approach to sex simply ensures that young people who say yes will be unprepared to prevent disease and pregnancy.

Aren't we, as parents, neglecting our responsibilities when we fail to ensure that our children understand how to protect themselves and their partners in their sexual relationships? We should not be lulled into believing that our schools will educate our children about sex. Bennett's guidelines still prevail in our schools, and they guarantee the failure of most public sex education to prepare our children for thoughtful and responsible sexual choices.

Bennett, together with Senator Helms, also suggested that we play down condom use because it may give teenagers the message that adults expect them to engage in sexual intercourse. How many teenagers would think that their teachers were encouraging them to engage in sexual intercourse if they discussed how condoms can reduce risks? The experience of young people has taught them that adults tend to discourage them from getting involved sexually at "too young" an age—which usually includes their current age. There are many reasons for having intercourse, but "my teacher encouraged me" comes very low on the list.

But just for the sake of argument, what if open discussion of condoms did encourage a few virginal teenagers to become sexually active—using condoms. If the teacher's presentation was that persuasive, surely it would also convince many sexually experienced teenagers to use condoms. And if using condoms prevented disease and pregnancy, that would not be a bad outcome. To judge the worth of sex education, we have to ask ourselves: *What should we be doing: trying to stop sexuality or trying to stop unsafe sexuality?*

Secretary Bennett did not want to talk about condoms in the schools because he was not searching for answers to our sexual problems with an open mind. He was convinced he had the answer, which was to spread the moral message of sexual abstinence. Being convinced you are right before looking at the evidence is the trademark of a prejudgment or prejudice. The irony is that this effort to prevent sexuality and its unwanted outcomes only serves to increase the odds of pregnancy and disease. But despite this fact, virtually no parents object to the dogmatic abstinent views that are so often imposed on our children. It is as if we all agreed that our public schools should indoctrinate rather than educate our children about sex.

I know that some of you think that, although it may be all right for young people eighteen or older to take some sexual risks, younger teenagers just cannot responsibly make such decisions. Research indicates, however, that those under eighteen in Canada, the Netherlands, Sweden, France, England, and virtually every developed country in the world are able to engage in sexuality *with far fewer pregnancy and disease outcomes than our young people.*[18] It is our young people who are so poor at responsible sexuality; therefore, it is vitally important that we find out why—and make some changes.

The clash between the restrictive traces of our Victorian past and our abundant sexual behaviors is the source of much of our sexual ambivalence. We need to discuss honestly and openly the internal conflicts that so many of us have. Instead, we hear self-righteous moralizing and we make jokes about sex, but we rarely talk frankly and sincerely about our feelings and thoughts. That unrealistic approach pushes our internal conflicts out of the range of our own understanding and control. As a result, it is very difficult for anyone in our society, teenage or older, to develop clearly thought-out sexual standards by which we can live. Several studies have shown that when those who have been raised very restrictively do engage in sex, they are very inefficient at protecting themselves from pregnancy and disease.[19] When thoughtful, careful, and concerned planning for sexual choices is lacking, we find that impulsive, emotional, and forced choices take its place.

Koop, Condoms, and Television

In the Reagan and Bush administrations, those who supported abstinence received favored treatment. For example, Secretary Bennett's educational brochure was distributed nationwide, while former surgeon general Everett Koop's very informative 1986 brochure on AIDS was never given national distribution, despite the fact that as surgeon general he was charged with protecting our nation's health. Two years later, in June 1988, a brochure on AIDS was finally funded by Congress—without the support of the White House—and was distributed to the nation's households. This congressionally funded brochure was well done, and it discussed homosexuality, condoms, and nonabstinent behavior—exactly what Congress had previously voted to ban. The sexual confusion of the nation is mirrored by such contradictory congressional actions.

According to many political analysts, the reason Surgeon General Koop had such difficulty in getting his 1986 pamphlet distributed was that his views were too "liberal" for the Reagan administration. Although Koop himself is a religious fundamentalist and a believer in abstinence, he noted in that pamphlet that if sex is not avoided condoms should be used:

> If you jointly decide to have sex, you must protect your partner by always using a rubber (condom) during (start to finish) sexual intercourse (vagina or rectum).[20]

Before becoming surgeon general, Koop was an active anti-abortion-rights campaigner. Reagan appointed him with the expectation that he would continue his restrictive approach to sexuality. When it came to promoting the health of the country, however, Koop was more a medical doctor and a realist than he was a dogmatist. He did not believe he had the right to impose his abstinence standard and let people die of AIDS for lack of condom protection. In this sense Koop took a pluralist stance, but he operated within a White House that took an absolutist stance and that saw abstinence as the only answer. There was a similar lack of support when President Bush took office, and so in May of 1989 Koop announced his resignation.

The White House was not Koop's only battleground. On February 10, 1987, Koop had asked the television networks to lift their self-imposed ban on condom advertisements because the "threat of AIDS is so great, it overwhelms other considerations." Network officials responded that they did not want to offend any segments of their audience and so would not lift their ban. Think of it: in a nation where before age twenty over 80 percent of our young people have had premarital intercourse, our television networks deem the advertisement of condoms to be offensive! Is it better to avoid offending some viewers and thereby save the networks some advertising dollars, or is it better to try to help people avoid AIDS or an unwanted pregnancy? The real offense in the stand taken by the television networks is to our intelligence and to our sense of morality.

In late 1988, the networks finally agreed to air a public service announcement about condoms. The U.S. Centers for Disease Control prepared the announcement but decided to avoid even using the word *condom*. They also failed to get the announcement shown during prime time. The final video portrayed a barefoot man sitting on a chair saying: "If I told you that I could save my life just by putting on my socks, you wouldn't take me seriously because life is never that simple." Then he starts to put a sock on his bare foot and says: "But watch . . . OK, you're right, that wouldn't really save my life. But there's something just as simple that could." Then you are to guess what that "something" is!

Imagine a car commercial never using the words "seat belt" and informing people that your suspenders will not save your life "but there's something else that could." How good would that be in promoting seat belts? Only in regard to sex would we even think of communicating in such an incoherent way, because we are still genuflecting before the Victorian fear of sexual honesty.

By way of comparison, here is a description of a 1987 British public service announcement on their "telly."

> The British spot shows a working-class couple making out on a sofa. Delighted when his girlfriend quickly agrees to his overtures, the young man is shocked and crestfallen when she assumes he has his "rubber-johnnies" with him. He pleads. She's unmoved, citing concern about contracting AIDS. "Nobody knows these days," she says, "so if you want humpy-pumpy, it's pop-it-in-a-bag time."[21]

Clearly the British have gotten over their Victorian past a lot faster than we have. They are living in the real world—while we are living in a world of dollar-oriented television and government prudery. As a result, the British are saving lives while our commercialism and self-righteousness place American lives at risk. In recent years our public-health condom commercials have improved, but there is still too much avoidance and caution. Recall that in 1994 Joycelyn Elders was forced to resign as surgeon general when she suggested that we pay attention to masturbation in our sex education curriculum.

Considering the lack of strong moral backing for our current sexual behavior and the fear and hesitancy of many to question our government's emphasis on abstinence, it is no wonder that virtually every country in the Western world has fewer unwanted pregnancies and less disease than we do. Despite our alarmingly high rate of AIDS and teenage pregnancy, people worry about offending others. Through public silence on the use of condoms, we all contribute to our sexual crisis. Where is our support for sexual choices that can enhance rather than endanger our lives? Why are we so afraid to speak out?

For example, no one has ever suggested advertising condoms on television to prevent the spread of the genital herpes virus; yet it is estimated that 25 to 60 percent of all Americans over the age of fifteen have been infected with that virus.[22] Most of these people do not yet show any symptoms. There is a heavy price attached to that show of timidity. We now know that the lesions of the herpes virus are a possible pathway for the entry of the Human Immunodeficiency Virus (HIV) that causes AIDS. Our inability to speak out about our sexual needs has put millions of us at extra risk of contracting AIDS.

The same public inaction applies to the plight of the three to four million women who are unknowingly infected with chlamydia each year. Chlamydia is our most common but least discussed sexually transmitted disease. How many of you have read any government warning about this disease? Yet it will leave many hundreds of thousands of unsuspecting women unable to have children, and thousands of infants will be born infected. Indeed, sixty percent of the women with chlamydia will pass it on to their newborns. Chlamydia is a key cause of the four-fold increase since 1970 in tubal pregnancies. A small number of women die from such pregnancies each year.[23] Most women will not even know they have the disease until years after the infection has already done its damage. Careful use of condoms would have prevented most chlamydia infections as well as those of gonorrhea, syphilis, and virtually all our sexually transmitted diseases. How could a democratic people not have promoted condom use decades ago when the Europeans were doing that very thing? What is even more amazing is that there still is opposition to promoting condom use today.

Planned Parenthood stands as one of the few exceptions to this reluctance to publicly request more help for those who are sexually active. In late 1986 Planned Parenthood, because of the almost 900,000 illegitimate births that year, asked the television networks to accept their advertisements for contraception. The networks refused to allow such ads.

Even in this request by Planned Parenthood, there was no assertion of the *joys* of sexual relationships but rather a request to avoid the *painful* outcomes of sexuality. Believers in abstinence assert the joys of their perspective. Why is it so difficult for those who believe in sexual standards other than abstinence to assert the joys of their perspective? Just being able to avoid disease and pregnancy is hardly a key motivation for getting sexually involved. Isn't it inconceivable that we would be pursuing sexuality with such vigor unless there were some superb rewards? Some may be having sex to keep a boyfriend but most are not. So why aren't we honest, realistic, and affirming of the physical and psychological pleasure that we seek so frequently in our sexuality?

We could be discussing a wide variety of safer sex practices, such as masturbation, old-fashioned heavy petting, or intercourse using a condom. Instead our politicians, schools, churches, and families most often just say no. The logic seems to be: Don't toss people a life jacket, for that may encourage them to go swimming. But our young people don't need our encouragement; as our sexual crisis proves, they're already in the water.

Will the Real Sexual Pluralists Please Stand Up?

I suspect most of you reading this book view yourselves as relatively open about sexuality. I would wager you favorably compare yourselves to your much more sexually restrictive parents. You probably also take pride in your willingness to talk about sexuality and to encourage sex education in the schools for your children. Most Americans look at themselves this way today. And, indeed, we really *do* emphasize the value of sexuality much more than we have in the past.

Nevertheless, I would suggest that most Americans do not fully appreciate just how much our Victorian background continues to handicap us in our approach to sexuality. The majority of even liberal Americans still are emphatic about their rejection of teenage sexuality, homosexuality, and much more. Is this moral stance the result of careful examination of these sexual choices, or is it based on the myopia produced by the long-out-of-date Victorian lenses we are still wearing? Anthropologist Gayle Rubin, an astute commentator on American society, describes the constraints that come with our Victorian heritage:

> This culture always treats sex with suspicion. It construes and judges almost any sexual practice in terms of its worst possible expression. Sex is presumed guilty until proven innocent. Virtually all erotic behavior is considered bad unless a specific reason to exempt it has been established. The most acceptable excuses are marriage, reproduction, and love.[24]

This attitude toward sex has an impact particularly on young people. It does not stop their sexual desires; rather, it pressures them to grab for sexuality without much forethought, as if sex were some illegal commodity that has to be quickly obtained and furtively consumed.

A pluralistic approach to sex would be far more effective in resolving our sexual problems. Pluralism means an acceptance of the rights of others to differ from you in their choices. It asserts that there is more than one way to achieve a moral life. Accordingly, it is recognized that no individual has the right to seek to impose one "moral" pathway on everyone; on the contrary, it is the right and the responsibility of all people to find what suits them best. For pluralism to work, a broad range of sexual choices must be accepted as legitimate. The dogmatic view that sees only one choice as right and all others as wrong must be rejected. In this book I will try to persuade you to become more pluralistic, to broaden the realm of acceptable choice, and thus to be better able to discover what sexual choices suit you best. And I will soon spell out the limits of what is acceptable in pluralism as in all sexual standards.

We Americans do take a pluralistic stance in religious and political choices. We say we believe that each religion has a right to its way of practicing its faith and that each political party has a right to its specific platform and legislative goals. You may think one religion or party is better than another, but you would never try to have your choice taught in the public schools and imposed by law on everyone. Such a pluralistic approach to important values is considered a fundamental part of our constitutional rights in this country.

But in sexuality we do not openly voice our support of sexual standards other than abstinence even when we believe in them. That lack of honesty and pride about our sexual choices results in our failure to support a pluralistic position on sexuality. In many ways most of us seem ashamed or afraid to go public with what we really think and feel in the area of sexuality, unless we happen to fully endorse the Victorian values of universal abstinence. Because our innermost feelings regarding sexuality are ambiguous and conflicted, we also hesitate to step forth and say we think premarital sex can be a good thing. So our public stance, one way or another, supports abstinence. Politicians know this. They avoid the issue and endorse only abstinence. Who speaks for the millions of Americans, young and old, who don't believe that abstinence is the only moral standard?

Only a minority of our teenagers abide by or believe in abstinence, but because of our conflicted culture they often don't clearly believe in any other sexual philosophy either.[25] They are hampered in their preparation for sexual choices by the continuous battle with the restrictive sexual stance of our traditional religious, educational, political, and family institutions. The media and other commercial enterprises, with their profit motive, do offer sexual titillation, but other institutions fail to fill the moral gap and define how we can make responsible and caring sexual choices. Our waffling, our internal conflicts, our ambivalence, and our dogmas about sexuality are major blocks to thinking clearly and to understanding today's grave sexual problems. We currently seem to act to encourage both the pleasures and dangers of sex, with little awareness of how to maximize the chances of obtaining one without the other.

Sexual Pluralism: A Chance to Say Yes or No

Promoting abstinence for young people in a small rural society where there is strong agreement on values might work. Abstinence might also work in an authoritarian society where young people were carefully watched, kept ignorant, and given little opportunity for any sexual rendezvous. But we are a democratic society and we have given our young people the freedom to interact with each other. We stress self-fulfillment and striving for what we value in life. In such a society, suggesting "Just say no" as *the* solution to our sexual problems is analogous to having a nation of swimming enthusiasts with a high drowning rate, and instead of providing training for safer swimming, advising the nation: "Don't go near the water!"

Of course, there are people who prefer abstinence but do *not* try to impose it on everyone else as the *only* right sexual behavior. Abstinence may best fit some people at a particular time of their lives. Such a *personal choice* is surely an option that must be fully accepted as part of any pluralistic approach to sex. Surgeon General Koop preferred abstinence, but despite his own preference, he accepted the right of others to have their own views on sex.

The mirror image of our dogmatic abstinence approach is the 100 percent sex-positive viewpoint. This approach is also dogmatic in that it demands universal acceptance of what is felt to be the best sexual standard for everyone. The sex-positive viewpoint contends that the basic nature of sex is good and pleasurable and that it is always worth seeking unless someone offers a strong reason in a particular case to avoid sex. In this "Just say yes" perspective, pleasure is to be fully pursued and precautions are rarely considered.

Clearly the nature of sexuality involves both the danger emphasized by the sex-negative philosophy and the pleasures praised by the sex-positive philosophy. The amount of danger and pleasure in any sexual encounter depends on a number of circumstances, not the least of which is gender. For women the chance of force being used in sex is far greater than it is for men, so the danger elements are more obvious. Since women are not treated as equal to men, they have more to lose in terms of their reputations if they transgress the restrictions placed upon them by society.

So, if contraception is not used properly, the woman is the one who gets pregnant. So the dangers of sex are more real for women than for men, and that must affect how they act and feel about sex.

Of course, if we really had a pluralistic system that encouraged equal choice, we would demand that men not use force, not condemn their partners for what they are both doing, and share the responsibility for contraception. Only in that way would women be as free as men to make the sexual choices they prefer and the system be truly pluralistic. If we want women and men to feel the same about sexuality, we must change the gender inequalities that exist in our social world. More about that in later chapters.

For both men and women, there are special times in their lives when their evaluation of the dangers and pleasures of sex will change radically. Events like falling in love or getting divorced can make a big difference in one's approach to sexuality. Societal changes also have an impact. Think of how the advent of herpes and AIDS created more awareness of danger—and how in the early 1970s the feminist movement made women more willing to challenge the sexual restrictions placed upon them. The last sexual revolution made us all more aware of the pleasures of sexuality, and the civil rights movement helped gays and lesbians feel freer to come out of the closet and declare the pleasure of their sexual lifestyles. The social setting of our lives is of prime importance, and later I will discuss ways of changing that social setting so as to better support pluralism.

All of us have to judge for ourselves how much importance we place on the dangers and the pleasures of sex at a particular point in our lives. To prejudge this and say that for all people regardless of their situation and personal characteristics, the dangers will almost always outweigh the pleasures or the pleasures will almost always outweigh the dangers is clearly presumptuous. Such an authoritarian approach to sex denies individuals the right to choose the types of sexual relationship they personally feel are worth pursuing. Are *you* willing to imprison yourself in someone else's sexual dogma and disenfranchise yourself from a free sexual choice?

The pluralistic approach to sexuality is broad enough to encompass the realities of sexuality and to be acceptable to a democratic people. In the dangerous and pleasurable world of sexual choices in which we live, safety depends upon concerned and responsible choices, and disaster awaits those who thoughtlessly promote the sexual dogmas of "just say yes" or "just say no." Thus, pluralism rejects all dogmatic philosophies of sexuality—positive or negative—that prescribe the same sexual behaviors for everyone. The essence of pluralism is individual choice, whereas the essence of dogma is thoughtless obedience to rules and the denial of individual choice.

In addition to rejecting dogmatic standards, sexual pluralism rejects the use of force or exploitation to achieve sexual satisfaction. As I will discuss in later chapters, *pluralism promotes the values of honesty, equality, and responsibility in sexual relationships.* To force or manipulate someone into a sexual encounter is to remove that person's freedom of choice and to violate these values of pluralism. Since pluralism is built upon the right of everyone to choose, it necessarily abhors rape and sexual encounters in which people lie about their motives or exploit their sexual partners. Therefore, it condemns the exploitation of a child to satisfy an adult's sexual desires.

But outside of force and exploitation there is *no specific sexual act* that we can assert will necessarily lead to harm. For example, you may want to restrict sexual choice to those who are at least eighteen because *you personally* don't trust younger teens to be responsible or you don't like to think of your teenage child having intercourse. In chapter 3 I will discuss the evidence showing that teenagers under eighteen can be sexually responsible. Some of you may be uncomfortable with that possibility. But please hold off judgment and perhaps I will persuade you to have more faith in the potential of our teenagers to exercise responsible choices if we but prepare them and let them know we believe in them.

Another behavior that surely stirs controversy is homosexuality. Homosexuality is an orientation that, in 1996, 60 percent of Americans say is "always wrong."[26] All civilizations have had homosexual relationships and many peoples, like the ancient Greeks, have praised such sexual unions. Although the U.S. Army discharges those who are openly gay and lesbian, the ancient Spartans built their army upon the homosexual loyalty of their soldiers to one another, and it became one of the most feared military forces of its time. There are also non-European cultures today that praise the virtues of homosexuality.[27]

In our own society, the recent Laumann et al. study reports that after puberty 9 percent of men and 4 percent of women had some sexual activity with someone of the same gender.[28] Even though a much smaller number eventually make homosexuality their main orientation, it is clear that same-gender sexuality is a rather common experience in our society, as in all societies.

Homosexual behavior may not be the ideal for most Americans, but why is there such hatred and fear of it? What harm do people see in such sexuality? I know many think that the risk of AIDS is a key reason for our homophobia, but AIDS cannot be the reason. Hatred and fear of homosexuality existed long before the 1980s and in fact was stronger in earlier decades, and it has lessened in the 1990s.

All cultures stress heterosexuality because it is linked to their marriage and family institutions. So it is rather amazing that so many people have so little confidence in the ability of heterosexuality to prosper if homosexuality were to be openly accepted. But when sex is viewed as dangerous and threatening and the safe haven of "proper" marital heterosexuality is seen as challenged by homosexual behavior, then irrational fears can easily develop. The passage of the Defense of Marriage Act by Congress and by many states in 1996 shows this fear. Those cultures around the world that are more sexually pluralistic and accept homosexual relations lack the anxiety reactions we have about homosexual behavior. Our anxiety and condemnation does not stop homosexuality. It does reveal how fearful we are of sexual choices, and most importantly, it creates much unnecessary misery for those who pursue homosexual relationships.

This pluralistic viewpoint may bother some readers, but if we are to rethink our approach to sexuality, a great many of our preconceptions about sexuality must be challenged. Besides the major sexual problems already mentioned, we will discuss pornography, sex therapy, and the role of religion in sexuality. We need to develop an overview of how sexuality operates in our society. I am convinced that a broader and deeper moral acceptance of sexuality is an essential first step in liberating ourselves from the quicksand of fear and repression that has produced the many sexual problems of the present day.

The Ideal Society and the Abortion Debate

The high level of emotions in our debates about various sexual controversies should make it obvious that we are not simply arguing about how to resolve those specific sexual problems. If we get emotional arguing about the morality of teenage sexuality or homosexuality, it is because these issues touch upon our most fundamental values. But what are those basic values in which our sexual debates are rooted?

I believe our controversies on sexuality grow out of the clash of two visions regarding what kind of ideal society Americans should be creating. The *pluralistic* lifestyle promotes broader sexual choices and increased equality between men and women in all their social roles. The alternative *traditional* lifestyle is based on restricting sexual choices and promoting a male dominant type of society.[29] The pluralistic ideal fits best in a society wherein many choices are possible because of equality of opportunity in the family, religion, politics, economics, and education. The traditional ideal envisions a society with fewer choices and more emphasis on respecting and operating within the existing customs and power groups. I want to be clear here that there are aspects of our traditions that I support, such as the values of honesty, equality, and responsibility in sexual relationships. But I see as detrimental the overall traditional emphasis on restraining people's choices in today's type of society. It is this overall restrictive character of our sexual and gender traditions that I reject and not our entire set of past customs.

The specific debates about sexuality may camouflage this fundamental clash of moral visions, but at the root of these controversies are different ideal social systems. *We are really battling about an overall philosophy of how people should relate to one another in all walks of life and not just in the sexual sphere.* By realizing this we can better clarify our own thinking and decide what sexual philosophy best fits our own personal view of a good society.

A quick look at the abortion debate will illustrate my point. There is often so much emotion in this debate that very little knowledge comes forth. But one thing is obvious from a wide variety of studies: those who are abortion rights opponents are more sexually restrictive, less in favor of equality for women, and more in favor of the status quo in general.[30] To help document this I analyzed national data from a 1996 representative sample of Americans. About 1,500 people were interviewed by professionals working for the National Opinion Research Center (NORC) at the University of Chicago. My analysis of their study found that abortion rights opponents compared to abortion rights supporters are more likely to:[31]

> be homemakers and not work outside the home,
> support abstinence before marriage,
> oppose the promotion of safe-sex practices by the government or the schools,
> oppose teenagers having birth-control information,
> believe that homosexual acts are always wrong,
> believe that explicit sexual films lead to the breakdown of morals,
> favor laws restricting explicit sexual films for all people,
> oppose equal rights for homosexuals,
> believe the Bible is the literal word of God,
> not promote the integration of a racially segregated social club,
> support the view that everyone should follow one moral standard,
> strongly support traditional homemaker roles rather than more flexible and equal roles for women,
> not allow homosexuals to teach and not allow books on homosexuality in the library.

Notice that abortion rights opponents generally oppose actions like increasing contraceptive availability even though that would reduce pregnancy and would therefore decrease the number of abortions. If the central concern of abortion rights opponents is really to stop "killing unborn babies," then why don't they do everything they can to reduce the number of unwanted pregnancies? When asked about this seeming contradiction, most of those opposing abortion back away and assert that young people shouldn't be having sex in the first place and if they do, they have to accept the consequences. That answer reveals that the main root of the abortion debate is not really about when life begins but how life should be lived.

Surgeon General Koop, himself a strong anti-abortionist, has criticized the abortion rights opponents for precisely this opposition to encouraging contraception. In a little known and very revealing speech he said:

> I have never said this before in public. I believe that the pro-life forces—and I use that as a very broad term to include everybody that is pro-life—I think that they have shot their wad in the sense that I don't think there is anything more that they can do that will change any more opinions. And therefore, the bottom line is that if you want to get rid of abortion in America there is only one way to do it: you get rid of unwanted pregnancy. And unfortunately many of the people who are most vociferous about their antiabortion stand are the very same people that have prevented research into contraception and the distribution of contraceptive advice to the people who most desperately need it. Until we face that issue as a society and get rid of that, we are not going to make progress about the abortion issue.[32]

In the NORC national survey several questions measuring gender equality were posed:

> Should women leave the running of the country up to men?
> Should a woman not work if her husband can support her?
> Would you vote for a woman president?
> Do you think men, rather than women, are better suited to politics?

In response to every one of these questions, those who oppose abortion rights were less willing to endorse equality for women. Seeing women as people who can be dedicated to a career and other interests outside the home makes abortion rights much more difficult to deny.

It is apparent that abortion rights opponents, compared with abortion rights supporters, are significantly less likely to tolerate a pluralistic view of sexual choice or an egalitarian view of women's role in society. Anthropologist Faye Ginsburg's book on the abortion debate in Fargo, North Dakota, fits very well with my thinking here. Ginsburg summed up her view of the Fargo abortion debate by noting: "Battles such as the one taking place over abortion are not only over that specific issue but over which interpretation of gender will prevail."[33] Clearly, two major philosophies of sex, gender, and overall lifestyle are being fought out with the symbolism of abortion. As I will show, the same is true in all our sexual-crisis areas.

The abortion debate has deliberately been kept away from these underlying philosophical differences because they could compound the divisiveness and make victory on the abortion issue more difficult. Both sides fear losing some adherents who support their position but not their underlying philosophy. But it still would help us personally in deciding issues like abortion to examine our private beliefs and feelings to see which underlying philosophy we are most willing to endorse.

Resolving Our Sexual Crisis

I suspect that many readers may feel ambivalent about these issues and would endorse some aspects of both the pluralistic and the traditional philosophies of sexuality. A large group of Americans are confused about how to handle these sexual dilemmas. All of us may feel this way at one time or another. However, the key to resolving our current sexual crisis is our willingness to get to the root of our ambivalence by examining our beliefs and feelings. Faced with the serious sexual problems that have been discussed in this chapter, we cannot afford to sit idly by and wait for it all to be resolved. If we care about our future and that of our children, we need to make the effort to lessen the pain by speeding up the acceptance of a pluralistic sexual philosophy.

There are those who caution us not to make waves, not to propose changes in our sexual customs that may offend some traditional beliefs. We have heard that often from our television networks and from our government. One other source is Elizabeth M. Whelan, president of the American Council on Science and Health, who expressed her views in a *New York Times* article. She was complaining about the "insensitivity" of many of the people she heard speak at the Fifth International AIDS Conference in Montreal—the same conference at which I had my luncheon encounter. Here are some of the "insensitive" proposals at that AIDS meeting that she believes will alienate thoughtful, "open-minded" Americans and thereby hurt *our* chances of coping with AIDS:

> Demanding full legal recognition of lesbian and gay relationships . . . the necessity of making condoms common items . . . getting songs about condoms in the media . . . artwork featuring explicit homoeroticism.[34]

Now Whelan is right that *some* traditional Americans will be offended by such proposals regarding homosexual rights and condom usage. But how can she call people who react this way "open-minded"? Why *should* we avoid offending those who reject the basic values we put forth? Who ever heard of a significant change that occurred without offending someone's traditional views? Did not the civil rights movement offend the traditional American view of black inferiority? Did not the women's rights movement offend the traditional American view of male superiority?

If you are dealing with a controversial topic like sexuality and if you want to change things, you must accept the fact that you will offend some people. And if you have something significant to say, isn't it worth saying even if it offends some people? To avoid offending all people's sensitivities is to support the status quo. We cannot do that in the midst of a major sexual crisis. Building a new sexual philosophy based on pluralism is a far more important goal than catering to the traditional values that are the roots of our sexual crises. By working to promote the guiding values of honesty, equality, and responsibility (HER) in all our major institutions, we can build a moral foundation for sexual choice.

There will undoubtedly be many major confrontations over the proper way to handle our sexual crisis. Some battles may be temporarily lost, like the 1996 Defense of Marriage Act's outlawing of homosexual marriage. But such decisions will increasingly irritate and motivate the ambivalent majority of Americans who are in many ways more in tune with the emerging pluralistic sexual philosophy. Despite the thrashing about by some dogmatic traditionalists, in their desperate efforts to halt the tides of change, the signs that the Victorian world view is doomed are clearly visible.

By now you know I have a point of view on how we can resolve our sexual crisis. I will examine with you the reasons why America is unable to cope with its many sexual problems and spell out in detail how I believe we can turn things around.

2

Alice in Wonderland: Sexual Upbringing in America

Is There Sex before Adolescence?

The scene is an Oprah Winfrey talk show and the topic is "Dial-a-Porn." Parents are talking about how their children have called Dial-a-Porn phone numbers and heard explicit sex talk. Repeatedly these parents emphasize the point that the "innocence" of their children was taken away forever by being exposed to such phone conversations. The audience is horrified by their stories and disgusted that things like this can happen. Oprah sums up the feelings being expressed:

> Once you are exposed to sex—you're never able to regain innocence again—from then on you have sexual thoughts—you have sexual feelings—innocence is forever gone. It encourages sexual curiosity that would not have been there.[1]

A similar kind of alarm concerning the loss of "sexual innocence" has also been voiced by Tipper Gore, wife of Vice President Albert Gore. Tipper Gore bought Prince's *Purple Rain* record for her then eleven-year-old daughter. When she played it, she, like Oprah, was shocked by what her daughter was hearing. In Tipper Gore's case the greatest shock came when she heard the lyrics to the song "Darling Nikki," which describe a woman masturbating with a magazine. Tipper, like Oprah, bemoaned the "loss of childhood sexual innocence" that such songs bring about.

> If you don't try to shield them from . . . all this explicit kind of stuff
> until they're ready to handle it, then you're robbing them of their inno-
> cence, their one time in life to be somewhat carefree.[2]

Tipper reacted by proposing that legislation be passed requiring recordings of rock music to be rated like movies, so parents would be able to
better control what their children heard. She founded the organization
Parents' Music Resource Center (PMRC) to help accomplish this purpose. In 1985, together with others like Susan Baker, wife of then secretary of state James Baker, Tipper persuaded her husband to conduct hearings in the United States Senate on rock music. Some record companies
were frightened that they might lose sales and offered voluntarily to put
warning labels on recordings with explicit sexual lyrics. Most of the
musicians strongly resented this impediment to the free flow of music.
Performers as far apart as John Denver, the late Frank Zappa, and Dee
Snider argued against enacting such restrictive legislation. Fortunately for
our First Amendment rights, and the diversity and quality of our music,
no "innocence protection" legislation was passed. But the attempt has
intimidated record companies and labels, or "Tipper Stickers" as they are
called, are now being "voluntarily" placed on many CDs.

Tipper Gore's reaction to "Darling Nikki" illustrates our fear of sexuality, our view of sex as dangerous, and especially our apprehension of
what might be released if children "who weren't ready" were exposed to
explicit forms of "it." Let's look at this realistically. We can't stop our
children from finding out about types of sexuality that we don't like. But
if we openly and honestly discuss sex with our children, we can help
make them responsible and caring in their own sexual choices regardless
of what today's world exposes them to. For example, if a mother dis-
covers her son listening to a record she doesn't like, that is a perfect
opportunity for mother and son to sit down and talk about why she
objects. She could suggest other music for her son. Wouldn't that contribute more to that child's development of a responsible approach to sexuality than blindly following some committee's judgment about what
record deserves a stigmatized label?

I wonder if it isn't Tipper who was not ready to handle "this explicit
kind of stuff," rather than her daughter. Comments like those of Tipper
Gore and Oprah Winfrey assume that children really are innocent of
sexual pleasures and desires unless they are exposed to sexual ideas by
hearing phone messages or recordings of rock music.[3] As I will discuss
shortly, we know that infants masturbate and children of all ages explore
each other's genitalia. So sex in children is far from dormant even if one
doesn't experience Dial-a-Porn or hear "Darling Nikki."

People like Oprah and Tipper seem to mean by "sexual innocence" the absence of things like sexual thoughts, genital responses, and the awareness of how one is sexually aroused. A lot of parents would probably feel more relaxed if childhood did not have any sexual component and if sexuality magically appeared at puberty or, better yet, at marriage. Many parents have mixed feelings about their own sexuality and any recognition of sexuality in their children may arouse their own unresolved anxieties.

But let's be honest about preadolescent sexuality—were you "sexually innocent" prior to reaching puberty? Is that an accurate view of *your* preadolescent sexuality? When you were a child wouldn't you have preferred learning more about the meaning of your sexual development rather than being blocked from such clarification by parents who were trying to keep you "innocent"?

We still don't want to believe what Sigmund Freud said in 1905 when he shocked Vienna and most of the Western world by asserting the reality of childhood sexuality. Here is what he wrote back then:

> Popular conception makes definite assumptions concerning the nature and qualities of this sexual impulse. It is supposed to be absent during childhood and to commence about the time of and in connection with the maturing process of puberty; it is supposed that it manifests itself in irresistible attractions exerted by one sex upon the other and that its aim is sexual union or at least such actions as would lead to union. But we have every reason to see in these assumptions a very untrustworthy picture of reality. On closer examination they are found to abound in errors, inaccuracies, and hasty conclusions.[4]

Almost all of the research of the twentieth century supported Freud's assertion that children were sexual creatures. Alfred Kinsey, almost a half century after Freud, shocked this country with his own revelation of sexual responses involving erection and lubrication not only in preadolescent children but even in newborn infants!

> What seem to be sexual responses have been observed in infants immediately at birth, and specifically sexual responses, involving the full display of physiologic changes which are typical of the responses of an adult, have been observed in both female and male infants as young as four months of age. . . . Masturbation (self-stimulation) is an essentially normal and quite frequent phenomenon among many children, both female and male [and] is not infrequently the source of orgasm among small girls. . . . Of the females in our sample, 27% recalled that they had been aroused erotically before the age of adolescence . . . 48% of the adult females in the sample had recalled some sort of pre-adolescent sex play.[5]

Other reports by social scientists, like Boston therapist Larry Constantine and Gustavus Adolphus College sociologist Floyd Martinson, support and elaborate upon these earlier reports.[6] Children's preadolescent sex play occurs both with the same gender and with the opposite gender. Actually, somewhat more of it involves sexual exploration with someone of the same gender. The vast majority of such play involves simply exhibiting one's own genitalia and/or touching the genitalia of the other child. Such preadolescent sex play is even more common among boys: 70 percent of the preadolescent boys in Kinsey's sample reported having such experiences.[7] Many of us seem to have forgotten our own preadolescence. Do we really need to be reminded that "doctor" is not just a role played in hospitals by M.D.s?

Around 1980 a study was undertaken by a group of five women educators and researchers who formed the "Study Group of New York." They asked 225 parents of children three to eleven years of age how they handled sexuality in their children. One of the topics explored was masturbation. A mother of a six-year-old boy commented:

> Oh, yes, he masturbates. He walks around with his little hand on his penis for hours. It started when he was a baby, I would say every night, going to sleep holding his penis.[8]

Here is a response of a mother of a ten-year-old girl:

> She feels very comfortable with her body. She can be sitting in the living room watching television and stroking her legs almost up to the vaginal area. I think mainly she does it in bed. It relaxes her to sleep. . . . So I definitely think that she masturbates.[9]

Not all parents were so tolerant. Some wanted masturbation to be more of a private matter. There were also parents in this study who clearly did not approve of masturbation by their small children, whether done privately or publicly. One mother said:

> As a Christian, I see that it's not a normal thing, because your body is not only something for pleasure. It belongs to God, and when you're married you enjoy that part with your husband.[10]

But those parents who accepted masturbation still exhibited some obvious anxieties about sexuality—for when they did discuss sex with their children, they most often failed even to mention the pleasurable aspect of sexual experiences. They wanted their children to emphasize relationships and affection, and so they hesitated to mention pleasure too prominently. Since intensity of bodily pleasure is the aspect of sexuality that most clearly distinguishes it from other activities, this hesitancy surely defeats any realistic preparation for sexual behavior. Children experiencing these bodily pleasures must wonder why their parents don't seem to understand what they are feeling!

The belief in sexual innocence is even harder to accept when one looks at older preadolescents. In the late 1970s University of Minnesota sociologist Gary Fine studied Little League Baseball players. These were mostly white, middle-class youngsters, eleven and twelve years old. Fine didn't believe that much sexual behavior beyond kissing and "above the waist" petting was occurring, but sex was a constant topic of conversation among these preadolescent boys. Here are some excerpts from Fine's study:

> I asked a group of boys what they did when they went out with girls. One twelve-year-old said: "Make out. Squeeze their tits." . . . One of Harry's friends says that Harry and his girlfriend sit in the back of the movies and give each other "mouth-to-mouth resuscitation."[11]

This sampling of evidence should make it clear that there is no period when there is an absence of sexual activity by children.

Nevertheless, child sexuality is not the same as adult sexuality because children lack the full set of social scripts about how sexual relationships should be carried out. But children do explore their own and other children's bodies, they do have pleasurable genital responses, and they learn what turns them on sexually. Clearly the way parents and others react to childhood sexual behavior will have an important impact on the child's adolescent sexual development.

For parents not to face the reality of child sexual explorations is to forego a major opportunity for a positive input into shaping their child's future sexuality. The very acts of denying childhood sexuality, trying to limit it, and not discussing sex, give the child the clear message that sexuality has something taboo and negative associated with it. Childhood is the perfect time for parents to give their children permission to explore sexuality, to give them a positive view about it, to open up a dialogue, and to help prepare them for establishing their future sexual relationships. One parent I spoke to made this point quite vividly. He told me that his father saw him playing with his penis and yelled at him: "Get your hand off of that!"

He promised himself he would be different and when he noticed his four-year-old son playing with his penis, he responded by saying: "I do that sometimes myself and it does feel good. But it's kind of a private feeling and best to do when you're alone."

Childhood sexual exploration should not be seen as a step toward sexual obsession. As all parents know, children have a limited concentration span in almost all of their activities. Talking about sex can easily get boring to a child if too much time is taken from other interesting activities. Since my professional work involves studying sexuality, I have frequently talked about sex with my three children, and I can testify that they showed no obsession with it. They would often say to me: "Okay, Dad, let's talk about this later. I'm going out to play now." Sex is just another activity that children are learning about and seldom does it become a key focus of a child's life. Finally, although I am surely not saying we should encourage sexual intercourse for preadolescents, it is important to note that their exploration of one another's genitalia is quite safe from the point of view of disease and pregnancy—a lot safer than during the teenage years.

Adult anxiety about childhood sexuality is thus not based upon any rational appraisal of what is happening in their child's life. Rather, because parents see sex as dangerous and threatening, they conclude that kids should be kept away from it. Of course, parents can have a realistic fear that other adults may take advantage of their child's lack of knowledge about sex and may sexually exploit the child. But if that is your concern, it follows that you should talk *more* about sex with your child rather than promoting ignorance by acting as if childhood sexuality is a disruption of some "natural state of sexual innocence." I will delve into this important point later in this chapter.

Parental Hang-ups about Sex

Even parents who accept a more modern view of sexuality are sometimes reluctant to prepare their child for sexuality. For example, the typical response I receive from *modern, liberal parents* is: "I am open about sexuality with my children and I will always try to answer any question at all that they raise about sexuality."

Consider whether we would wait for questions to be raised in any other area of great importance to our children? We don't wait for children to ask before teaching them how to tie their shoes, or how to add, or why not to play in the street. How well would children know how to read if we waited for them to ask us before we taught them how to read? We think these are things they should know and we make sure they know them, *whether they ask about them or not.*

There are a number of reasons that childhood sexuality is so difficult for many parents to deal with. One reason is that if children's lives are viewed as having a sexual dimension, then we must face the reality that children will act on those feelings and masturbate or play childhood sexual games exploring one another's genitalia. To acknowledge the reality of childhood sexuality means that we must face up to the unresolved conflicts we feel about managing and experiencing sexuality. For example, some married people feel guilty about masturbating. Maybe when we were kids our parents disciplined us for exploring our playmates' or our own bodies and that may still be an upsetting issue. Perhaps also we don't want our kids to be aware that we are doing some of the same things they do.

How can we deal with a preadolescent's openly pleasure-centered type of sexuality when we are not at ease with openly discussing the pleasure dimension of our own sexuality? Facing up to the reality of the pursuit of sexual pleasure by our children may well challenge us to examine our own ambivalent views about sexual pleasure. What better escape than to tell ourselves that children benefit by being kept as "sexually innocent" as possible?

These are just a few of the reasons that the myth of childhood sexual innocence has a strong emotional appeal, which makes many of us want to believe in it despite the fact that Freud, Kinsey, Constantine, Martinson, and most other researchers say this belief is false and potentially harmful.[12] Like so many mythical beliefs, this one earns its way by easing our personal anxieties.

Miriam Feldman, a Minneapolis medical writer who writes about AIDS, is a perfect illustration of the point about parents I am making. As the mother of a seven-year-old girl, she talks of the "little things that set off the alarms in my mind." She illustrates her feelings by noting how she responded when her daughter recently picked up an AIDS pamphlet with a picture of a condom:

> I snapped it out of her hands the moment I realized what it was. Then I thought, "What happens when I am not there to edit the world for her?" . . . How much does she really need to know about AIDS? . . . Now I worry that I may have to explain more than the rudiments . . . I'm not advocating a return to the days when sex was something unspoken or whispered. Yet I wish I could shield my daughter a bit longer from the realities that we must face because of AIDS. I wish she could share some of our innocence. There was an aura of mystery to sex then . . . as long as she is missing teeth and wishing for dolls and for some time after that—I will try to edit the world for her.[13]

If this is the reaction of a medical writer who is well educated about sex, imagine the response of millions of parents who are not so well educated. We literally seem to walk in fear that our children will learn about sex.

The myth of childhood sexual innocence is a refuge sought by many parents. It comforts some to believe that if children wish for dolls or building blocks, they can't be sexual. Children know this isn't so. Isn't it time for grown-ups to become more aware of what their children already know?

What Nonindustrial Societies Do

But how different are American parents from parents in other societies? Are there any societies that do acknowledge childhood sexuality and actually accept it openly, or even encourage it? First we'll look at the sexual customs in some nonindustrial societies and then turn to some comparable modern industrial societies.

Many nonindustrial societies accept children having sexual intercourse as early as ages seven to ten. One of the most famous examples of this was reported about seventy years ago by the Polish anthropologist Bronislaw Malinowski.[14] During the First World War Malinowski found himself as an alien in England and persuaded the British to drop him off at the Trobriand islands in the Southwestern Pacific Ocean for the duration of the war. It was a stroke of luck for him. He spent four years there and established himself as an expert on Trobriand culture for the rest of his long career. In his accounts of Trobriand life, he noted that between the ages of eight and eleven most boys and girls started having sexual intercourse with one another. As long as these boys and girls avoided their brothers and sisters, this behavior was perfectly acceptable to the adults in that society.

In Mangaia, near the Cook Islands in the South Pacific, preadolescent masturbation is openly acknowledged. Children also privately play at copulation. Just prior to puberty at about ages twelve or thirteen training for sexual intercourse begins. In this society it is customary for an older male to circumcise a young boy and then to give him the first instructions regarding intercourse. The young boy is further trained in the art of coitus by an appropriately related kinswoman or some other older experienced female. The boy is taught how to hold back his orgasm until the girl has had two or three orgasms of her own. An adult woman instructs the girl about sexual intercourse and teaches her how to achieve multiple orgasms.[15]

What about childhood homosexual behavior? Is that too seen as acceptable in some societies? In the highlands of New Guinea, north of Australia, there is a tribe called the Sambia.[16] Gilbert Herdt, an American anthropologist lived with the Sambia from 1974 to 1976 and described their childhood male homosexual behavior. In this society, childhood heterosexual play is strictly forbidden. In this sense, they are quite Victorian. However, what they substitute is anything but Victorian. At about age seven or eight, each boy joins an all-male group of older teenage boys. The preadolescent boys are taught that they should fellate the older teenage boys. The practice is supported by the belief that only by swallowing sperm can a young male develop his own sperm. In short, then, this homoeroticism is viewed as "the royal road to Sambia manliness." Without it fatherhood is thought not to be possible. When the young man gets married, in almost all cases, this same-gender behavior ceases. Gilbert Herdt estimates that over 95 percent of Sambian men are exclusively heterosexual after marriage.

Interestingly, homoerotic sexual behavior that to us would be taken as a certain sign of homosexuality is seen as an essential part of *heterosexual* socialization in this culture. Childhood sexuality, too, is accepted as normal as long as it is *not* heterosexual. Americans who wish to prevent heterosexual childhood behavior would never consider the Sambia method of substituting homoerotic behavior even though it is much more effective than our Victorian measures. In any case, it is clear that the notion of a period of childhood sexual innocence would be seen as quite ridiculous to the Sambians as well as to the other cultures that I have mentioned.

There are no reports of children becoming "addicted" to their sexual behavior in Sambia or in any of the other cultures that I have read about.[17] Childhood is often seen as a time for sexual pleasure as well as for many other sources of pleasure. In fact, in a number of societies the name for the period of childhood and early adolescence means "the time for pleasure." Contrast that with our approach to childhood sexuality and you will see who is running scared from childhood sexual explorations.

The point I am making is *not* that we in America should copy any of these other cultures, but rather that other societies do prepare their children for their future sexual lives in much more direct ways than anyone in our society even proposes. Preparation of some sort is essential. Before they leave their teens about 80 percent of American youngsters will have had sexual intercourse. Our failure to take advantage of preadolescence to prepare our children for adolescent sexuality is, in my view, a tragic attempt to avoid the erotic reality of our society. The disastrous consequences of this in terms of early teenage pregnancy will be commented upon in the next chapter.

It is important to realize, however, that preadolescent sexual exploration is not given carte blanche in any society—it is always limited in some way, even in the societies I have mentioned above. Adult exploitation of children is not accepted. But permission is given in all those societies to engage in acts that will prepare children for adult sexuality. In

America we still avoid preparing our children for the reality of sexuality in today's complex society. Pluralism asks parents to grant permission to their children for sexual exploration involving masturbation and examining genitalia and to use those occasions to discuss the meaning of sexuality with them. Most parents do not do a good job at this and, as I shall discuss in the next chapter, that builds the foundation for a myriad of very serious sexual problems in the teenage years. If we were really as sexually open and honest as we think we are, we could never be this inhibited with our children.

What Other Industrial Societies Do

I imagine many of you are thinking that these nonindustrial societies are so exotic that it is hard to see their relevance for our society; it would be more relevant to know how the sexual upbringing of American preadolescents compares with that of preadolescents in other developed countries. One of the very few studies that makes this comparison examined children's sexual thinking in four modern countries. The research was carried out by two Australians—Ronald Goldman, a psychologist, and his wife, Juliette Goldman, a sociologist. The Goldmans compared the thinking of Australian children about sex to that of children in North America (United States plus Ontario, Canada), England, and Sweden, using a total sample of 838 children ages five to fifteen.[18] Many of the children's responses were quite revealing of the sexual attitudes in their societies. For example, only half the American children, compared to almost 90 percent of the Swedish children, were aware that sex was pursued for reasons other than reproduction. This means that Swedish children were much more likely to know that pleasure and enjoyment was a major reason for having sexual relationships. For example, at age nine, 60 percent of the Swedish children, compared to only 4 percent of the North American children, listed enjoyment as a purpose of sexual intercourse! The Goldmans comment:

> There is a clear progression with age of those who see the function of coitus to be enjoyment. More Swedish children express this earlier at 9 years, compared with the majority of the English-speaking 13-year-olds who do not achieve this view until that age.[19]

It is also important to note that Swedish children do not run out and have sexual intercourse at age nine just because they know about the pleasurable aspects of sexual intercourse. In fact, as I will discuss in the next chapter, teenage sexual behavior in Sweden is far *more* responsible and problem-free than in our own country.

Swedish children knew about contraception earlier than children in the other societies studied by the Goldmans. Swedish children also had the lowest scores when boys and girls were measured for "aversion" to each other. In addition, they were the best informed concerning the origin of babies. This was so even though in all countries every child in the sample had a younger sibling, and so had a chance to learn about birth. Despite this, many of the five- to seven-year-old children, particularly in America, thought babies came out of their mother's anuses. An inch or two off can make a world of difference in their understanding of childbirth.

It was most informative to find that children in all cultures, but especially in America, felt that their parents were hung up about sexuality. The Goldmans put it this way:

> One fact is abundantly clear. Children perceive it is the adults who have hang-ups about sex, and adults who deliberately or unconsciously withhold the information and knowledge the children seek.[20]

Perhaps the most critical finding of all was that American children had the least and the longest delayed sex education of the four cultures. Our children also had the least adequate vocabulary with which to talk about sex. Without an adequate vocabulary, clear thinking is impossible. Imagine trying to talk intelligently about driving a car without a vocabulary of terms that have clear, shared meanings like gas pedal, brakes, steering wheel, and car keys. What if we called the gas pedal "it" and the brakes "that thing"? When we needed to stop, we would say: "Get your foot away from 'it' and put it on 'that thing'!" We'd have a lot of accidents that way and there would be even more reckless drivers.

That is very often the way we talk about sex with young children, and to them it sounds as if we're talking about a part of life that is not very nice and whose existence we'd rather not openly discuss, unless some problem forces us to. It is precisely these restrictive sex attitudes that breed an abundance of future sexual "accidents" for ourselves and our children.

Our notions that children "aren't ready" to discuss this or that aspect of sex seem largely based on the fact that many adults aren't ready to talk with kids about sex. Swedish children demonstrate that kids at early ages can comprehend complex notions about many aspects of sexuality. Our unwillingness or inability to be honest with our children about sex and to prepare them realistically for the sexual world in which they will live has produced more harm than any of our words ever could. To illustrate the harmful consequences of our attitudes let's examine the sexual abuse of children to see how our approach to childhood sexuality contributes to this tragic problem.

What You Don't Know Will Hurt You

Even those professionals who set up preventive sex abuse programs for our public schools often seem unable to be open and honest about sexuality with children. Sociologist David Finkelhor from the University of New Hampshire, a recognized expert on the study of the sexual abuse of children, has written:

> There has long been a consensus among professionals in the field that one thing that inhibits children from telling about abuse is that they do not have a vocabulary or past experience for discussing sex-related matters. . . . This avoidance of explicit sexual content must be patently obvious to the children. Even in some wonderfully creative prevention programs, what they are seeing once again is adults using euphemisms and circumlocutions to talk about sex. The message behind the message for some children may be that, in spite of what adults say, they still do not want to talk in plain terms about sex. . . . It is possible that when adults talk to children only about avoiding the coercive forms of sexuality they leave children with the impression that sex is primarily negative. . . . It is possible that through some of these programs children come to feel uncomfortable or guilty about childhood sex play they may have engaged in. Programs often try to leaven their approach by talking about positive touch, but almost never do they discuss what might be positive sexuality.[21]

The fear that public schools would not permit a more outspoken prevention program is one reason for the sexual timidity in these abuse prevention programs. Yet Finkelhor and others are convinced that children cannot be protected from sexual abuse in a setting where adults are afraid to talk openly with children about sex. One price of our myth about the value of childhood sexual innocence does appear to be increased risk of childhood sexual abuse. This is so because sexual ignorance offers the weakest protection against sexual abuse.

In an ideal program we would discuss the feelings involved in sexual experiences and present an open and honest view of a wide range of sexual acts like masturbation, oral sex, anal sex, and intercourse. Contraception, including condoms, would be talked about even though we don't expect many preadolescents to have intercourse. Condoms, like tampons, are best discussed prior to their being needed, rather than afterwards. In discussing sexuality with children we have to take the point of view of the participant in a sex act. What does that person seek? What are the pleasures and risks? What are the different moral views on that act?

This sort of sophisticated understanding by our children from the very youngest ages on may not be easy for some adults to accept, but the alternatives in terms of sexual abuse and many other sexual problems are horrendous. In America today we are dealing with children who are likely to engage in masturbation and eventually in oral sex and intercourse. We must keep in mind that we are dealing with sexual creatures who by the time they enter grade school are quite aware that their genitalia have some special significance.

Promoting abstinence offers some parents a refuge from having to face an ongoing open dialogue on sex with their children. They can simply give their children one answer to all sexual acts: Just say no! But we must realize that we cannot prepare our children for the sexual reality they will face in our society as long as we think abstinence is the *only* standard that adult society will openly endorse.

For the great majority of our young people abstinence is an outmoded standard that they will surely discard. Most parents today did not themselves abide by an abstinence standard and they probably expect their children to have intercourse at some time before marriage. It is time that we face our obligation to be honest and realistic with our children about sexuality and talk with them about our sexual feelings and thoughts. I am convinced that such an approach to sexuality would lead to a tremendous increase in our ability to produce adolescents who are sexually responsible and know how to control the outcomes of their sexual acts.

We can't arm children against being sexually abused by an adult by simply preaching abstinence as the only right standard. We can arm them only by giving them realistic preparation for future sexual choices and empowering them with the right to think sexuality through and to say yes or no to various sexual choices as they get older. Most importantly, that empowerment would include the ability and the awareness to object to an adult who is trying to sexually abuse them.

The importance of preparing our children about sexuality was brought out in an article by Dr. James Krivacska.[22] He was president of the New Jersey Association of School Psychologists and chair of program guidelines for the National Association of School Psychologists. Dr. Krivacska emphasized that children have no innate competence to judge what is "good touch" and what is "bad touch." They need to become aware of what is appropriate sexual expression before they can adequately judge sexual abuse. So we need to educate children about appropriate sexuality and discuss sexuality more openly with them if they are to be able to develop awareness of sexual abuse. Without this all our warnings will only add to the shame and disgust that is connected to sexuality. The Sex Information and Education Council of the United States has issued a booklet on how to accomplish sex education for children from birth to age five.[23] So we are moving slowly in that direction.

Our Panic Response to the Sexual Abuse of Children

The major research on sex abuse of children shows the commonness of all forms of sexual abuse. David Finkelhor, Co-Director of the Family Research Laboratory at the University of New Hampshire, notes that, based on nineteen surveys, 20 percent of women and about 7 percent of men were sexually abused as children.[24] A large proportion of that abuse was perpetrated by people known to the child, like friends or relatives, and in a significant minority of cases the father or stepfather was the abuser. About 20 to 25 percent of childhood sexual abuse of females involves vaginal penetration or oral-genital contact.[25]

Sociologist Diana Russell from Mills College in the San Francisco Bay area studied sexual abuse of children with emphasis on father/daughter incest. Russell found that 2 percent of those growing up with a natural father were sexually abused as were 17 percent of those growing up with a stepfather.[26] Sociologist David Finkelhor, the specialist in the area of child sexual abuse whom I mentioned above, has estimated that for the country as a whole about 1 percent of women are sexually abused in some fashion by their fathers.[27] The type of abuse varies from fondling to sexual intercourse. Finkelhor's 1 percent estimate amounts to about one million American women aged eighteen and over who have been sexually abused by their fathers! If these estimates are anywhere near the mark, father/daughter incest is far from a rare phenomenon.

But we don't like to believe that father/daughter incest occurs with such a high degree of frequency—it makes too many of us feel like a potential victimizer or victim. Even Sigmund Freud came to reject the accounts of his female patients because he could not believe that father/daughter incest was as common as he was being told in therapy sessions. He finally decided that his patients' assertions of incest were fantasies based on their unconscious desires to have intercourse with their fathers. (Talk about blaming the victim!) Out of Freud's inability to accept father/daughter incest came his notion of the Oedipus and Electra complexes. Here is how Freud put it:

> Almost all of my women patients told me that they had been seduced by their father. I was driven to recognize in the end that these reports were untrue and so came to understand that the hysterical symptoms are derived from fantasies and not from real occurrences. . . . It was only later that I was able to recognize in this fantasy of being seduced by the father the expression of the typical Oedipus complex in women.[28]

Today there are many who, like Freud, still prefer to deny the reality of such incest; however, the evidence is overwhelming. Unfortunately, father/daughter incest is a reality, not a fantasy.

Our avoidance of facing up to sexual abuse often leads to hysteria and irrational acts when it becomes clear that it has actually occurred. The sensational 1984 Scott County, Minnesota sex abuse case is a good illustration of precisely this point. Twenty-four adults from the small town of Jordan, Minnesota, were legally charged with molesting children and most Minnesotans reacted with great emotion. The allegations contended that there were two interlocking rings of sexual abusers. Altogether sixty-nine people were suspected as child molesters and sixty children were thought to be victims. One man, a garbage collector with a history of sexual abuse, admitted guilt and was sentenced to forty years in the state prison. Of the other adults charged, one couple went to trial and was acquitted. Twenty-two other cases were dismissed when Scott County District Attorney Kathleen Morris dropped all charges. One of the reasons for dropping the charges was the constant questioning of the children involved. One eleven-year-old boy was questioned by therapists, social workers, and detectives a total of seventy-four times! For three months he denied being sexually abused, but then he changed his story and said he had been abused.

The media covering the event reported that:

> A psychiatrist who studied the cases said the children have suffered more because of the investigative techniques used by authorities than they did by being molested—if any were sexually abused at all.[29]

Many of the parents tried to sue Kathleen Morris and Scott County, but it was ruled that county officials were immune because they were "just doing their jobs." Nevertheless, the Minnesota Supreme Court did reprimand Morris for the way she prosecuted her cases of alleged sexual abuse of children.[30]

Children had been separated from their families—at times for over a year. The aftershocks for children and parents were dramatic. Dr. Jonathan Jensen, the Director of the University of Minnesota's Child Psychiatry Outpatient Clinic, together with Dr. Barry Garfinkel, wrote a report about the Scott County experience. They described the atmosphere in Scott County as that of a witch hunt and charged that the children involved had been put into conflict with their parents and the rest of society.

> In the Scott County system, the procedure of removing the child from the home for a long period of time, changing the child's identity with a new name, separation from siblings, change of religion, and instructions not to reveal any identifying information about themselves produced a strong undermining of the children's personality structure. . . . An entire County organization failed to understand the impact of these procedures on child development.[31]

Other types of sexual abuse cases also seem to involve a great deal of mishandling and emotion. The widely publicized McMartin Preschool case in California began in 1983 and finally in 1990 the not-guilty verdict on fifty-two of the charges was handed down. The case cost an estimated thirteen million dollars and a second trial on some remaining charges led to a mistrial. The district attorney's office made perhaps the most serious error in referring the frenzied parents of children who might have been abused at the McMartin Preschool to a little-known sex-abuse center. There 384 children were interviewed by social workers who were not trained in proper methods for a criminal investigation. The sex abuse center reported that they believed that more than 340 of the children had been sexually abused! However, these social workers employed a very leading type of questioning and so it was unclear whether they had blurred the line between fact and fancy in the children's minds. After the McMartin not-guilty verdict, several jury members commented publicly that one of the main reasons for their verdict was that they had very little confidence in the results of the interviews of the children because of the leading method of questioning.

There are other cases where overzealous child protection workers have led and prompted answers from children and where there has been carelessness in accusations of abuse.[32] We are having these difficulties in part because we haven't yet developed clear guidelines for child protection workers. Besides more accurate methods of interviewing children, everyone involved must be aware that differences in sexual values may well enter into judgments about whether something is "sexual abuse."

For example, in a day care center a situation might arise where during a nap period a girl is privately masturbating herself to sleep. If the day care worker permits such behavior, is that sexual abuse of children? What should the day care worker do? Is the day care worker doing enough if she or he checks with the child's parents to see whether they accept that behavior in their child? Should the day care worker just insist that such behavior stop? Should she educate the children about sexuality and if so, using what guidelines?

In good measure your answers to such questions will depend upon whether you believe in the sexual innocence of children and therefore see sexual acts as destroying a child's innocence or whether you see sexual displays and explorations as an expected part of preschool children's lives. We must have open discussion groups of parents, child protection workers, and social scientists so that we can learn how to judge what "sexual abuse" is. Then instead of panicking, we can determine exactly what has happened and what we should do about it

No one can deny the lasting trauma that sexual abuse of children can produce. We must encourage children to come forth and tell us about acts of sexual abuse and we should not assume their charges are just childhood fantasies. But it is equally true that we must avoid allowing our emotional reactions to add additional harm. Certainly we must act when we suspect there may be child abuse, but let's think of the children's welfare first and not allow our own emotional response to the abuse to lead to extreme actions that will only increase the harm to the children.

If we discussed sexuality with our children more openly and honestly, we would not only strengthen them against being manipulated but we would get more in touch with their feelings and our own feelings about sexuality. If abuse occurred, we would then be better able to focus upon minimizing the harm to the child instead of creating a witch hunt.

The Production of Sex Abusers: Father/Daughter Incest

But how do we stop producing adults who abuse children? That is surely a central concern. We need to know more about the people who sexually abuse children. What attitudes toward sexuality do sexual abusers have? To help answer these questions, I spent several months sitting in on five therapeutic groups treating sex offenders at the University of Minnesota. Most of the men had been sent there for group therapy by the court because of incest offenses. They were given the option of spending two years in therapy groups or staying in jail for that same length of time. In order to produce change the therapy groups had to probe deeply into the motives and feelings of the men and that process was often quite unnerving for the offender. Accordingly, some men chose to stay in jail rather than undergo therapy. Sitting in on these therapy groups helped to develop my own ideas about the causes of sexual abuse.

The two leaders of each of the five sex offender groups would routinely ask the eight or ten men in their group why they had committed the sex offense. In most of these cases, the offense was incest with a preadolescent daughter. I was struck by the explanation given by "Bill" in one of the first groups I attended. He explained that he was often very sexually turned on and he needed an outlet beyond his wife. The group leader asked him why he didn't masturbate to relieve himself instead of having sex with his daughter. Bill was taken aback by that suggestion and blurted out: "No, not me! The way I was raised made it clear that masturbation was bad for a boy and even worse for a grown man. I sure as hell wasn't going to do that."

Although many of these men spoke in an earthy and open fashion about sex, it was most often in a way that indicated they viewed sex as a "dirty" practice, but their "natural" desires drove them to do it anyhow. The typical beliefs of these sex offenders caused them to picture sex as a "drive" controlling them, rather than a choice they were making. Sex was bad but they had to have it. Although there is surely no view of sex held by all the offenders, this sort of "3D" view of sex as dirty, dangerous, and degrading was very common.

Despite the fact that these men believed in the power of the male sexual drive, they were not usually very aggressive, macho men. Other researchers like anthropologist Paul Gebhard, an associate of Alfred Kinsey, also reported that incest offenders were often ineffectual, nonaggressive, and dependent men. These were men who were not, in their own minds, living up to the masculine image they admired. Their incestuous behavior may have been their distorted way of proving to themselves that they were indeed "real men."

If a man is raised with the idea that almost all forms of sexuality are "dirty" but quite compelling, then he has very few guidelines for how to act sexually outside of marriage. In his view *all* sex outside of marriage is considered "bad," so all nonmarital sexual acts get lumped together as "dirty," even though he knows he will engage in some of them because of his irrepressible "sex drive." Just how does such a man judge the relative worth of each of these forbidden sexual acts?[33] Faced with this situation he may resort to whatever sexual outlet offers the least resistance, and that may well be his own or someone else's child.

In all areas of social life, gross imbalances in power generate abuse of the less powerful. If men accept a traditional male role, then they feel they naturally have authority over their children and their wives. Children become a type of property of their fathers. The more powerful a man is, the more means he has at his disposal to do anything he may desire to those with less power. It was the former secretary of state, Henry

Kissinger, who said, "Power is the greatest aphrodisiac." Having power makes the possessors of power feel that they can *demand* whatever sexual pleasures they desire and it coerces others to do what is desired.[34]

Power differences are present in magnified ways in father/daughter incest. In this case, gender, age, and authority differences converge to create a formidable power imbalance—one that is prone to produce sexual abuse. One particular incident that happened during my group observations brought this vividly home to me.

A new member joined one of the sex offender groups—I'll call him "Jim." One of the group leaders asked Jim how he now felt about his sexual abuse of his two daughters—"Mary," age nine, and "Cindy," age eleven. Jim's response was a revelation of his inner attitudes toward his family: "Everything was going along just fine until Cindy called the cops. When she did that, she took my power away from me! She shouldn't have done that!"

The key phrase that struck me was: "She took my power away from me!" To Jim, the power he had in his family authorized him to do what he wanted sexually to his daughter. He defended his sexual relations with his daughters by saying that he really cared for them, and he asked how he could do them any harm just by teaching them a little about sex. "Sex with me was one hell of a lot better for them than it will be when they grow up and guys start grabbing them and trying to do all kinds of things to them."

The joining of sex negativism with male dominant gender roles is an explosive mixture. The negative "3D" view of sex does not afford much insight into how to make sensible sexual choices for it is all forbidden territory. Such men learn to think of sex as a dangerous, degrading, and dirty emotion that drives them to act sexually. When this view of sex is coupled with a belief in male dominance, some men may feel justified in yielding to their desire to have sex even with their own child.

Massachusetts psychiatrist Judith Lewis Herman agrees that sexual restrictiveness and male dominance are two of the key causes of sexual abuse. Herman obtained in-depth information on forty women in therapy who had experienced incest with their fathers and compared them to twenty other patients who had not experienced incest.[35] Although this comparison is important, it consists of a sample of white middle-class women who are going for therapy, and so her findings may not represent all types of father/daughter incest in this country.

Herman found that the incestuous fathers were hard working and often successful men who were trying to fulfill the traditional male role of breadwinner. However, these fathers seemed to lack confidence and acted meek and ingratiating when they were with men of higher authority.

In addition, fully half of these fathers were physically abusive to their wives. All the wives were homemakers and only a few ever worked outside the home. In addition, these wives were often ill, both physically and emotionally, and thus not fully available to protect their daughters. When the daughters did tell their mothers about the incest, the mothers did very little. These family characteristics were much less likely to be present in the comparison group of twenty women who had not been sexually abused by their fathers.

The bulk of the father/daughter sexual contact involved masturbation and oral sex. Force was rarely used. Incestuous fathers often told their daughters that they were teaching them about sex and getting them ready for marriage (just like the excuse I noted from a father in the sex-offender program). Thirty-two of the forty daughters were the eldest daughters or the only daughters and many of them played a sort of wife-substitute role that came to include sexual relations.

The long-range price paid by the daughters was high. After the abuse, many had sex without contraception with almost anyone who wanted them, some tried suicide, others ran away from home or were raped by other men, and almost all developed very low self-esteem. Nevertheless, the daughters had high regard for their fathers and had great difficulty in challenging their fathers' authority. At the heart of such sexual abuse is a conflict between wanting to obey their fathers and feeling that what they were doing was very harmful—a most difficult conflict for a young child to resolve.

One of the most provocative findings concerns the sexual attitudes in these incestuous families. Many of these families were churchgoing and conventional to a fault. Usually, both the mother and the father had restrictive attitudes toward sexuality. Female bodies in particular were considered "dirty." Sex was a taboo subject at home:

> The fathers conveyed to their daughters the sense that sex was evil and shameful, at the same time that they continued to display their own sexual preoccupation with their daughters. Some daughters perceived that their fathers were essentially blaming them and holding them responsible for the sexual interest they aroused.[36]

These fathers emphasized that sex was difficult to control and this became even clearer as their daughters began to date. The fathers became very jealous and restrictive and warned them to beware of their date's sexual aggression!

Herman's study concludes that one major reason for this sexual abuse is the authority traditionally granted to fathers to dominate their families.

That authority is seen by some fathers as giving them a license to do whatever they wish with their daughters. Herman feels this traditional father authority role must change before we will see a reduction in the sexual abuse of daughters.

> As long as fathers dominate their families, they will have the power to make sexual use of their children. Most fathers will choose not to exercise this power. But as long as the prerogative is implicitly granted to all men, some men will use it.[37]

It seems clear to me that the view of children as property, as completely controllable by adults, encourages the sexual abuse of children. What Herman is saying here about fathers and daughters fits very well with that explanation. As I mentioned at the beginning of this chapter, if we want to reduce exploitation of children, we have to empower children. Young people need to know that they have real choices to make in the area of sexuality. To do that we must develop a pluralistic rather than a dogmatic approach to sex. Forbidding or ignoring all child sexuality does not give a child control over his or her sexuality. In line with Dr. Krivacska's views, I believe that only when children are given the right to say yes to some forms of sexual exploration will children feel that they have the responsibility and the ability to say no to other sexual practices.

There is another type of sex-offender background that is often mentioned by therapists who treat sex offenders. It may not be as common as the sex-negative, male-dominant background, but it is worth mentioning. Sex offenders do at times come from a sexually unregulated family environment where just about anything goes. That sort of "normless" family environment can be accompanied by poverty, alcoholism, and a lack of any predictable structure. Included in that chaotic environment is the sexual abuse of children. In addition to father/daughter abuse, there is a good deal of sexual abuse of boys by their fathers and stepfathers.[38] I have focused here on father/daughter sexual abuse because that is the much more common form of abuse both in a chaotic environment and in a traditional family environment.

In summary, the evidence is persuasive that at least one of the major causes of the sexual abuse of children lies in traditional beliefs about sexuality and male dominance that are too narrow to provide fathers with an understanding of other less destructive ways of coping with their desires for sexuality and power. Ironically, it is the traditionalists who are the most emotional in condemning the sexual abuse of children. These same traditionalists fail to see how often their own footprints lead up to the scene of that crime.

Sexual Pluralism: Pathway to Nonabusive Sex

Few human societies and no other species on this planet raise their off-spring with such inept preparation for sexuality as we do in America. We often call ourselves "liberated" and "modern," but we have seen how hesitant we are to inform and discuss sexuality with children. We are particularly reluctant to point out the positive aspects of sexuality. We fear that if children know that sex is pleasurable, they will pursue it constantly during all their waking hours—if not also in their dreams.

Many people say sex is too emotional, too embarrassing, and too complex to deal with dispassionately and rationally. How can we possibly get people to think about sexuality in a reasoned manner? It may not be easy, but it can be done and it must be done if we are to help our children. The starting point has to be the acceptance of a pluralistic view of sexuality. We have to reject the dogmatic sexual philosophy that states that it is always dangerous to encourage open discussion of sexuality with preadolescents. To impose such "sexual innocence" on all children, to forbid masturbation, to avoid discussion of sexual feelings, or to condemn sexual exploration is to guarantee that a child will develop a negative view of sexuality and learn more sexual customs from the street than from his or her parents. The way out of our sexual impasse is to reject traditional restraints on children's sexual education and to accept the importance of socializing our children to sexuality *from birth onward.*

Let me state clearly that I am not talking of encouraging children to have sexual intercourse with one another. On the contrary, what I am suggesting here is a way of avoiding sexual abuse. I am talking about our willingness openly to encourage our children to learn more about sexuality. In that way we can empower them to make better choices during childhood and to use their sense of sexual awareness to avoid being exploited by others during childhood as well as later in life.

As I've noted, many parents minimize discussing sex with their children out of the same mistaken fear that Oprah Winfrey and Tipper Gore have, namely, that they will "start" their children's sex life. But as we've seen, *our children's sex lives are on "start" when they are born.* We can show our children that sexuality, like other childhood pleasures, such as desserts or watching television, can be managed. It is our fear and not our children's lust that most needs control.

We all make sexual choices from birth onward when we masturbate, when we play "doctor," and when we kiss or touch each other. The most important thing is not that we try to prevent or deny the reality of these behaviors but rather that we give our children guidelines for understanding and regulating these sexual experiences. Children need this parental support for exploring and understanding their own sexuality. Parental denial of sexuality loads childhood sexuality with the baggage of guilt and repression, which they may carry throughout life. Parental acceptance gives children a belief that they can manage their sexual behavior in ways comparable to the management of other important parts of their lives.

Some of the acts of our children will be homosexual. Such acts are commonplace during childhood. Surely some children will come to prefer homosexual acts over heterosexual acts. Homosexual behavior occurs in all major civilizations and it is a perfectly normal behavior, according to the American Psychiatric Association. Here, too, the best way to help the child and the parent is to encourage open discussion of what is being experienced and what it means to both the child and the parent.

We don't lose control by empowering children with sexual rights; we gain control, for it is we, the parents, who give our children permission. If our children move in directions we think harmful, we can redirect them but only if they view us as part of the learning process rather than as a repressive element in their lives. We abdicate our responsibilities as parents if we deceive ourselves into thinking we are prolonging our children's sexual "innocence" by not dealing openly with their sexual choices. Instead, we need to pass on to our children the pluralistic values of honesty, equality, and responsibility as guides to their own sexual acts.

Our children will be sexual whether we participate in helping them learn about sex or not. We can neglect our responsibility to sexually educate our young children. We can make them naive; we can make them vulnerable to abuse; we can set them up for many future sexual problems; but no matter how hard we try, we cannot make them "sexually innocent."

3

Teenage Sex:
A Time for Acceptance

The Swedish Model

In September 1975 I began a ten-month sabbatical in Uppsala, Sweden, with my wife and our three children. I had been invited to teach and to do research at Uppsala University because of my interest in Swedish sexual customs. This was a chance to learn about them firsthand.[1] As I began to compare Swedish sexual customs with our own, I gained new insight into our restrictive and unrealistic ways of looking at teenage sexuality. This was dramatically illustrated by an incident that occurred during the year of my visit.

My wife had organized an open discussion between American and Swedish students and their parents. Most of the students attending were young teenagers. One hotly debated topic concerned the proper age for first sexual intercourse. A number of Swedish junior high school girls were arguing that age fourteen was old enough while their mothers argued that they should wait until they were sixteen. I knew right then that I was in a different culture. Not many American parent-child groups would have a public discussion with these opposing positions. Picture the reaction if this debate were raised at your local PTA!

As the discussion proceeded, an American female college student who was spending the year in Sweden stood up and said, "I find this discussion very upsetting! I think you have all lost sight of the value of saving sexual intercourse for marriage. Marriage is the proper place for starting sexual intercourse. It's not a matter of whether you are fourteen, sixteen, or any other age—it's a matter of being moral and waiting until you're married!"

61

The Swedish parents were stunned into silence for a few moments. Swedes are generally not as confrontational or argumentative as Americans. Then one Swedish mother asked the American student, "Do you know that in our country most women do not marry until they are over twenty-five years old? Are you proposing that our young women wait all those years for their first sexual intercourse?" The student responded, "Yes, that is exactly what I am saying. Marriage is the only proper setting for sexual intercourse!" I thought to myself: "Okay! Now we'll see some real verbal fireworks." But the Swedish mother just looked at the American student, paused for a moment, and then calmly said: "How quaint!"

The American student's view was so foreign to this Swedish mother that it was not seen as threatening; rather, it was seen as odd and unrealistic. Swedes have a strong belief in the right to sexual privacy and would therefore hesitate to interfere with any freely chosen sexual act. The imposition of abstinence on others would be seen by most Swedes as grossly inappropriate. This does not mean that Swedes are orgiastic liberationists in their approach to sexuality. On the contrary, they prefer stable "relational" sexuality to casual "recreational" sexuality. Furthermore, they certainly aren't fully liberated from their own traditional past. The traditional influence was obvious at the meeting—there were very few fathers there and the question of age at first intercourse for boys was not even raised.

Swedes generally view sexual intercourse as a natural and expected occurrence during the teen years. Rather than trying to prevent it, they prepare their young people for their first sexual experience. In that sense there is less of a clash between Swedish parents and their teenagers. As a result of their more realistic approach to preparation for and acceptance of teenage sexuality, their overall pregnancy rates are only one third of what ours are.[2] This should give us pause to wonder why we continue to try to block teenage sexuality rather than to prepare our teens for the very real possibility that they will participate in sexual intercourse.

I think the way in which the Swedish public schools try to deal with sex offers much for Americans to think about. During the year I spent in Sweden, I spoke with one of the key people who helped organize their then newly revised sex education curriculum, Carl Gustav Boethius, an active member of the Lutheran Church. Swedes have several decades of experience with sex education, having required sex education in their schools since 1956. Boethius explained to me that the new sex education report was a result of ten years of work (1964–1974).[3] The goal was to instill a broad knowledge and appreciation of a variety of sexual behaviors from early ages, starting if possible in preschool. They haven't yet achieved everything they've aimed for, but understanding their goals can be very useful for us in America.

One fundamental issue concerned how to handle moral values in sex education in the public schools. The solution the Swedes adopted still impresses me as an excellent one. The Swedish Sex Education Commission decided that they would do more than just present the facts about sex. Instead, those fundamental values on which Swedish society is in strong agreement would be presented by the sex education teachers as an essential part of sexual behavior. *The key value in Sweden is to link sexuality with concern for the other person's welfare.* There is a general pluralistic approach stressing tolerance for different sexual choices. Personally I would pick three values as most important for the achievement of pluralism. I have mentioned these values in both chapters 1 and 2. I believe both Swedes and Americans can best promote pluralism by emphasizing sexual relations that incorporate *honesty, equality,* and *responsibility.* These three values form the acronym *HER* and are the heart of my view of sexual pluralism. I believe the Swedes would agree with me.

Swedes feel that open and frank discussions between people planning to have sex are necessary to ensure that both parties understand what is intended. Mind reading should not be necessary in a sexual relationship. Treating one's sexual partner as an equal is another very important value in Sweden. Women and men are to be equally valued and to be equally allowed to assert their wishes. Responsibility and concern for the welfare of both partners in regard to pregnancy, disease, and emotional outcomes are also key values. On the negative side, the harmfulness of exploitation or the use of force in sexual relationships is very strongly emphasized. Making love is seen as a private celebration and one person should not unduly pressure another to participate in such an event.

As part of the value of responsibility, the Swedes promote condom use and do not, as we so often do, belittle the effectiveness of condoms in order to try to discourage teenage sex. As the story I related at the start of this chapter indicates, Swedes have much less of an "abstinence only" bias than we do. Condoms have been publicly advertised on billboards in major cities for a long time. In the early 1970s, one famous Stockholm billboard displayed a drawing of a smiling penis with wings, hovering over a flower. Underneath were written the words: "Don't Pollinate. Use Condoms." And condoms were not hard to get. They were available on many downtown streets in outdoor machines as well as in a large variety of stores.

It is ironic that in America we make cigarette machines available everywhere regardless of the fact that smoking is responsible for over 400,000 deaths annually (more than one of every six deaths in the United States), but where we could *reduce* death and disease by increased presence of condom machines, we often hesitate to act. Only recently have packages of condoms come out from behind the counter and ceased to be treated as if they were a dangerous prescription drug. The message in the United States is: "Stay away from this dangerous and degrading act"; in Sweden it is: "If you show concern for your partner, we will do all we can to make it possible for you both to enjoy the benefits while avoiding the dangers of sexuality." Does our approach to sexuality properly express your priorities?

But even in pluralistic Sweden there are controversial issues about which people disagree. Consequently, on issues like teenage sexuality and homosexuality, alternative perspectives are presented in the classroom. Teachers are not to present any one side as *the* morally correct position. The goal is to encourage students to take a more thoughtful approach to the entire area of sexuality, to expand their range of acceptable choices, and to create a more pluralistic sexual philosophy. However, in order to achieve this in Sweden or the U.S., I believe all sexual choices must conform to the basic values of honesty, equality, and responsibility. Abiding by these positive values guarantees that force and exploitation in sexuality will be avoided. *A person cannot be honest, equal, and responsible and still force or exploit someone else. Therefore, honesty, equality, and responsibility are the very foundation of the pluralistic approach I described in chapter 1.*

In line with their pluralistic approach, Swedish law accepts prostitution on a one-to-one basis where two people freely agree to have sex for money. But Swedish law does not accept a pimp who controls prostitutes and profits from their work, because there is little honesty, equality, and responsibility in the relation of the pimp to his prostitutes. Even in Sweden their pluralistic program has not been fully implemented and there is a need for much more training of teachers to be competent to use the program. But the model is there and, most important, there is a shared desire to put this program fully into operation.

How do you personally react to this Swedish approach? Certainly, many American parents would feel quite threatened by such an open system. Some parents are frightened by freedom of choice that might lead their children to seriously consider any sexual possibilities other than what they think are the "proper" ones. But surely we know that children will learn of many sexual alternatives from their peers and from the media. If you don't openly and reasonably discuss more than abstinence with your child, then when your child is tempted to change sexual standards, and they will be—you will not be seen as a safe person with whom to talk. The more pluralistic parents are, the more they will be relevant to a wide range of sexual choices and the more influential they will be in encouraging their children to choose wisely.

I would strongly propose, in line with the Swedish approach, that all schools and our parents take a pluralistic stance and frankly and realistically discuss a wide variety of sexual practices with our children. We can show our children how to make sure that their sexuality shows a concern for the other person. In my view, we would reduce our rate of teenage pregnancy if we were more able to bring the full discussion of sexual choices into the light of an animated class or home discussion. This is surely more effective than continuing our badly failing efforts to impose abstinence on teenagers.

Sexual Dogmatism vs. Sexual Pluralism

An interesting controversy in New Hampshire involved then governor John Sununu (later President Bush's White House chief of staff, now on CNN's "Crossfire"). The event dramatically underscored the vast differences between American and Swedish attitudes toward sex. The clash centered on how to deal with homosexuality in high school sex-education classes. A great many Americans seem to be uncomfortable in calling homosexuality "normal." Despite the fact that the American Psychiatric Association no longer labels homosexuality as an emotional disturbance, we are often fearful of that sexual orientation. This became obvious in 1988 in Dover, New Hampshire, where an education manual started a state-wide uproar because it did not share the public's bias and condemn homosexuality.

This education manual was written for high school sex-education teachers and published by the Prenatal and Family Planning Program of Strafford County, New Hampshire. In the manual the authors state that homosexuality is an integral part of a gay or lesbian person's identity and thus is normal for those individuals. The clinic was attempting to make life safer and less stressful for those teenagers who can become victimized by homophobic hatred.

The political reaction was immediate and explosive. Senator Gordon Humphrey (R-NH) called for a federal investigation of the clinic, proposed federal legislation barring federal funds from any project that viewed homosexuality as normal, and condemned the clinic with the following comments: "The program deserves worse than an F. It should be immediately expelled from New Hampshire. . . . Homosexual conduct is morally wrong."[4] Governor Sununu noted: "It is not the kind of a document that I would like governing any kind of programs that my kids would be exposed to."[5] The Strafford County Commissioners stopped funding for the entire Prenatal Family Planning Clinic and *all* its programs. As a result, the clinic's contraceptive programs for low-income pregnant women were without funds.

Chuck Rhoades, the executive director of the Strafford County Clinic, sent me a copy of his April 18, 1988, letter responding to the county commissioners who had cut off his funding. In it he explained to the county:

> This curriculum is a manual for teachers, designed to be used in a sex education program for young people ages 14–18 where their participation is voluntary and their parents have given their written permission for their children to participate. . . . [The manual] explicitly recognizes that sexual orientation is one aspect of being human, and that there are heterosexual, bisexual, and homosexual people in every society. The curriculum also recognizes that some young people know from a very early age that they are only attracted sexually to the same gender and that these young people are often the targets of prejudice, hatred, and even violence from their peers and the larger society. These negative attitudes are commonly referred to as homophobia. All mainstream medical, psychological, educational, sociological and legal organizations support the position that homophobia is the problem, not homosexuality.

The National Organization for Women (NOW) supported the clinic in its fight and NOW President Molly Yard commented that the Strafford County Commissioners were "very prejudiced, bigoted and intolerant of people who are different from themselves."[6] The American Civil Liberties Union also came to the support of the clinic and finally reached a settlement with the New Hampshire Attorney General's Office. The state agreed to resume funding if no public funds would be used for the production of the controversial manual. Governor Sununu was angered by the agreement and tried to find another organization to take over the clinic's operation completely.[7] But that did not materialize and the issue seemed finally settled. The six months of conflict had surely stirred up homophobia and heterosexism, but hopefully it may also have caused some people to think through their unreasonable fears about accepting individuals with different sexual interests from their own. Our difficulties with and negativism about homosexuality are still with us. Witness the heated reaction in 1994 in Queens, New York, over teaching about homosexuality. Even the actress Ellen Degeneres received criticism in 1997 for coming out as a lesbian on her TV show and in real life.

Where would you have come down on teaching and talking about homosexuality? Why do so many people fear telling their children that homosexuality is a legitimate sexual orientation held by some people? Do we really believe that just calling homosexuality a legitimate orientation would all of a sudden persuade our children to become homosexual and would nullify all the heterosexual pressures of society? If change of sexual orientation were so easy, why would people remain homosexual despite the immense pressure from all quarters to be straight? It is not our intellectual processes that lead to our fears. If our sexual philosophy were more pluralistic, we would have more confidence in our own choices and would allow others the right to live as they choose. The fear of someone being different from us is rooted in the dogmatic, absolutist belief that there is only one right way to behave sexually. Once we discard this belief, we will not find it so difficult to grant equality to others who are different.

Compulsory abstinence (as opposed to sexual pluralism) continues to dominate our public school sex education system even as we approach the next century. The Sex Information and Education Council of the United States (SIECUS) and the Alan Guttmacher Institute—a highly regarded, independent corporation for research, policy analysis, and public education—conducted two studies on sex education.[8] It found that the emphasis in public school sex education classes was on AIDS. Also, abstinence was the strategy almost always recommended for avoiding AIDS. The same strategy was also recommended for avoiding pregnancy. Sex was treated just as alcoholism is in our schools. It is seen as a dangerous and uncontrollable addiction—too dangerous for any high school student to be able to handle. The Reagan administration's chastity approach, which I commented on in chapter 1, has left its mark on our public schools, even as we close out this century.

It would be a far more realistic strategy to recommend that students be given instructions on how using condoms and spermicides can make having intercourse a great deal safer; they would thereby learn how to protect themselves and their partners. Such preparation would help students cope with the sexual choices that perplex them today. But in our public schools preparation for sex is forced to take a distant back seat to abstinence or the prevention of sex. When condoms are mentioned, they are often criticized for being very risky and difficult to accept. In fact we have only a minority of states that insist that information about family planning be covered. A few like Michigan, in addition, recommend birth-control clinics in all middle or high schools.[9] In my own state of Minnesota, the Twin Cities' schools have clinics but most of the suburbs do not, due to the strident opposition of a few anti-abortion-rights groups and others. Most states avoid the controversial issues involved in teaching children how to save their own lives and those of their sexual partners. We pay the cost for this in the lives of our children.

Despite this restrictive public education policy, national polls show that the great majority of adults believe that birth-control information should be available to teenagers and a majority also agree that it should be available to fourteen- to sixteen-year-olds even if their parents do not approve.[10] But once again there is little willingness shown by politicians, school principals, or parents to go public and support such a program. The power of our Victorian past to sabotage the present is disturbing. Can anyone really morally defend this avoidance of teaching our children to protect themselves from disease and pregnancy? To refuse to educate youngsters about condom use and other contraceptive methods is to expose them to a life-threatening risk. How can we think of that as proper sex education?

The nineteenth-century dream of promoting abstinence has led to the twentieth century's nightmare of rampant teenage pregnancy and disease. We have never in the two thousand years of Christianity had a society in which the majority of people practiced abstinence and we surely will not have it now. Only in America (even in the Clinton administration) is there a government-supported program to stop teenagers from having sex. When will we learn to accept our right to make sexual choices? We cannot deny sexuality and so we must find the courage to deny others the right to dictate our child's sexual lifestyle!

Peggy Brick, past president of SIECUS, has commented on the failure of adults to endorse sexual pleasure for adolescents. This is a serious gap, for whether adolescents are abstinent or not, sexual pleasure is a major reality in their lives:

> Here is our nemesis: the failure of most adults to acknowledge, or apparently even care about, the role of pleasure in adolescents' experience of their sexuality. Even adults who discount the usefulness of "just say no" are unlikely to advocate *good* sex for teens. . . . We must validate sexuality as part of being human—even during the adolescent years.[11]

Instead of trying to stop teenage sexuality, we need to accept our children's search for sexual pleasure. It is our role as parents to train our children so that they will abide by the important values of honesty, equality, and responsibility and demand that their partners do the same in whatever type of sexual relationship they enter into. We drop friends when they show little concern for our feelings and needs. We certainly should do the same with our sexual partners if they cannot or will not develop those mutual concerns.

If we gave top priority to this concern for the values involved in a sexual relationship, we could alter the nature of teenage sexuality far more than any government "chastity bill" could. The burden of learning how to be sexually honest, equal, and responsible could be lightened by *open* discussions with teachers, parents, clergy, and friends. Peer groups of trained students could also help lead discussion groups and throw additional light on the important decisions that must be constantly made in the area of human sexual relationships. A few schools have tried these approaches with great success, but most schools are waiting for more support from parents and other adult groups. It is time to dump the dogma of chastity as the only choice. As Faye Wattleton, former president of Planned Parenthood Federation of America, said: "Just saying no prevents teenage pregnancy the way 'Have a nice day' cures chronic depression."[12]

But before we can believe in pluralism we must be personally convinced that choices other than abstinence are morally acceptable for some teenagers. We don't have to think of all choices as of equal moral value, but the choices have to be seen as acceptable. As a first step it would help to stop thinking of first coitus as the *loss* of virginity and instead see it as the *start* of a broader, more potentially rewarding sexual life. Treating girls and boys more equally would help accomplish this. We hardly ever talk about a boy's "loss of virginity." How fair is it to train our sons to be sexually freer than our daughters? After all, these young men are going to have sex with someone's daughter. Introducing more honesty, equality, and responsibility into our sexual lives and theirs is surely preferable to the impulsiveness, deception, and irresponsibility we currently practice.

We need to get away from our focus on *prevention* of sexuality and concentrate on *preparation* for this exciting part of life. Of course, young people can choose to be abstinent, but we should also grant them the right to choose to have sexual relationships if they can carry on a HER relationship. The media should encourage birth-control advertisements whether they offend a small group of people or not. We should warn the media that their restrictions on contraceptive advertisement is morally offensive to a much larger group of people who are just now learning to speak up. As parents, teachers, politicians, and religious officials we can speak publicly for pluralism and thereby help to limit teenage pregnancies. *If we restrain our own anxieties in the interest of promoting our children's informed choices, the pluralistic approach will grow.* Pluralism will expand our tolerance at the same time as it prepares our children for making honest, equal, and responsible sexual choices. Wouldn't this approach be a major improvement over what we now do?

But Can Teenagers Really Be Ready for Sex?

There can be no exact age at which everyone is "ready" for intercourse. Many European countries set fifteen as the legal age for premarital intercourse. This age limit conveys the message that adults are uneasy about anyone engaging in sex *before* this age while at the same time it empowers young people to make up their own minds *after* that age. In our country, fifteen is the age when our youngsters get their automobile driving permits and at sixteen they have their licenses. If we can train them to avoid the risks of driving, perhaps we can do the same for sexuality.

As I see it, the irresponsible thing is not that our youngsters would decide to have intercourse at fifteen. What is far more irresponsible is that we as adults have not prepared them for that very *possible* choice. In a pluralistic perspective, competence to choose is deemed far more consequential than is choosing any one particular sexual standard.

In 1996 a representative national sample of fifteen hundred adult Americans was asked if premarital intercourse for teens fourteen to sixteen years old was "always wrong." Sixty-nine percent said it was. But when the wording was changed to ask about premarital intercourse for a "man and a woman," only 24 percent said it was always wrong.[13] Obviously the older you are the more acceptable premarital intercourse becomes. During the last sexual revolution there was a notable drop in the age at which sexual intercourse began. Today, before they are eighteen the majority of our young people have had sexual intercourse. That change has precipitated a strong public debate about contraception, abortion, and sexual rights, particularly for teenagers under eighteen.

The age at which young people are seen as no longer "too young" depends a good deal on your image of sexuality. The more you focus upon the difficulties in managing the pregnancy and disease risks of sexuality, and the "moral" tie of sexuality to marriage, the longer you're going to want young people to wait. On the other hand, if you stress the pleasurable aspects of sex, the psychological rewards of intimacy, and the ability of people to manage the consequences of sex, then you will accept sexual relationships at younger ages. It all depends upon your personal perspective and how you mix the colors of danger and pleasure in your portrait of human sexuality.[14]

Where do you come out on this issue? Is thirteen or fourteen too young? How about fifteen, sixteen, seventeen . . . ? To the pluralist the young person must be old enough so that he or she can freely choose and not be exploited. Only by preparing our children and then observing when we think they are capable of exercising sexual choices can we intelligently make a decision as to when they are "ready." The most important thing is that this is *not* a decision that we can impose on a child. We cannot control our child's sexual behavior. All we can do is prepare our children for honest, equal, and responsible sexuality, no matter when it occurs. Those are the values we try to incorporate in all human relationships. *Isn't it time to make sex moral and not just dogmatic?*

The conflicted and dogmatic way we teach children about sexuality in America is obviously not working. Our pregnancy rate for girls under age fifteen is *several times* the rate of most developed countries![15] In 1994 we still had almost 13,000 births to teenagers under age fifteen.[16] If we want to stop such disastrous unwanted consequences, we need to make some serious changes in our approach to sexuality.

The reaction by a mother who wrote to Ann Landers about her fifteen-year-old daughter's contraceptive usage is unfortunately typical of many Americans:

> I don't know what to do next. I just discovered that our beautiful 15-year-old daughter is sexually active. I also found that she is on birth control pills. I have been completely incapacitated since I found the evidence. I can't do anything but think about how badly we have failed. I can't talk to my husband about it. He would go to pieces. Our whole lives have revolved around this child. We have tried hard to be good parents. We supported her school activities and let her know that she could come to us with anything. I had several talks with her about premarital sex. She was brought up to be a good Christian, I am devastated. Help me.[17]

Note that not a word is said about being thankful that the girl is on the pill. The mother is just overwhelmed by her strong negative feelings toward premarital sex. She clearly doesn't believe in her daughter's ability to handle it. The amazing thing is that her daughter had the good sense to protect herself by using a contraceptive. The pill, however, offers no protection against a wide range of sexually transmitted diseases ranging from gonorrhea to AIDS. Condoms used together with foam spermicide are protection against both pregnancy and disease, and they are available without prescription in drug stores. But you can be sure that this mother would never have talked about contraception in a frank, open manner with her daughter.

This mother feels that she has failed because her daughter did not blindly obey her sexual rules. She says that she told her daughter that she and her husband were willing to talk with her about anything. But it must have been obvious to the daughter what her parents would have said if she had expressed any interest in having intercourse. Her mother's goal was prevention and thus preparation for choice was out of the question.

To illustrate what kind of "talks" some people have with their children about premarital sex, here is a quotation from the files of psychologist Catherine Chilman, whose work on teenage sexuality is a classic in the field:

> My parents were cold and harsh and very bossy. I rebelled as a teenager but they wouldn't let me date. They never discussed sex except to say "don't." I soon got into drugs and sex. I got birth control pills and my mother found them and took them away from me. I told her I would get even and get pregnant. So finally she gave the pills back, calling me a dirty whore.[18]

The daughter in this last quote sounds difficult to live with, and the mother seems to be authoritarian. But even in such a situation what good would it do to prohibit contraceptive use? Isn't it precisely such rebellious children who are the most in need of protection against their tendency to take risks? The fundamental question that parents must answer is: What takes priority—exercising sexual control over their children or teaching them to make responsible sexual choices? Most parents have opted for control and in doing so have increased the odds of high-risk sex if their children follow the pressures of their friends and choose to have intercourse.

The American Teen Pregnancy Factory

The media have told Americans over and over that our teenage pregnancy rates have been constantly rising. There is no question that our rates are far higher than those of other Western countries, but it is *not* the case that they have been constantly increasing.

One of the best scientific studies we have comes from a blue-ribbon committee of experts, the Panel on Adolescent Pregnancy and Childbearing, which spent two years reviewing, analyzing, and discussing what we know about teenage pregnancy. They concluded that teenage pregnancy rates *for sexually active women* had *gone down* between 1974 and 1984 and that the 1960s probably was the decade with the highest rates! Teenage pregnancy rates fell again in the 1990s.[19] This may surprise some readers. Let me explain.

There have certainly been increases in the *number* of teenage pregnancies from 1960 to the mid 1970s. However, keep in mind that during those years there were vast increases in the percentage of women having premarital intercourse and thereby putting themselves at risk for becoming pregnant. Roughly speaking, in 1960 about 20 percent of all single fifteen- to nineteen-year-old women were nonvirginal; by 1970 the percentage was about 30 percent; and it was almost *50* percent by 1980. That 50 percent rate for teen nonvirginity has not significantly changed since then.[20] But the size of the teenage female population doubled between 1950 and 1980, from about five million to about ten million. So, since there is a much greater number of fifteen- to nineteen-year-old women and a much higher proportion of them are sexually active, we would certainly expect a greater *number* of pregnancies during those years. But if we ask what *proportion* of this much larger group of sexually active teens became pregnant, the answer is that the *proportion* of nonvirgins getting pregnant has actually gone *down*.

There were changes in sexual behavior that could have led to an increase in the percentage of sexually active teens getting pregnant. For example, during the 1974–1984 time period the number of sexual partners each woman had was rising, as was the frequency of intercourse, and women were starting intercourse at earlier ages.[21] The major reason for there being no rise in pregnancy rates had to be a counterbalancing improvement in the use of contraceptives by these teenage women. As evidence of this, I would note that a very large proportion of unwanted births to teenagers are to women who *never use contraceptives*. The percentage of teenagers never using contraceptives went down from 36 percent in 1976 to just 15 percent in 1982.[22] So we were indeed getting better at contraceptive use. The improvement was, I believe, in large measure due to increased acceptance of premarital intercourse by young people during the last sexual revolution. That acceptance helped legitimize preparing for intercourse by taking precautions against conception. Just imagine how much more could have been accomplished if our political and religious leaders had actively promoted safer sex instead of just trying to stop sexual intercourse? How many millions of unwanted pregnancies could have been avoided?

In the first edition of this book (1990) I predicted that teenage pregnancy rates would go down in the 1990s.[23] The most recent data from the government indicate that there has indeed been a significant drop in teenage pregnancy rates from 1991 to 1996.[24] The 1995 National Survey of Family Growth (NSFG) shows that the percentage of fifteen- to nineteen-year-old females who are nonvirginal is at 50 percent. This rate is the same as that in the 1979 Zelnik and Kantner national survey.[25] Our condom usage at first coitus has increased dramatically over the few past decades. In the 1970s 18 percent used condoms at first coitus. In the 1980s it was 36 percent, and in the 1990s (1995 NSFG) it is 54 percent. This is a major reason for the drop in the teenage pregnancy rate. The percentage of females using any contraceptive method at first coitus in the 1990–1995 period has risen to 76 percent. That percent would have been about 50 percent as recently as the early 1980s. So despite the fact that over three-quarters of our nineteen-year-old women have had premarital intercourse, there is strong evidence that they are taking more contraceptive responsibility and promoting condom use as well as other methods. The view of teenagers as incapable of contraceptive responsibility is increasingly being challenged by the latest research findings.

But while our teenagers are better today at preventing pregnancy, they are still woefully inadequate compared with their fellow teens in other countries. In this country we have had about one million teenage pregnancies each year since 1973. About a half million of those pregnancies end in abortion or miscarriage. The other half million are live births. These births are divided roughly into about 150,000 births to young women who were married at the time of their child's birth and about 350,000 to women who were not.[26] This rate of abortions and births for our teenage population means that over 14 percent of our sexually active teenage women gave birth in any one-year period. This is the highest rate of teenage births in the Western world![27]

By the time our young women are twenty-five years old their pregnancy rates are no longer higher than those of women in other Western countries.[28] But as I noted, in their early teens their rate is much higher than that in other Western countries.[29] So it takes our young women ten very dangerous years to finally achieve the same degree of safety enjoyed by women in other Western societies. What more evidence do we need of our failure to teach our young women how to protect themselves? *Telling our teenage women to "just say no" to sex very often has the effect of "just saying yes" to pregnancy.*

Canada, the Netherlands, and Sweden: How We Compare

Why are all other Western countries so much better at preventing pregnancy? The best international study of teenage pregnancy was done by the Alan Guttmacher Institute during the mid-1980s; it compared teenage pregnancy in the United States with thirty-seven countries. There was also an in-depth comparison of the United States with Canada, England, France, the Netherlands, and Sweden. This study can greatly improve our understanding of why we suffer from a tragic lack of leadership in regard to teenage pregnancy.[30]

The Guttmacher Institute analysis was undertaken by teams of researchers who visited these other countries in 1984. The objective was to find what factors distinguished countries with low pregnancy rates from those with high rates—like the United States. In all of the six countries examined in depth about the same proportion of teenage women have intercourse. Of these countries Canada, the Netherlands, and Sweden throw the most light on our problems and, I believe, they are of most interest for the present discussion. Let's start with Canada.

Canada is the country we Americans probably know the best. Still how many Americans have even heard of what the Canadians call the "quiet revolution" (*la révolution tranquille*)? Quebec was a province dominated for centuries by conservative religious forces. Then in the late 1960s the "quiet revolution" began. Progressive and feminist forces united and radically changed public attitudes regarding sexuality. Quebec enacted legislation supporting abortion, encouraged the formation of family planning clinics with contraception for young people, and also greatly expanded their public sex education. They even founded the first Department of Sexology in North America at the University of Quebec in Montreal. Today our rate of teenage pregnancy is almost four times that in Quebec. If we compared only those women under age fifteen, the differences would be even greater.

The Guttmacher Institute study describes some of the changes that occurred during this "quiet revolution":

> Attitudes towards fertility control play a central role in the new liberated spirit of Quebec. The province historically had an extremely high fertility rate and large families. . . . Fertility control is seen as part of a revolt against the church and the burden on women of large families . . . the fertility rate of Quebec in 1982 was the lowest in Canada . . . Quebec moved rapidly from being more conservative than other provinces to being similar to or slightly more liberal with regard to sexual matters.[31]

In Quebec, as in the United States, traditional religion in the past had rejected the view that teenage women have the right to decide their own sexual futures and to take responsibility for their sexual decisions. The result was a soaring teenage pregnancy rate. *Lack of empowerment to make personal decisions means lack of taking responsibility for those decisions.*

I found precisely this same outcome in a study I conducted on Minnesota college women. Together with two colleagues at the University of Minnesota, I surveyed almost five hundred coeds to learn what characteristic distinguished those women who were most likely to seek contraceptive advice from those who were not. We found that those women who felt they had the right to decide to have intercourse were the most likely to try to protect themselves with contraceptives. Those women who felt intercourse was wrong thought they had to be "swept away" before having intercourse and were the least likely to use contraceptives.[32]

William Fisher, a Canadian sociologist from the University of Western Ontario, presents other relevant findings on this point in regard to Canadian students. In his study of college students, he found that those students who showed a fearful and negative reaction to sexuality were the poorest at anticipating when they would engage in sexual intercourse and the poorest at protecting themselves with contraceptives when they did have sex.[33] The simple lesson seems to be that you will not plan for what you feel you have no right to choose to do. But you may well still do it!

I can best portray how sexually restrictive training in the modern world can lead to tragic outcomes by quoting for you the words of "Betsy," a sixteen-year-old American girl studied by psychologist Paul Abramson of UCLA. Betsy travelled the well worn "forbidden" and "swept away" pathway to unwanted pregnancy and abortion. Here is her story in her own words:

> Each time after John and I had intercourse, we would talk about it. And each time we would vow not to do it again. As such, we would go for a week with only petting, but then we would resume having intercourse. You know, I enjoyed sex very, very much with John. He had a large penis but intercourse was never painful. In fact, I was always very well lubricated. Yet, there were other complications. You see, we never got together to have intercourse, that is, we could never plan it. I guess this is what I needed to do because of my religious beliefs. So naturally, we never had any birth control at our disposal because that would mean planning or premeditation. It would just have to happen, that is, it would have to get to a point where we were so totally out of control that we couldn't turn back. Actually, we were usually so hot and turned on that we couldn't stand it.[34]

Religious and other ideologically restrictive views of sexuality do prevent *some* women from having intercourse. But, as the case of Betsy indicates, men and women with this background often do engage in intercourse and then they are at very high risk.

The Netherlands also witnessed a change in religiosity similar to what happened in Quebec. Like most of the Western world, the Netherlands had a sexual revolution starting in the late 1960s. The result was that birth rates declined, contraceptive use increased, and the people became more open about discussing sexuality. The condom is very widely used in the Netherlands, and Dutch media, unlike our television networks, now do help promote the use of condoms and other contraceptive methods to control unwanted births and sexually transmitted diseases. As was the case in Quebec, the Netherlands became more secular and less religiously traditional in a very short period of time—about five to ten years.

The Dutch have the lowest adolescent pregnancy rates of the six countries examined in depth in the Guttmacher Institute study. They are a pragmatic society and accept what "works" to prevent unwanted pregnancy. Their teenage birth and abortion rates are both much lower than ours. One reason their pregnancy rate is lower is the fact that 75 percent of their teenagers use contraceptives at first coitus. The U.S. figure for contraceptive use at first coitus was 50 percent until 1988, when it rose to 67 percent and, as I've mentioned, it is 76 percent as of 1995. So it took us fifteen years to catch up with the Dutch, who by now surely have made advances. Dutch teenagers are likely to avoid the ineffective method of withdrawal; instead they use the pill and condoms. Note that the methods that are the most effective require forethought and planning and that means acceptance of the right to choose to have intercourse.

It is worth noting that men in the Netherlands, compared with men in the United States, have a much stronger sense of responsibility about not getting their partners pregnant. This, of course, is a very powerful factor in lowering unwanted teenage pregnancy. The Dutch have a high regard for individualism and parents have come to accept, but not to encourage, sex for their teenage children. Of great importance is their endorsement of a pluralistic society. They consciously seek to promote a society that makes room for a variety of perspectives and they give their adolescent children far more preparation for sexual choices than we do. The result is that their early teenage pregnancy rate was but one-sixth of ours in the early 1980s.

It is also enlightening, in terms of teenage pregnancy, to compare our society with Sweden's. As noted at the beginning of this chapter, the Swedes have a more open acceptance of sex education for their children than we do. Sweden has the earliest average age at first coitus of the six countries in the Guttmacher study—16.7 years of age. Like all of these countries, the proportion of sexually active women is similar to ours, and yet their pregnancy rates are but one-third of ours. Their rates would be even a smaller fraction of ours if we compared only women under age fifteen.

Contraception seems to be the key to lower pregnancy rates in Sweden as it was in the Netherlands and Quebec. Two-thirds of Swedish women used contraceptives at first coitus even in the early 1980s and they, too, use the more effective methods. Swedish school nurses send students to the youth clinics for contraceptive help during the regular school hours. The Guttmacher researchers note that in Sweden, as in the Netherlands, there does not seem to be as much "moral ambivalence" about teenage sexuality as there is in the U.S. These other countries have no fantasies about many teenagers postponing sexuality.

The great majority of births that occur outside legal marriage in Sweden are wanted births in stable cohabiting relationships. Cohabitation in Sweden is accepted as an alternative to legal marriage.[35] Those who do have *unwanted,* out-of-wedlock births in Sweden, as most everywhere, are usually the most economically deprived and the very young. As I described earlier, the Swedish government has an effective program to encourage contraceptive use and to give free contraceptive services to young people. An expanded program went into effect in 1975 and was followed by a major drop in teenage pregnancy. The Lutheran Church in Sweden is not very influential in today's secular society, as shown by the fact that very few Swedes are regular churchgoers, and even those who are active churchgoers have almost the same rate of premarital intercourse as nonattenders.

After analyzing these and other societies, the Guttmacher Institute researchers concluded that dogmatic views restricting openness and pluralism about sexual options definitely hamper the control of teenage pregnancy:

> In the U.S. . . . there is much ambivalence: sex is romantic but also sinful and dirty; it is flaunted but also something to be hidden. This ambivalence is less apparent in the European countries where matter-of-fact attitudes seem to be more prevalent. . . . It stands to reason that where sexuality as a whole carries less emotional baggage, sex and pregnancy among teenagers are likely to be dealt with more realistically . . . a society's openness about sex may be an especially important factor influencing adolescent fertility and pregnancy.[36]

Many Americans argue that we should not be more open about sex because teenagers are too immature to handle it and that contraceptive availability would encourage more sex and would only make things worse. In their summation the researchers debunk many of these widespread beliefs.

> To summarize, . . . the studies provide convincing evidence that many widely held beliefs about teenage pregnancy cannot explain the large differences in adolescent pregnancy between the United States and other developed countries: teenagers in these other countries apparently are *not* too immature to use contraceptives consistently and effectively;

the availability of welfare services does *not* seem correlated with higher adolescent fertility; teenage pregnancy rates are *lower* in countries where there is *greater* availability of contraceptive and abortion services and of sexual education; adolescent sexual activity in the United States is not very different from what it is in countries that have much *lower* teenage pregnancy rates; although the pregnancy rate of American blacks is much higher than that of whites, the white rate is still much higher than the overall teenage pregnancy rates in the other case study countries.[37]

These findings strike at the root of the beliefs so often used in America to support a restrictive approach to sexuality; yet most parents, politicians, and religious leaders have not spoken out in favor of greater open preparation for sexuality. How much more unwanted pregnancy will it take to convince our people?

The Guttmacher researchers sum up their major conclusions and suggest that two overall factors are the key to our very high rate of births to teenage women: "An ambivalent, sometimes puritanical, attitude about sex, and the existence of a large, economically deprived underclass."[38] These conclusions lend strong support to the perspective we've been developing.

The Guttmacher Institute people make the following suggestion:

Increasing the legitimacy and availability of contraception and of sex education in its broadest sense is likely to result in declining pregnancy rates, without raising teenage sexual activity rates to any great extent. That has been the experience of most countries of Western Europe, and there is no reason to think it would not also occur in the United States.[39]

Previously in this chapter I mentioned another major report on teenage pregnancy by the Panel on Adolescent Pregnancy and Childbearing. The recommendations of this fifteen-person expert panel are in agreement with the conclusions of the Guttmacher Institute. They recognize the reality of adolescent sexuality and our inability to prevent initiation of intercourse. They note that "making contraceptive methods available and accessible to those who are sexually active and encouraging them to use these methods diligently is the surest strategy for pregnancy prevention."[40] But we in America still do not seem to be hearing the message and we continue to act in ways that promote the teenage pregnancies that we do not want. What better evidence of our crippling internal conflict could there be?

The Rich Get Richer and the Poor Get Pregnant

All social classes contribute to our high rate of teenage pregnancy, but those living below the poverty level have especially high rates. Lack of power to influence their lives is a key cause of this. To understand the language of power and how it relates to pregnancy, listen to the words of a fifteen-year-old girl cited in Catherine Chilman's book on teenage pregnancy. Professor Chilman, cited earlier, is a psychologist now retired from the University of Wisconsin in Milwaukee. Her fifteen-year-old respondent, "Suzie," explained to her why she doesn't use contraception: "I would just as soon get pregnant because my grades at school will force me out anyhow . . . I'll probably die young, so what difference does anything make?"[41] What these comments so pathetically indicate are feelings of hopelessness and powerlessness. Suzie's views are an illustration of a fatalistic philosophy of life so very common in the youth of our lower social class.[42] In essence, the attitude is "what will be will be; there's nothing that can be done about changing the world, so accept your fate and make the best of it."

Those who are economically better off endorse the dominant American belief that there is plenty of opportunity, and if people work hard, they can shape their futures according to their desires. That perspective makes more sense if you're a white, middle-class man but if you're a black, lower-class woman, it just doesn't mean much. The economically deprived really cannot do very much about their future and a "why care what happens" attitude should not surprise any of us. A major study in New York City also found this same resignation to fate among the impoverished: "Regardless of how accessible abortion services are, teenagers in poverty will be less likely to seek abortion than their more educated, and financially better off, counterparts."[43]

The Panel on Adolescent Pregnancy agreed with such conclusions and strongly encouraged enhancing the life options of those teenagers living in poverty as a way of counteracting the growth of fatalism and better controlling teenage abortion and birth:

> Research has shown the deleterious effects of poverty on those caught in its cycle: attitudes of fatalism, powerlessness, alienation, and helplessness that are perpetuated from one generation to the next. . . . Teenagers need a reason to believe that parenthood is inappropriate at this point in their lives. Accordingly, one important strategy for reducing early unplanned pregnancy is to enhance their life options, by encouraging them to establish career goals in addition to parenthood and by helping them understand the value of educational attainment and

employability skills. This strategy is aimed at reducing adolescent fertility by nurturing the motivation to prevent untimely and unplanned parenthood.[44]

Most Americans believe in working hard and making it on your own, but they have also recognized the need to help out those whose opportunities are far from equal.[45] Despite those altruistic feelings, in the 1980s the federal government did very little to help the poor and we now have over 14 percent of our nation living in poverty in one of the wealthiest countries in the world! Many of our cities today have created Third World ghettos within them with excessive rates of disease, poverty, and homelessness, inhabited heavily by women and children. Can we accept this in a society that prides itself on its humanity?

For the millions living in poverty the alternatives to having a baby out of wedlock are far less attractive than they are to those living in the suburbs. Males who can earn a decent living are in short supply and marriages break up at a very high rate either by desertion or divorce. So poverty lowers the reasons for trying to confine births to marriage. It is difficult to argue with the harsh realities of poverty in our ghettos and extol the great advantages of having babies in marriage. What this means in plain terms is that the range of choices open to those living in poverty is far narrower than that of those who are better off economically. Our poverty rate is very high for a Western country, and for a country as wealthy as we are, it is, as Senator Paul Wellstone has recently said, unconscionable. To offer choices is to offer hope and so a pluralistic philosophy demands that we improve the lot of our fellow citizens and thereby help to reduce the number of unwanted babies coming into our world.

We don't really have a choice about paying the cost—either we do that now in welfare, job retraining, day care, free contraception, and other ways or else we will pay for it later in taking care of the unwanted children and the immense problems they will bring as they grow up.

Shutting Down the Pregnancy Factory

My recommendations about promoting condom use and empowering teenagers to make responsible sexual choices may raise the anxiety level of some of my readers—particularly those who are parents of young teenagers. But these suggestions are realistic and pragmatic. As I have shown, scientists from a wide variety of backgrounds are in agreement on them. Similar suggestions have been put forth in earlier years by others. For example, sociologist Hyman Rodman, then Director of the Family

Research Center at the University of North Carolina in Greensboro, made comparable recommendations in a book on teenage sexuality in 1984.[46] Rodman made three recommendations which basically asked for (1) legislation giving minors the right to consent to reproductive health services at age fifteen, (2) the development of sex education programs sensitive to all value positions on sexuality, and (3) greater federal support for reproductive health services available to adolescents. Such recommendations are precisely the type of changes that the Guttmacher Institute and the Panel on Adolescent Pregnancy and Childbearing later concluded were necessary. People are becoming increasingly favorable to such suggestions, but, until AIDS, very little could penetrate our protective deafness in the area of sexuality.

The evidence is overwhelming that we can produce teenagers of *all* ages who can intelligently handle the range of sexual choices that confront them in their social world. We are not doing that now. We practice unsafe sex as a society if we do not prepare our youth for the real world they face. Our society must erect a safety net for its youth if we are to prevent the worst possible outcomes.

When polled, the majority of teenagers today say they have never discussed contraception with their parents. Our culture produces so much mistrust and ambivalence about teenagers using contraceptives that our contraceptive clinics must work very hard to counteract this if they are to teach young women how to protect themselves.[47] In order to remove our social roadblocks against contraceptive preparation, we need a major revision of our philosophy of sexuality. We have to think of sexuality in a more pluralistic way. Pluralism would empower teenagers with sexual choices and sexual responsibilities.

There are some good signs. For example, we find that condom use has increased significantly and that positive attitudes toward condoms has likewise risen among both men and women.[48] Even teenage males have sharply increased their use of condoms. If we are to control unwanted pregnancy, these more realistic and positive approaches must be vigorously promoted to counteract the widespread sexual ambivalence and negativism that still exist today. More of how we can do this in later chapters.

Contraceptive awareness can become a natural part of young people's growing up, if we simply make the effort to protect our children. The vast majority of parents say they favor this, but a vocal minority remains opposed and continues to make politicians and administrators of our public schools fearful of change.[49] Surely, abstinence should remain as *one* of the legitimate choices, but we cannot accept it as a compulsory or imperialistic standard for all teenagers.

We must more fully legitimize the possible choice of premarital intercourse and thereby encourage our young people to become more responsible for their own sexuality. This is a moral choice that all of us can make. We can try to shape our society to help us control teenage pregnancy. We must try to change our society to reduce poverty and the hopelessness that accompanies it. We can raise youngsters from infancy onward in ways that prepare them for the sexual choices they will face and we can encourage them to make those choices in line with our shared pluralistic values of honesty, equality, and responsibility (HER). We can deepen our trust in our teenagers' ability to choose wisely in accord with the values we have given them. If we believe in our teenagers' ability to act with care and concern, they will believe in themselves.

We don't really have many other options. Some parents may not like such an acceptance and empowerment of teenagers for sexual decisions. But we have made a total mess of trying to stop teenagers from having sex. The rest of the Western world has found that preparation, empowerment, and expecting responsibility works. Isn't it time for us to close the floodgates of unwanted pregnancies and create a safer and more morally responsible teenage generation?

4

The Stalled Sexual Revolutions
of This Century

Revolutions: One Isn't Enough

One day back in 1973 historian Carl Degler was sifting through the materials in the archives of Stanford University's library. To his surprise he found a manuscript by a medical doctor who had started a study of the sexual lives of married women in the year 1892! The author was Clelia Duel Mosher, M.D., born in 1863. She began her research as a student of biology at the University of Wisconsin and finished it at Stanford University. She never published her study and just tucked it away in Stanford University's archives at the end of her life in 1940. When it was discovered thirty-three years later, it was indeed like an archaeological find—the oldest recorded study of sexual practices in America, gathering dust in the archives at Stanford!

Most of the forty-five women Mosher interviewed were, like herself, born before 1870. They were highly educated women for their times; over three quarters of them had been to college or normal school. When Stanford historian Carl Degler read Dr. Mosher's findings, he was taken aback by the strength of the sexual interests of these Victorian women. Over 40 percent of these wives reported that they usually or always had orgasm in sexual intercourse and only one-third reported that they rarely or never had orgasm during sexual intercourse. Their rate of sexual intercourse was five times a month—not so low even by today's averages of almost seven times a month.[1] There were clear signs that, at least for these women, Victorian restraints were not fully dominating their sexuality. They were, of course, more sexually constrained than we are today, but they also showed that even a century ago sexual intercourse in marriage was for many women far more than just a "wifely duty."

Later in her career, when she was sixty-three years old, Dr. Mosher taught a class in Personal Hygiene at Stanford University. It was the 1920s and "the times they were a-changin'." The premarital sexual escapades of this generation far exceeded the moderate pursuit of marital sexual pleasure by her nineteenth-century sample of women. This new generation was born in the first decade of the twentieth century and came to maturity in the 1920s. She sensed the difference and wrote in her notes:

> These lectures in Personal Hygiene are exhausting me. . . . Where should I draw the line? My Victorian sense of decent reticence is constantly shocked although my secretary says I have given no sign . . . it is a new age, new thinking, new ideals . . .[2]

Dr. Mosher was lecturing to the "flaming youth" of the 1920s. This century's *first* sexual revolution was in progress. According to the data gathered by Kinsey, the percentage of women born between 1900 and 1909 who had intercourse before marriage doubled from 25 percent to 50 percent! The premarital nonvirginity rate for men in that same birth cohort held relatively stable at about 80 percent.[3] This birth cohort was the generation that created the sexual revolution of the 1920s and shocked pioneer sex researcher Clelia Mosher. It may also shock today's baby boomers to realize that these were their grandparents!

Still, despite some sensationalized reporting, the 1920s were not a time of orgiastic sexuality. Most of the increased sexuality occurred in stable, affectionate relationships. Men moved more toward intercourse with women for whom they cared rather than with prostitutes or casual sexual partners. During the 1920s, these young revolutionaries fashioned a more egalitarian version of courtship and sexuality—one that continued to evolve during the rest of the century.[4]

The 1920s were a turning point in our society. As University of California historian Paula Fass sees it: "The twenties [were] a critical juncture between the strict double standard of the age of Victoria and the permissive sexuality of the age of Freud."[5] Fass describes the overall spirit of the 1920s:

> Did the young use sex and morals as a basis for conscious generational revolt? On the whole the answer would appear to be no, although their sexual attitudes and practices did distinguish them from their elders and made them appear rebellious. They welcomed the lingering naughtiness of which they were accused, but more in the spirit of play than with any serious display of anger. As eager capitalists, the young were anything but rebellious in social and political questions.[6]

There are some remarkable similarities in the social forces that propelled the sexual revolution of the 1920s and those involved in the second sexual revolution which began in the late 1960s. Both revolutions involved a major war, a dramatic rise in divorce, and increased equality between men and women.

World War I ended in 1918. It was the first war in which American troops had been sent to Europe. The war provided a more panoramic view of the world to millions of American men and women. "How you gonna keep 'em down on the farm after they've seen Paree" was not just a line from a World War I song. It reflected the realization that the war had enlarged our awareness of possible lifestyles and that the nineteenth-century wall of Victorianism had started to crumble.

The Vietnam war, starting in the mid-1960s, helped to propel us into the *second* sexual revolution of this century. That war produced a profound disruption of our customary ways of viewing the world. It was the most unpopular war in our history, and young people felt justified in criticizing our involvement. Anyone over thirty can recall the scores of protests, often followed by violent confrontations with police and national guardsmen. The tragedy at Kent State epitomized the public turmoil in that war:

> On April 30, 1970, President Nixon announced that American and South Vietnamese forces were moving against enemy sanctuaries in Cambodia. Minutes after this announcement, student-organized protest demonstrations were under way. . . . On May 2, the ROTC building at Kent State was set afire. On May 4, Kent State students congregated on the university Commons and defied an order by the Guard to disperse. Guardsmen proceeded to disperse the crowd. The students then began to taunt Guard units and to throw rocks . . . the three ranking officers on the hill all said no order to fire was given. . . . Twenty-eight guardsmen have acknowledged firing from Blanket Hill . . . the firing . . . lasted approximately 13 seconds. The time of the shooting was approximately 12:25 P.M. Four persons were killed and nine were wounded.[7]

The Vietnam war increased our willingness to criticize our society. Our view of what was right and wrong was changing. Many people reasoned that if our country could be wrong about Vietnam, than it could be wrong about other things like family, religion, and certainly sexuality. This critical stance helped prepare the fertile soil in which the second and much more angry sexual revolution was starting to grow.

The 1920s' sexual revolution set the direction of change, which during the next few decades transformed the public view of sexuality, and helped to clear the path for the sexual revolution of the late 1960s. But as

I have noted, there were significant differences in the tone of these two sexual revolutions. One shorthand way to grasp the difference is to listen to the popular music of each time period. For example, the lyrics of Cole Porter's 1928 hit "Let's Do It (Let's Fall in Love)" portrays the jocular sexual atmosphere of the 1920s in comments about the birds and the bees and springtime. Contrast that with the Beatles hit of 1968 "Why Don't We Do It in the Road."[8] The Beatles were not talking about birds or bees or springtime. They were directly talking about "doing it." The mood and type of emotion involved in these two revolutions are revealingly written into these contrasting popular tunes of the two eras.

In both the 1920s' and the 1960s' sexual revolutions, there was a move toward greater equality between men and women. In 1920 the Nineteenth Amendment enfranchised women after more than seventy years of political struggle. The 1920s, like the 1960s, were a time of economic prosperity and expansion. Women were entering the labor force in growing numbers and their incomes slowly began to increase their social power. In addition, women were going to college in greater numbers than ever before, and that, too, was destined to increase their influence and change the image of the "gentler sex." Dr. Beatrice Hinkle, a physician and psychoanalyst, writing in 1924, summed up some of these early changes:

> One thing however is clearly evident: Women are demanding a reality in their relations with men that heretofore has been lacking, and they refuse longer to cater to the traditional notions of them created by men, in which their true feelings and personalities were disregarded and denied. This is the first result of the new morality.[9]

Most of us have forgotten that it was during the 1920s that feminists made their first unsuccessful attempt to pass an Equal Rights Amendment granting legal equality to women. By the end of the 1920s the feminist movement declined somewhat in influence. But it was only a pause, not an ending. The rush into the labor force by women, which started in World War II and continued into the 1960s, reignited the drive for greater female power and aided the revival of the feminist movement in this country. The 1960s, like the 1920s, also showed a sharp rise in the percentage of women in our colleges. The expectations men and women held for each other continued to alter in accordance with the new opportunities to meet and to get to know one another on the campuses and in the workplaces in our country.

Gender Equality: The Mother of Change

Each sexual revolution moved us closer to an egalitarian relationship between men and women in all spheres of life. Still we must admit that even in the late 1990s we've got a long way to go before even coming in sight of full equality between the genders. Evidence of this is that women in 1997, in the last few years of the twentieth century, comprise only 11 percent of Congress and at work earn 30 percent less pay than men do; furthermore, there are very few female rabbis or ministers and there are no female priests. Finally, even in nurturing institutions like the family, men still dominate.

But we have made some progress in gender equality. This is illustrated by the analysis of survey findings on changes in attitude that have occurred since the 1960s done by sociologist Arland Thornton of the University of Michigan.[10] A large sample of mothers in 1962, and then again in 1985, were asked to respond to the following statement: "Most of the important decisions in the life of the family should be made by the man of the house." In 1962 only 32 percent of the mothers disagreed with this statement. By 1985, 78 percent of this *same group of mothers* disagreed!

A picture of change over a shorter period of time can be seen in a different study, using a nationally representative sample. It looked at women under the age of thirty in 1977 and compared their responses with women in the same age group in 1985. Here are their responses to three questions on gender equality:

1. "It is more important for a wife to help her husband's career than to have one herself." In 1977 only 59 percent disagreed but in 1985, 83 percent disagreed.

2. "A preschool child is likely to suffer if his or her mother works." In 1977 only 47 percent of these women disagreed and in 1985, 65 percent disagreed.

3. "It is much better for everyone involved if the man is the achiever outside the home and the woman takes care of the home and family." In 1977, 57 percent disagreed but by 1985 the percent of women who disagreed jumped to 72 percent.

Finally, as an example of political changes in gender attitudes, in 1972 only 74 percent of a national sample representative of the country said they would vote for a woman president. But by 1996 that percentage had risen to 93 percent. All these findings document the fact that sizable changes in attitudes have occurred and these trends seem to be continuing at the present time.

When male and female roles change rapidly, there is always a price to pay. Major changes in the divorce rate are almost always an unambiguous sign of rapid social change. In both sexual revolutions, the divorce rate soared skywards. Between 1915 and 1920 our divorce rate increased 50 percent. That is a relatively moderate increase compared to what has happened recently—between 1963 and 1979 our divorce rate more than doubled![11] When there are extensive changes in the way men and women relate in the workplace, the schools, and elsewhere, they can no longer depend on conventional ways of interacting with each other in marriage. Each couple must privately negotiate new ways of getting along. That process is often accompanied by conflict, and more than occasionally it breaks down and ends in divorce.

We are still working out what is expected in the roles of husband and wife. Whose job comes first? Who cooks? Should a couple have children and when? Who initiates sex? Who gets up for the 2 A.M. feeding? Who pays the bills? Whose career comes first? These all become issues that need to be discussed and resolved. Sociologist Lynda Holmstrom, writing in 1972 during our years of rising divorce rates, reported on an in-depth study of twenty dual-career professional couples. One woman whose marriage broke up depicts the conflict of a modern wife with a traditional husband:

> One of the problems was that he wasn't very flexible in anything. I had to do everything. Well, I . . . don't mind doing work. But to be expected all the time to do all the work without any cooperation I think is not fair.[12]

Divorce rates have been stable or slightly down during the entire decade of the 1980s and in the 1990s have dropped a bit more. Maybe we are getting better at our new marital negotiations and expectations. But new problems have arisen. As sociologist Lenore Weitzman has pointed out in her award-winning book *The Divorce Revolution,* the new "no fault" divorce laws did not take into account the sacrifices made by wives for their husbands' careers.[13] After a divorce, a husband still has his career, but his wife often has a house that she can no longer afford to keep. This situation has pressured women to prepare better for their economic futures just in case a divorce does occur. Seeking economic independence has an impact on many parts of the female role—including the sexual. Economic autonomy reduces dependence on others and makes sexual assertiveness a much less risky procedure.

The family may still be the number one priority for most women, but the ability to earn money is running a close second. Given the poor record of child-support payments, being employable becomes essential. One divorced wife in California described her economic plight to sociologist

Lenore Weitzman this way: "There is no way I can make up for twenty-five years out of the labor force. . . . No one wants to make me president of the company just because I was president of the PTA."[14]

High divorce rates have given many people more years during which they are not married and thus more time to rethink their sexual standards. And thought is the enemy of habitual ways of behaving in sex and everything else. Those who have been through a divorce know that dating is not what it was the first time around. It's much like having a second baby—everything is speeded up and one has a better idea of what to expect. Divorced people are more open in acknowledging their sexual interests and are more aware of what they do and don't like in dating. Sexual standards often change after a divorce. For both men and women it is common after a divorce to have a period of time during which sex takes over center stage.

Sociologist Robert Weiss studied the transition to being single again. He reports what one of his divorced men told him:

> At first I went around screwing everything I could get my hands on. You go through that stage. And then you ask yourself why you did that. And then you realize that sex isn't all you want out of a relationship. And then you can start having normal relationships with people. But it took me a year, a year and a half.[15]

Divorce adds a variety of new family forms—single parents, stepparents, and even parents who marry each other a second time. About half of today's children will at some time in their lives live with only one parent. These experiences change our conception of marriage and the family. People are more likely to think about the possibility of having more than one marriage, for they know that half of those who marry today will divorce. A recent study found that fully a third of the high school senior women and 45 percent of the high school senior men in this country are unwilling to say that they will stay married for life.[16]

About 10 percent of our young people will never marry—most of them by choice. Another 10 percent will most likely never have children—some by choice and some due to repeated postponements that exceeded the time on the biological clock. The average age at first marriage has increased from twenty for women and twenty-three for men in the early 1960s to over twenty-four for women and twenty-six for men in 1996—the oldest ages at first marriage in the twentieth century!

All these changes do not mean that young people don't want to marry, that they don't want to have children, or that they don't value marriage. What the sexual revolutions did was increase the value of other choices and legitimize a wider range of choices relating to marriage. But almost all young people continue to expect to marry *someday* and have children *someday.*

Nevertheless, there is more than one script to read from today. Young people can now think about whether they want to marry, have children, remarry, live together, focus on a career, or just put off deciding anything. *The age of pluralism is arriving in our gender roles.* It makes life more interesting and exciting but also less secure and less predictable. Choices increase the ability to find a rewarding fit between lifestyle and personal values, but they also increase the need for awareness, understanding, and hopefully a bit of luck in making those choices.

Sexual practices have also become more pluralistic. One prime example is cohabitation. Young people now feel they have the right to live together without being married if they so choose. In the late 1960s there were about five hundred thousand unmarried couples living together in America. By the mid-1990s that number had reached three and a half million. It is estimated today that over 40 percent of those who marry have lived with each other before marriage. Cohabitation grew as a sign of the greater acceptance of premarital intercourse. Instead of sneaking back to their own separate quarters in the middle of the night, young people increasingly decided to be more honest about their sexual relationships and to stay together. They reasoned that if having sex with someone they cared about was acceptable, why not throw off the Victorian hypocrisy and live together?

Premarital sexual intercourse changed dramatically during the last sexual revolution. During the 1970s the percentage of women having intercourse before they married rose sharply from the 50 percent level that had been reached in the 1920s' sexual revolution. Since the late 1970s the percentage of women having premarital intercourse has surpassed the 80 percent mark and is now approaching 90 percent.[17] For men, over 90 percent had premarital intercourse, only a small rise from the 80 percent figure prevalent in the 1920s. In addition, as we discussed in the last chapter, women were starting to have intercourse at much earlier ages.

Sexual attitudes, too, had changed a great deal. In a national study I conducted in 1963, only 23 percent of Americans accepted premarital intercourse under some conditions, but by 1975 that percentage had risen to over 70 percent and in 1996 it was 76 percent.[18] Choice had become legitimate in the area of premarital sexual intercourse. Sexual attitudes on extramarital sexuality change much more slowly, but here too there seems to have been some change: more people feel that if a married couple is in the process of divorcing or if they have an agreement to accept affairs, then extramarital sexuality may not always be wrong.[19]

During most of this century, the entire Western world has been moving in the same direction toward gender equality and sexual permissiveness. The greatest amount of equality has occurred in Sweden and Denmark and the least in Spain and Ireland. We fail somewhere in between in our degree of progress toward overall sexual and gender equality. But we are all together, travelling in the same direction; only the speed of movement varies.

The Leadership Role of the Baby Boomers

The pacesetters of the sexual revolution of the late 1960s were the so-called baby boomers. They are the progeny of the millions of men and women who after World War II produced large families so quickly that startlingly high birth rates resulted. Our families had been getting *smaller* for over one hundred years, but from 1946 to 1964 American women gave birth to an average of four million babies a year. That amounts to almost twice as many babies *for each woman* of childbearing age as are born today. This dramatic rise in birth rate is what has come to be known as the baby boom. There are seventy-six million baby boomers, and if you were born between 1946 and 1964, you are one of them.

When the massive baby-boomer cohorts began to reach adolescence in the 1960s, they changed our outlook on youth. Politicians very quickly recognized a large potential constituency and in 1971 passed the Twenty-Sixth Amendment to the Constitution dropping the voting age to eighteen. The majority of states followed by lowering the legal drinking age (now restored to twenty-one by pressure from the Reagan administration). Most states then also lowered the age for all legal rights to eighteen. Business saw the great wealth this vast group of youngsters had to spend and catered to their interests. These early baby boomers were joined year after year by more fellow baby boomers like wave after wave, crashing against the shore of conventions until they permanently transformed the shape of our lifestyles.

The mothers of these baby boomers were themselves changing in ways that helped prepare their children for their future revolutionary role. During the 1950s and especially the 1960s, the mothers of the baby boomers joined the labor force in unprecedented numbers.[20] There were many reasons for this change—money for their larger families, interests in the world outside the home, the desire to be more economically independent, the desire to have a higher standard of living, and the availability of jobs in our expanding economy—all were motivations for change. Day care centers began to grow all over the country and grandparents filled in when needed.

It is remarkable that in 1950 just 12 percent of the mothers of preschoolers were employed, whereas today the figure is about 60 percent. The employment of mothers of preschoolers indicates there has been a significant change in the way people conceive of a woman's role. It shows that motherhood, though still of primary importance, can be modified because of the desire to work outside the home. That alteration decreased the difference between men and women. Men have long been allowed both family and employment as acceptable parts of their gender role.

The Victorian family with its dominant husband and full-time housewife had ironically been dealt a lethal blow at the very time that we were glorifying parenthood in the baby-boom years. It certainly isn't easy for women to combine parenthood and full-time employment, but neither was it easy to meet the demand that every woman be a full-time mother regardless of her ability or interest in doing so and despite whatever career interests she might have. Of course, pluralism would allow a woman to choose *for herself* to be a full-time housewife or any other lifestyle. There is a price to pay for every societal arrangement, but at least now a woman has more choice in her lifestyle.

The employed mother played a key role in the sexual revolution that began in the late 1960s. For one thing, her employment meant that her child probably had a greater variety of role models. Children were exposed to other adults who gave them choices that parents alone might not. Accordingly, such children were likely to become more autonomous —more desirous of running their own lives. In particular, those children had a more varied model of the role of mothers. That more flexible view of mothers expanded the acceptance by both boys and girls of female autonomy—the freedom of women to choose what they wish to do with their lives. *Now, despite Sigmund Freud, autonomy rather than anatomy was becoming destiny for women!*

The increased autonomy of baby boomers themselves meant that they did not simply pass on the traditions of their parents but were more likely to be innovative and to scrutinize their traditions carefully. And they did indeed do just that. They experimented with new sexual scripts—some wisely and some not so wisely—but they strove for a much higher degree of overall equality between men and women. The baby boomers were the generation for which our second sexual revolution was waiting. They took another giant step away from our Victorian traditions. Without a doubt, there were increases in crime and drugs and other things we are not so proud of. But they were a charismatic generation that established changes for younger and older Americans and energized our entire society. They redesigned our concepts of sexuality and gender equality in their own image. But as I shall comment upon later, unfortunately they never really finished the job. They left us as "liberated Victorians"—not fully able to enjoy our liberation or to escape our Victorianism. But they set the stage for the third sexual revolution that I will speak about later.

The Mythical Place of the Pill in the 1960s Revolution

The media and even many experts have spread the word and convinced many people that changes in gender equality and the autonomy that those changes brought were not the key causes of our sexual revolution. Here are the words of historian Bradley Smith:

> The event that was to have the greatest effect upon sexuality in the United States and, ultimately, in the world was the release of the birth control pill. . . . Young women who would never before take a chance on sex with their boyfriends for fear of pregnancy . . . adopted new attitudes towards sex. . . . The resulting freedom changed the sex habits of the nation.[21]

Smith is thus arguing that gender equality and autonomy were themselves the consequences of the development of the contraceptive pill. In this view, the pill is seen as the central force that produced the sexual revolution and the related changes in our society. The reasoning is that with the pill available the main reason blocking women from sexual equality was removed. Even in 1985, Sally Olds, a respected and well-known freelance writer, was taken in by this view:

> The turbulent 1960s ushered in the sexual revolution. . . . Advances in contraceptive technology made this surge in sexual activity possible, and may even have spurred the entire rebellious era by turning at least one oft-repeated maxim on its head, that "bad" girls were sure to get "caught."[22]

We have also had support for this view from the famous sex therapists Masters, Johnson, and Kolodny:

> The pill made premarital sex considerably safer and permitted millions to think of sex as relational or recreational rather than procreative . . . the availability of the pill provided a sense of freedom for many women and probably contributed more to changing sexual behavior than has generally been imagined.[23]

Lots of people believe this explanation and it sounds persuasive. But let me indicate why it's really not a very accurate picture of what happened.

Those who believe in the revolutionary power of the pill are pre-suming that before the sexual revolution of the 1960s women were ready and willing to have intercourse if only their worries about pregnancy were alleviated. That makes female sexual motivations much like a car with an engine running but blocked from movement by one obstacle, fear of preg-nancy. Just remove that road block and it will surely push forward. But the major block for women was not their fear of pregnancy. Women throughout this century have been subjected to a restrictive sexual upbringing. Accordingly, they have been programmed by society to start premarital sexuality, if at all, cautiously and only with the justification of serious emotional commitment. The evidence indicates that this upbringing and not the fear of pregnancy is the basic cause of female sexual resistance.

The Kinsey data gathered mostly in the 1940s supports my perspec-tive. In the Kinsey sample the primary reason for women restricting pre-marital coitus was "moral objections." That was cited as a "definite reason" by 80 percent of his sample, whereas fear of pregnancy was cited as such by only 21 percent of his sample. I should add that 32 percent of the women said that lack of sexual responsiveness was a reason for restricting coitus.[24] This lack of primary emphasis upon pregnancy doesn't mean that it was not a concern and unimportant. But for most women, whether virginal or not, moral objections drilled into them by our society were by far the more important reasons for their reluctance to have sex.

Another way to see the flaws in the "powerful pill" view of our last sexual revolution is to ask what if the pill did launch the last sexual rev-olution? If so, then today, thirty years later, we should surely find that most women starting to have premarital coitus would be on the pill. But if that were the case, we wouldn't have the Western world's highest rate of unwanted pregnancy. There is far from universal use even today. The latest data from the National Survey of Family Growth (1995) showed that only 15 percent of the women having first sexual intercourse in the 1990s were on the pill.[25]

Reluctance to have uncommitted premarital intercourse was instilled in women throughout this century by their parents and by our patriarchal traditions. In a formal sense both men and women were supposed to be abstinent before marriage, but in reality the harsher restraints and punish-ments were imposed upon women. Limiting the sexual experience of women gave husbands more confidence that their wives and girlfriends would be loyal and faithful to them. In effect this was an expression of the power of men over women. Of course, wives in our male-dominant society would not have the power to insist on equivalent behavior from their husbands.

But insisting that women be chaste doesn't stop men from having sex. Men would simply persuade some women to violate their standards and then blame the women for the transgression. That practice is the heart of the ancient double standard and I bet it still sounds familiar to almost all readers. The sexual revolution of the 1960s did somewhat mute the difference in sexual restrictions between men and women, but the difference is still very real even for young women in the 1990s. Unfair? of course, but social customs are not built on the principle of fairness—they are based far more on who has power. Just ask blacks, Jews, Hispanics, Catholics, or any other minority group about that.

Women even today feel that they cannot be as free as men for they must avoid the appearance of being too cavalier about sex. We don't live in isolation from our fellow humans. Their opinions of us and especially the wishes of those close to us influence us more than does a new contraceptive advance. A changed attitude of acceptance of sexuality among the key people in one's life makes it far easier to accept sex than does the advent of a new contraceptive technique.

Contraceptive methods are not new. In the eighteenth century, Casanova recommended that lovers use a lemon rind over the cervix to prevent pregnancy. At the 1876 Philadelphia World's Fair the most popular exhibit was the display of the new vulcanized rubber condom.[26] The diaphragm and pessary cap came into use in the 1880s. The condom, if properly used, is quite effective in preventing births.[27] The British cut their birthrate in half between 1876 and 1936 using the methods mentioned above. In our own country Jewish couples have had zero population growth rate for several generations by using these same methods. The revolutionaries of the 1920s and the 1960s did not have to wait for effective contraceptive methods. If they wanted to use them, they were already here. What they needed in order to be sexually freer was a change in the equality and autonomy our basic social institutions granted to women. Accompanying such egalitarian changes is the acceptance by one's friends and family of the right to have sex. That group support is the vital element needed for any lasting change in sexual behavior.

"Swept Away": The Escape from "Being Used"

Even today women don't fully accept their right to have sex. Dr. Carol Cassell, a well-known sex educator, has written in depth about the ways in which women in our society have been trained to feel the need to be "swept away" by passionate, romantic feelings in order not to feel "used" and to justify their sexual interests. That need was built into women by our society. I call our society's approach the "dirty glass of water" view of sexuality. Sexuality is perceived as too dirty for women to ingest unless they add a magical elixir that will purify it. The magical potion that can make the sexual water digestible is called passionate romantic love. It is mainly women who are seen as needing this special purification. In accord with my own views, Cassell describes the sexual plight of all too many women even today:

> Despite the sexual revolution, the pill, slogans of sisterhood, and media assurance that "we've come a long way," we are still not sexually free or emotionally satisfied. . . . Swept Away is a sexual strategy, a coping mechanism, which allows women to be sexual in a society that is, at best, still ambivalent about, and at worst, condemnatory of female sexuality. It is a tactic, employed unconsciously by women to get what they want—a man, sexual pleasure—without having to pay the price of being labeled wanton or promiscuous. Swept Away is, consequently, a counterfeit emotion, a fraud, a disguise of our true erotic feelings which we've been socialized to describe as romance.[28]

The persistence of the "swept away" phenomenon tells us that equality in sexuality is very hard to achieve in a society where the power of men and women is still unequal.[29]

To be sure, we have moved somewhat toward greater overall gender equality and accordingly there are more women today who feel that they do not need to be swept away in order to justify their sexuality. They may require love or friendship or just physical attraction, but in all these cases they take responsibility for their choices and do not feel the need for the excuse that they were emotionally swept away. Over fifteen years ago sociologist Lynn Atwater from Seton Hall University studied fifty wives who were having extramarital affairs. She documented the importance of sexual pleasure to these women and emphasized their desire to avoid being swept away:

> They specifically rejected traditional romantic feelings, as well as the traditional words, "in love," to describe their feelings. They did not use passion to excuse their involvements . . . women demonstrated an evolving script of female sexual expression with a common theme of female-centered sexuality, of enjoyment of oneself, of not living vicariously through one's partner . . . sexual involvement based primarily on erotic attraction to the male body, and, especially an emphasis on particular sexual activities like cunnilingus, extensive body contact, and kissing.[30]

Surely many more women would pursue sexual pleasures if they were treated as equals by men and therefore did not have to be concerned so much about whether their sexual behaviors might alienate some men. However, women would still have their requirements for a good sexual relationship beyond the physical. We all want women and men to act responsibly and honestly with each other. But if we want to achieve that important goal, we will have to equalize the distribution of power between men and women. That involves far more than simply giving women greater rights to have sex. Many women have learned that they can be free sexually but will still not be treated equally by men. Several feminist writers have noted the clash between sexual equality and inequality in social power:

> For women, sexual equality with men has become a concrete possi-
> bility, while economic and social parity remains elusive. We believe it
> is this fact, beyond all others, that has shaped the possibilities and poli-
> ties of women's sexual liberation.[31]

As long as women have less power they will feel the need somehow to please and attach themselves to these more powerful creatures called men, and sex will serve as a commodity in that pursuit. Inequality can easily lead to distrust, force, and manipulation between men and women. Women will see sex as a service to men as long as they are doing sex "his way and for him." When they have the feeling of power to pursue sex for their own satisfaction and not just for their partner's satisfactions, then the concept of sex as a service and being used will become rarities.

When there is inequality of power, men can pressure women into sexual encounters and sex can easily be used by women as a lure and a means of trying to balance power differences that exist. With unequal power the implied message from men is: "If you want me around, you better do what I want." The counter message from women is: "I have the key to your sexual satisfaction and I want some guarantees in return before I do what you want." This is hardly a sound basis upon which to build sexual relationships involving care and concern for each other.

Matriarchia: Sex in a Female-Dominated Society

Some readers, no doubt, may still be skeptical and think that sexual differences between men and women are just "natural." Well, come with me on an imaginary journey to a mythical society and I think I'll convince you otherwise. Picture yourself in a society called *Matriarchia* in which women dominate in every major institution—they hold the top political offices; they are the religious leaders; they are the leaders in the economy; they even are expected to lead in their marriages. Men are raised knowing that they have less power than the women with whom they will eventually mate. Women are the initiators in sex just as they are in every area because they are the most powerful group.

In such a society what would men do to protect the little power they did have? Men in that society would feel that their sexual attractiveness was one of the few assets they had that was valued by the more powerful group of women, and they would play those cards very carefully. Women in that type of society could easily use a man sexually and quickly turn from one man to another. So a man would have to be careful not to squander his one source of influence. Men would try to make women assure them in some way that they weren't just being used. Men in such a matriarchal society would surely be far less sexually assertive than they are in our type of society. They would see sex as a service to the women they were involved with. The risks involved in sexuality would be far greater for men in this society than in our own.

In Matriarchia women would not just sit by and let men use their masculine wiles to lure them into sexual bargaining. Women would use their greater power to get what sex they wanted. If they felt that men were not treating them right, some of them would gang up on a man and force him to perform whatever sexual acts they desired. At the same time, these women would demand faithful partners but also insist that some men be available to them for quick pleasures. To ensure male sexual restraint, women would connect sexuality to romantic love for men and tell men that when they are swept away by love for a particular woman, then and only then can they enjoy themselves sexually. Any man who violated that romantic code would be condemned and labeled a "slut." But, of course, the ruling women would not place any such negative labels on themselves.

You may be thinking that only women can get pregnant and that makes for a fixed difference between men and women. But that factor is controllable today by contraception and in my mythical society of Matriarchia, it would be the men who would be given the lion's share of the work connected with raising children. Given that duty, no matter who got pregnant, it might well be men more than women who would worry about pregnancy!

How many men reading this account would like to live in this type of society? The mirror image of that society is the heritage of women in most cultures in the world. It is not the "nature" of women to be less sexually assertive. Rather, it is the nature of human beings with little social power to be generally less assertive.

Women are not content with this state of affairs. Listen to three feminist authors commenting on women's views on sexuality:

> We are drawn, as women have been for ages, to the possibility of celebrating our sexuality without the exclusive intensity of romantic love, without the inevitable disappointment of male-centered sex, and without the punitive consequences.[32]

If we keep women economically and politically weaker than men and make sexuality the only valued currency of exchange for women, we can be sure women will be cautious in their spending habits. No two groups of people will ever look at sexuality in the same way unless they are valued in the same way by the society in which they live. If we want women and men to have equal rights to sexual expression, then we must work to create equality in the overall society between women and men. Gender equality can bring into being the values that should go with sexuality, which were discussed in the last chapter: honesty, equality, and responsibility. Social psychologist Warren Farrell is nationally known for conducting hundreds of groups of men and women dealing with gender roles. Farrell's views parallel mine on the importance of economic equality:

> I'm not saying sex should be unconditional. I am saying both sexes should have about equal conditions, which will only begin to happen when both sexes equally share responsibility for initiating—which will only happen when both sexes share equal responsibility for earning the income.[33]

To sum up, the degree of equality between men and women is the crucial determinant of whether a woman enfranchises herself with the sexual right to utilize contraceptive protection.[34] The popular view of the cause of the last sexual revolution has got things in reverse. A contraceptive advance does not legitimize your sexual rights. Believing in your sexual rights legitimizes the use of whatever contraceptive methods are available.

The Homosexual Revolution: Out of the Closet and into the Streets

Contrary to what many people think, we did not have only a heterosexual revolution in the late 1960s. There was also a very important revolution involving homosexual men and women. There were some moderate gay rights movements in the 1950s and 1960s, but they only laid the foundation for what was to come. The significant gay liberation revolt began with the Stonewall riot in New York City in 1969. At that time it was routine to harass the patrons in gay bars, but something different happened that summer night in Greenwich Village. As historian John D'Emilio describes it:

> On Friday, June 27, 1969, shortly before midnight, two detectives from Manhattan's Sixth Precinct set off with a few other officers to raid the Stonewall Inn, a gay bar on Christopher Street in the heart of Greenwich Village. . . . New York was in the midst of a mayoral campaign—always a bad time for the city's homosexuals. . . . Patrons of the Stonewall tended to be young and nonwhite. Many were drag queens and many came from the burgeoning ghetto of runaways living across town in the East Village. However, the customers at the Stonewall that night responded in any but the usual fashion. As the police released them one by one from inside the bar, a crowd accumulated on the street. Jeers and catcalls arose from the onlookers when a paddy wagon departed with the bartender, the Stonewall's bouncer, and three drag queens. A few minutes later, an officer attempted to steer the last of the patrons, a lesbian, through the bystanders to a nearby patrol car. "She put up a struggle," the *Village Voice* [July 3, 1969] reported, "From car to door to car again." At that moment, "the scene became explosive. Limp wrists were forgotten. Beer cans and bottles were heaved at the windows and a rain of coins descended on the cops. . . . Almost by signal the crowd erupted into cobblestone and bottle heaving. . . . From nowhere came an uprooted parking meter used as a battering ram on the Stonewall door. I heard several cries of "Let's get some gas," but the blaze of flame which soon appeared in the window of the Stonewall was still a shock. . . . Reinforcements rescued the shaken officers from the torched bar, but their work had barely started. Rioting continued far into the night, with Puerto Rican transvestites and young street people leading charges against rows of uniformed police officers and then withdrawing to regroup in Village alleys and side streets. By the following night, graffiti calling for "Gay Power" had appeared along Christopher Street. . . . For the next few hours, trash fires blazed, bottles and stones flew through the air, and cries of "Gay Power!" rang in the streets as the police, numbering over 400, did battle with a crowd estimated at more than 2,000. After the second night of disturbances, the anger that had erupted into street fighting was channeled into intense discussion of what many had begun to memorialize as the first gay riot in history. . . . Before the end of July, women and men in New York had formed the Gay Liberation Front. . . . Word of the Stonewall riot and GLF spread rapidly among the networks of young radicals scattered across the county and within a year liberation groups had sprung into existence on college campuses and in cities around the nation.[35]

The gay liberation movement built up the identification of gays with one another. The conflict unified homosexuals, gave them a sense of belonging, and thereby a sense of common identity. Historian John D'Emilio summed it up by noting that: "Gay liberation transformed homosexuality from a stigma that one kept carefully hidden into an identity that signified membership in a community organizing for freedom."[36]

In the 1970s thousands of young gay men and lesbian women left their small towns and headed for the cities. Pulitzer Prize winning author Frances FitzGerald described the changing scene, particularly in San Francisco, in this way:

> The gay liberationists called upon homosexuals to make an open avowal of their sexual identity. "Coming out" symbolized the shedding of self-hatred, but it was also a political act directed toward the society as a whole. . . . "We're the *first* generation to live openly as homosexuals," Randy Shilts said. "We have no role models. We have to find new ways to live."[37]

Gay organizations and publications grew in many cities, but nowhere did they flourish as in San Francisco. In the 1970s gay men by the tens of thousands migrated to the city by the bay. It is estimated today that about a third of the adult men in San Francisco are gay. When the AIDS epidemic hit, San Francisco had a politically powerful gay community that fought its way through the conflicts of those early epidemic years and came out with an organized way of coping. In contrast, cities like New York with larger gay populations but with less open gay identity were much less effective in the early handling of the AIDS crisis.[38]

It is important to note that it was not until the late nineteenth century that the term homosexual was applied as a label for a "type of person." Until then homosexual behavior was simply an act that violated Christian teaching—similar to adultery, masturbation, or fornication. It was not believed that it took a special type of person to do any of those acts. We need to regain that belief because there is no one type of homosexual person. A homosexual orientation, important as it may be, is but a part of a person's makeup. The same is, of course, true of heterosexuals. One doesn't really learn very much about a person by being told that he or she is a heterosexual. Things like our social class, politics, religion, job, and basic values determine much more about what kind of person we are than whether we are heterosexual or homosexual.

As a result of the sexual revolution, bath houses and gay bars multiplied in all major cities and gays increased their pursuit of sexual pleasures. In homosexuality, as in heterosexuality, our society's gender roles are a powerful determinant of behavior. Many gay males tend to orient themselves to sexuality just as heterosexual men do—emphasizing physical pleasure—whereas a great many lesbians approach sexuality like heterosexual women do—emphasizing emotional involvement with each other. But having said that, I must add that especially during the last ten years gay males have radically changed their behaviors and lesbian females today do not fit so neatly into any one "feminine" pattern. Therapist Margaret Nichols notes how lesbians moved in a new direction:

> Tastes in erotica became more varied and not limited to "warm" sex and many women began to prefer sex that included activities heretofore considered to be outside the boundaries of "normal" female sexuality: rough sex, "dirty" sex, role-polarized sex, "promiscuity," anonymous sex, sex without love, and sadomasochistic sex. By the mid-1980s, some women were producing pornographic magazines for lesbians such as *On Our Backs* (a takeoff on a well-known feminist newspaper called *Off Our Backs*).[39]

For lesbians the broader societal influence was visible in the fusion for many women of lesbian identity with feminism. Sisterhood was often more important than erotic pleasures, and the bond to women and the freedom from men was primary. Lesbianism, in this sense, developed the "male-free" potential of women. In contrast, the middle-class, college-educated women who founded the National Organization for Women (NOW) in 1966 were mostly heterosexually oriented feminists. Most feminists are not lesbians, but a great many lesbians do identify as feminists.

The lesbian feminist position is well put by Lillian Faderman, a professor of English Literature at California State University at Fresno:

> There is a good deal on which lesbian-feminists disagree, such as issues concerning class, whether or not to form monogamous relationships, the virtues of communal living, whether separatism is necessary in order to live as a lesbian-feminist, the nature of social action that is efficacious, etc. But they all agree that men have waged constant battle against women, committed atrocities or at best injustices against them, reduced them to grown-up children, and . . . a feminist ought not to sleep in the enemy camp.[40]

Lesbian feminists want to see a dramatic change in men's treatment of women before they will be willing to sanction heterosexuality. Many other feminists believe that "sleeping in the enemy camp" is an advantage that can encourage change toward greater gender equality.

The increased formation of gay and lesbian identities and the attempts to liberate heterosexuals from biases about gays and lesbians were essential parts of the homosexual revolution in this country.[41] As British social scientist Jeffrey Weeks sees it, the homosexual revolution of the 1970s had the objective of encouraging the realization by heterosexuals of the sexual diversity that exists in all societies, and helping to build possible ways that heterosexuals and homosexuals could coexist.[42]

It seems that just as straight women sought equality in the heterosexual revolution, the goal of the homosexual revolution was for homosexuality to be recognized as a legitimate option and for homosexuals to be treated as equals rather than as inferiors. In this sense, for both homosexuals and heterosexuals, the last sexual revolution was a movement toward greater social equality with sexuality serving as one of the lead vehicles in that pursuit.

The Deadly Mixture of Victorianism and Liberation

The rapidity of change during the sexual revolutions of this century left many with the illusion of being sexually liberated from the past. After this roller-coaster ride of social upheaval, we might well feel that everything has indeed changed. In reality the sexual revolutions of the 1920s and 1960s, instead of destroying our Victorian heritage, suppressed large segments of it in our collective psyche. The two revolutions were partial revolutions—what one might call "stalled revolutions" waiting to be finished. Without a doubt, there was considerable change, but much remains the same. The excitement of increased sexual liberation has blinded us to the sex-negative Victorian feelings residing within us. By and large, we have retained our dogmatic stance against gender equality, homosexuality, and teenage sexuality, and we continue to harbor remnants of an overall degrading and fearful view of sexuality.[43]

Each new sexual problem that arises, like teen pregnancy or date rape, breathes new life into those Victorian feelings about the degrading, demeaning, and dehumanizing qualities of sexuality. As a result instead of a reasoned response, each new crisis panics millions of Americans into emotionally running away from their newly won sexual freedoms. We have become a nation of fair-weather sexual liberals. At the first sign of a sexual storm we retreat to a more traditional position. Victorianism, though weakened, is far from dead in America. Why else would so many Americans at the end of the 1990s still think that homosexuality is immoral and so many women feel the need to justify their sexuality by being "swept away"?

Changes in sexual behavior and attitudes take time to be fully digested and to become a natural part of our lives. It is one thing to accept intellectually a new behavior and quite another to accept it emotionally. The forty years between our two sexual revolutions were a time for consolidation of our thinking, feeling, and acting in the sexual realm.[44] The dramatic changes of the last sexual revolution left us with a new consolidation problem. The sexual revolution ended in the late 1970s and only moderate changes have occurred in sexual behavior or attitudes during the decade of the 1980s. Both the remnants of our Victorianism and the societal inequalities between men and women have blocked our making further progress toward the goal of pluralism until the 1990s.

The Victorian sexual philosophy in America is part of a traditional approach to life in which male dominance is accepted and the inequality between men and women is considered proper. One basic reason why Victorianism is so difficult to eradicate is that it has the support of those who endorse the traditional philosophy in our country. But, as I will show, the 1990s offered a major opportunity for promoting a more gender-equal lifestyle and strengthening our new sexual philosophy of pluralism. The widely shared values of HER can guide our sexual acts in this pluralistic context.

Many Americans have allegiances to both our traditional *and* our pluralistic sexual philosophies. Because of this internal conflict we have fallen behind most other Western nations in gaining control over our sexual problems. One thing is clear: we need a more pluralistic view of sexuality. We need to broaden, not narrow, our sexual choices and we need to empower, not restrict, ourselves. Our freedom to make wise choices depends on our moving in this direction. It is imperative that we promote more HER values in all our basic institutions: political, economic, religious, educational, and family. Only in this way can we promote a pluralistic approach to sexuality. Despite our two sexual revolutions, many Americans are still uncomfortable in dealing with their sexuality. We are in a sense "liberated Victorians." In today's world, as the next chapter will document, that can be a fatal mixture.

5

AIDS, Condoms, and the Epidemic of Sexual Myths

"Sinful" Diseases

On July 4, 1976, as we celebrated the two-hundredth anniversary of our Declaration of Independence, the HIV virus that causes AIDS was insidiously making its way into the bloodstream of our nation. Hundreds of ships and thousands of visitors crowded into New York to celebrate our bicentennial. People poured in from every continent of the world and opportunities for international sexual and drug exchanges were very easy to come by. The celebrations lasted for many days. William Darrow, a veteran sociologist formerly at the Centers for Disease Control (CDC), believes that it was during those celebrations that the HIV infection was spread to a sufficient number of American homosexuals and intravenous drug users to start the epidemic in our country.[1]

Five years later on June 5, 1981, the CDC issued its first report on several cases of an unusual new disease, soon to be called: Acquired Immune Deficiency Syndrome (AIDS). During the five years from the initial spread of the Human Immunodeficiency Virus (HIV) in 1976, enough individuals had come down with AIDS to attract the notice of the medical community. Our two-hundredth birthday party had left us with an incredibly deadly hangover that will leave its mark on us well into the next century.

The late Randy Shilts, a San Francisco *Chronicle* reporter, in a poignant and informative political analysis described what happened after 1981 when the first cases of AIDS were reported. He carefully documented the lack of governmental support and leadership in dealing with

AIDS.[2] Shilts believed, and I agree, that if the disease had shown up initially in white, heterosexual, middle-class people, public concern and governmental support would have materialized long before the public sense of urgency was aroused by Rock Hudson's death in October 1985 or Magic Johnson's disclosure of his HIV-positive status in 1991. Shilts noted that even our blood banks refused to act and screen blood to be used for transfusions by checking for hepatitis. It was known that about 90 percent of the patients with AIDS also had hepatitis, and so such screening would have been quite effective. As a result of this hesitation, thousands of Americans and most of our hemophiliacs who rely on blood transfusions became infected with the HIV virus.

The public reaction to AIDS has been ambivalent and moralistic. Allan Brandt, a professor of the history of medicine at Harvard University, reports very similar moralistic reactions by Americans as they confronted other sexually transmitted diseases (STDs) over the past one hundred years.[3] Brandt points out that in the early decades of this century doctors and others wrongly informed the public that syphilis could be contracted by eating and drinking with infected people. Radio networks in the 1930s were even more resistant than television networks are today to talking openly about sexuality. Brandt describes how CBS refused to allow the words syphilis and gonorrhea to be spoken on the radio by the New York State commissioner of health:

> In November 1934 the Columbia Broadcasting Company scheduled a radio address by New York State Health Commissioner Thomas Parran Jr. on future goals in the area of public health. . . . Moments before airtime, CBS informed him that he could not mention syphilis and gonorrhea by name; in response to this decision, Parran refused to go on. . . . In a press release issued by his office the next day, he commented that his speech should have been considered more acceptable than "the veiled obscenity permitted by Columbia in the vaudeville acts of some of their commercial programs."[4]

In 1936, when Parran became Surgeon General of the U.S. under President Franklin D. Roosevelt, he organized a national effort to contain syphilis and gonorrhea and pressured the federal government to take more responsibility for controlling those diseases. Surgeon General Koop in the late 1980s was following in Parran's footsteps by his courageous efforts to provide government assistance in the fight against AIDS and his attempt to persuade the television networks to accept public health announcements and condom advertisements. The tragedy is that fifty years later such a battle was still necessary. The sensitivities of network customers and sponsors' dollars still carry more weight than the lives of our fellow citizens! That sort of callous, self-interested judgment illuminates what the real priorities of our television networks are.

I recall a personal incident that illustrates how our media prudery continued on radio into the 1960s. I was interviewed about my first book in 1960 by the then well-known radio personality Mary Margaret McBride. Just moments before the program began, she walked over to me and requested that I not use the words coitus or sexual intercourse on the air. I listened in amazement, for my book was a study of our premarital sexual standards concerning sexual intercourse and I could not clearly describe my book without using those words. I decided I would simply not abide by her request because I felt she had no right to restrict my comments about this important topic. The high priority she gave to fear of alienating her sponsors and segments of the audience was not my priority. I was interested in getting people to think, not in being sure that no one would be offended. The program was live and there was little she could do to stop me. Needless to say, it was my first and last interview on her show.

The manner in which our newscasters discussed AIDS between 1981 and 1985 is reminiscent of the Victorian radio standards I am talking about. Our television and radio announcers spoke then of "bodily fluids" as the cause of an HIV infection. Did they mean urine, tears, drippy noses, saliva, vaginal secretions, semen, or what? Furthermore, no one spoke of anal intercourse as riskier than vaginal intercourse because no one had the guts to use those terms on television! But after Rock Hudson's death, the public demanded to know more. The word spread that in Africa HIV infection occurs almost exclusively through heterosexual intercourse and *not* from homosexual acts or intravenous (IV) drug use. So the people in power felt at risk and things began to change in our country. Gradually after 1985 radio and television announcers began to talk in plain English in place of the Victorian gobbledygook they had previously used. Magic Johnson's bold announcement in 1991 of his HIV status as well as his outspoken support of HIV/AIDS research and knowledge helped move us forward.

A great many hospitals in earlier decades refused admission to patients with "venereal" diseases like syphilis and gonorrhea. Hospitals are freer today, but we still have doctors and nurses who refuse to treat AIDS patients even though they treat others with much more infectious and quite dangerous diseases like hepatitis. In the 1930s many viewed sexually transmitted diseases as due to "promiscuity" encouraged by the sexual revolution of the 1920s. Unlike other diseases, sexual diseases were seen as the individual's fault. Despite our somewhat more liberal atmosphere, today similar charges are leveled at people with AIDS.

We have all heard people blame those who have contracted AIDS. We don't often hear about people being blamed for contracting diseases that are not spread sexually. We would not think of saying to a polio victim, "It's your fault you can't walk. You shouldn't have gone swimming" or to a dying influenza patient, "You shouldn't have gone to that party where you picked up the bug. You deserve whatever happens." Consider also that the majority of those who have developed AIDS and died contracted the virus before we really understood the mechanism of transmission, so they had no idea that any disease so deadly was possible. Sexual diseases, in the view of many, carry the special stigma of sin and blame. The Victorian message that comes across is: "You behaved badly by having sex in an immoral fashion and so you deserve whatever you get."

Because of this moralistic response, the effective control of sexually transmitted diseases, even with our wonder drugs, has been inferior to that of other diseases. As Allan Brandt has so eloquently noted, there can be no "magic bullet," no effective cure, of any sexually transmitted disease as long as we block rational, efficient handling of sexually transmitted diseases by viewing them as "the wrath of God." Just what kind of God would give HIV infections to newborn babies, to hemophiliacs, to people unaware of how the disease is contracted, or more to the point, to anyone?

Patrick Buchanan, a former speech writer for Presidents Nixon and Reagan and a presidential candidate in 1996, is a good example of the people who take a judgmental stance on AIDS. Here is his "warm-hearted" response to AIDS sufferers: "The poor homosexuals—they have declared war upon nature, and now nature is exacting an awful retribution."[5] In the same vein, Jerry Falwell, the Baptist minister who headed the Moral Majority and who gave the benediction at President Reagan's renomination in 1984, showed how his narrow-minded moralism overwhelmed whatever Christian compassion he may have felt: "When you violate moral, health, and hygiene laws, you reap the whirlwind. You cannot shake your fist in God's face and get by with it."[6] William F. Buckley Jr., the conservative commentator, not to be outdone by the inhumanity of his fellow right wingers, recommended that there be mandatory testing for AIDS and that those found positive be tattooed on their forearms and their buttocks! Senator Jesse Helms suggested quarantining all people infected with AIDS, thereby unwittingly aligning himself with Castro in Cuba, where that is the official policy![7]

The very concept that there are special diseases associated exclusively with sexuality is quite misleading. The same diseases can be transmitted in a number of ways. To help correct this misconception the name "venereal disease" was changed in the 1970s by the Centers for Disease Control to "sexually transmitted diseases" (STDs) to indicate that these are diseases that, *in addition to other ways,* are often transmitted through sexual relations. We know, for example, that infection with HIV does occur in babies born to infected mothers, in people receiving infected blood transfusions, and occasionally in health workers who accidentally stick themselves with infected needles.[8] People often call these victims "innocent"—implying that if you got the virus through sex you are "guilty." These are words that would warm the heart of Senator Helms and make Anthony Comstock's ghost smile!

Even more commonly, infection with HIV occurs in thousands of intravenous drug users when they share HIV-infected needles with other users. Since these people are also doing something we think of as "bad" they, too, are blamed. Innocence is removed from those who behave in "immoral ways." We should remember that none of the victims of HIV were trying to get infected. Sure, some of them took great risks of infection through their behavior, but "risk taker" is quite a different label from "sinner." When we mix up those two labels, we're likely to prevent adequate treatment of AIDS.

Harvard historian Allan Brandt, to whom I previously referred, encourages us to avoid moralizing about AIDS. He notes that the medical problem is not how to encourage celibacy, but rather to discover how to avoid infection:

> AIDS has again raised the historic debate of addressing the problem of sexually transmitted diseases from a relatively dispassionate, instrumental standpoint versus the notion that only a proper moral standard will prevent their spread . . . social values continue to define the sexually transmitted diseases as uniquely sinful—indeed, to transform disease into an indication of moral decay. . . . It thus seems naive and wishful to assert that we have conquered the Victorians within ourselves, for underlying tensions in American sexual values persist, tensions that are brought forward in our approach to AIDS as well as other venereal diseases.[9]

The World Health Organization (WHO) has recently estimated the spread of the HIV virus in the world. They estimate that in 1980 there were about one hundred thousand people in the world infected with this new virus. In 1997 that estimate is twenty to thirty million people. To meet such an awesome threat we need pragmatism and pluralism, and to develop those qualities we'll have to jettison our Victorian self-righteousness.

A Therapeutic View of Wet Toilet Seats and Dry Sex

Traces of our alarmist, restrictive, Victorian view of sexuality can be found even among our so-called liberal sex therapists. The 1988 "crisis" book by world-famous sex therapists William Masters, Virginia Johnson, and Robert Kolodny is a prime example.[10] Their book stresses the risks in any heterosexual relationship that does not involve love and long-term commitment. Their position on love and commitment is a popular one in our country and it is not new for them. They had for some years before stressed the great importance of stable commitment to achieve what they call a "good" sexual relationship, and they highlighted the risks in un-committed sexual relationships.[11] In their "crisis" book they are merely being more forthright in stressing the great dangers they perceive in those less committed sexual relationships.

Most people in our country would agree that sex in a stable, affec-tionate relationship is of greatest value and is to be preferred. Some of my early work has documented and explained this American preference.[12] But there is less agreement by the public as to how to evaluate the very common types of sexuality that happen outside such deeply committed relationships. For example, is sex acceptable with someone you like but know you will leave when the summer ends? What about the value of sex in a weekend relationship with an attractive and interesting partner? What is the value of a lasting sexual relationship with someone you don't love but you like a great deal? These are very common settings for sexual encounters, and they are centered on pleasure and friendship rather than on love relationships; yet we should not forget that many of today's love relationships may well have begun as one of these other types of sexual relationships.[13]

Today, love relationships occupy only a part of the ten or fifteen years of dating that most people are involved in before committing themselves to marriage. We cannot pretend that pleasure/friendship relationships do not occur. We also know that such relationships are very likely to con-tinue to occur, regardless of the threat of AIDS. So it is all the more remarkable that Masters, Johnson, and Kolodny dismiss the physical and psychological rewards that so many people seek in such relationships by painting an extreme, inaccurate, and alarmist picture of the risks of con-tracting AIDS. They say:

> The AIDS virus is now running rampant in the heterosexual community
> . . . the fact is that it is theoretically possible to become infected with the
> AIDS virus from skin contact with a contaminated toilet seat.[14]

But Masters, Johnson, and Kolodny's own estimate is that one *unpro-tected* act of vaginal intercourse *with an infected partner* has just a one in five hundred chance of passing on the infection. This level of risk, which is only present if one is involved with an infected partner, does not seem at all to fit with their panicky view of the ease with which one can pick up the AIDS virus even from toilet seats. Sex, whether inside or outside of stable, committed relationships, *has* become more dangerous. But the real question that each of us must ponder is: has sex become *too* dangerous for us to be sexually involved on a pleasure/friendship basis or even on the basis of love, or can one reduce the risks to levels acceptable by using condoms and spermicides? As I shall show, contrary to public thinking, having many casual sex relationships when condoms are used is far safer than having long-lasting relationships when condoms are not being used.

There are those who say that if homosexuals have learned to radically change their sexual behavior, then heterosexuals will do the same. But much depends on perceived risk. Gay males know that their prevalence rate—the proportion of the gay male population that is infected—averages about one person of every five. Even so there are segments of the gay population still taking the same risks they were in the 1970s. Most have changed by using condoms for anal intercourse and making some reductions in number of partners, but only a small proportion have chosen to abstain from sex or stay with one sexual partner for the rest of their lives.

Now, "low-risk" heterosexuals (not IV drug users) have a prevalence rate much smaller than gays.[15] So the pressure for change is far less among heterosexuals. Even so, some heterosexuals are changing their sexual behavior, choosing partners more carefully, and using condoms more. But the overall rate of heterosexuals having intercourse and the number of partners do not seem to have altered very much since 1980.[16] My comments here should not be construed to mean that I think nothing needs to be changed. I feel strongly, as I will soon suggest, that condom use is the essential change to promote. But the romanticized suggestion that people should have sex only with those they love does not help at all, for it is not responsive to real human behavior and to how we are likely to get people to change. As I have noted, gays have not responded with large increases in abstinence or in monogamy, but they have responded with more caution. Surely that is the realistic direction to pursue for heterosexuals.

Another illustration of a far-out remedy came from the late sex therapist Helen Singer Kaplan, a Clinical Professor of Psychiatry at the New York Hospital-Cornell Medical Center. Her professional influence on sex therapy is second only to that of Masters and Johnson. She responded to the AIDS crisis by proposing a radical restriction on sexual behavior, which she recommended to *all* women. Her stand on the issue of AIDS fits with the type of alarmist approach found in the Masters, Johnson, and Kolodny book. Given her stature as a sex therapist and her influence on the public, her approach to the AIDS crisis is well worth examining.

Dr. Kaplan addresses her book to heterosexual women and warns them of the risks of contracting the AIDS virus from a variety of body fluids (blood, sperm, saliva, urine, and tears). Her tone is that of an authoritarian doctor giving a prescription to a naive patient. She advises women to avoid "wet sex," which includes being kissed on the nipples, deep mouth kissing, oral sex, intercourse, anal sex, and contact with sperm. The prescription is to practice "dry sex"—this permits only some sexual behaviors like rubbing up against each other, massaging each other, and masturbation. "Dry sex" is to continue until at least six months have passed after a negative test for the HIV virus. Of course, during those six months neither partner can have any "wet sex" with another person. At the end of those six months, a second HIV test is taken and if negative, and the partner is still interested, they can commence "wet sex."

Kaplan warns women that even "dry sex" requires safety precautions, and she advises the following after a woman has masturbated a man:

> You must wash immediately and disinfect the places where his semen wet you . . . only let him ejaculate on the dry parts of your body. . . . Scrub with soap and water in addition to disinfecting the area with undiluted rubbing alcohol or a dilute solution of Lysol . . . if you do not wash it off it will stay on your hands and if you bite your nails, or eat something with your fingers a few hours later, some virus might have survived and you could become infected.[17]

This is what Kaplan calls "great safe sex." Does that sound like great sex to you? How many people would abide by such a regimen? Her suggestions may be good for the Lysol company but they are impractical for most American women today. Imagine combining Kaplan's "Lysol washing" approach with Masters, Johnson, and Kolodny's "toilet seat" warning. You would have to be careful not only about semen spilling on you but also about sharing the same toilet seat. Wouldn't that make for a lovely evening?

Worse yet, Kaplan, like Masters, Johnson, and Kolodny, exaggerates the failures of condom use. No one promotes condoms as a 100 percent guarantee against infection—there is no way to engage in sex with anyone, including your spouse, and have a 100 percent guarantee against infection. But while no strategy is perfect, you will greatly decrease the likelihood of infection if you use condoms, especially if you are repeatedly having sexual intercourse with a partner who happens to be infected.

William Darrow, the sociologist formerly at CDC, whom I spoke of earlier, reports that studies of couples in which only one partner starts out infected show that with repeated, unprotected intercourse over a period of months or years, in almost half the cases the infection spreads to the other partner.[18] Of course, it is possible to become infected from just one sexual contact, and there is an artificial insemination case in the CDC records where that did occur. The use of condoms and spermicides would naturally greatly reduce, though not eliminate, the risk of transmission if one did have sex with an infected person. The fact that so many people know their partner has an HIV infection and still do not use condoms is potent testimony to the lack of public training in our culture for responsible sexual behavior.

The consensus today among epidemiologists is that although the risk is surely present for heterosexual transmission of the AIDS virus, it is an unlikely event for those who do not have partners in high-risk groups, such as intravenous drug users or bisexuals. Of course, one can't be sure that all partners will be low-risk people. A person might accidentally get mixed up with a group of high-risk people who inject drugs or are bisexual and that would increase greatly the chance of being with an infected partner. This is all the more reason to use condoms consistently. But while there surely is reason to be cautious concerning partners, there is little reason to recommend, as Dr. Kaplan has, that *all* women respond to this risk by practicing "dry sex" monogamously for at least six months with any new partner.

The decision whether to have intercourse with condom protection and spermicides, to restrict yourself to "dry sex," or to abstain depends on the value you place upon sexuality, the kind of partners with whom you are likely to interact, and the level of risk taking with which you are comfortable. Not all women would reach the same decision. Dr. Kaplan assumes she knows what is best for American women and in doing so she is prescribing *her* values and *her* risk-taking philosophy for all American women to follow.

Some women living in a high intravenous drug culture may find Kaplan's suggestions persuasive. Many other concerned, sexually active women may at first be attracted to Kaplan's "dry sex" recommendations; but upon reflection I believe it will become apparent to most of them that her approach is more a hazard than a help. In my opinion, only a minority of such women will abide by her "dry sex" guidelines for very long, and for the women who don't, Kaplan offers little else besides anxiety. Most importantly, by recommending an unrealistic course of action and exaggerating the risks of other methods, such as condoms and spermicides, she may well discourage the use of these safeguards and thus increase the risks of infection.[19] Kaplan has painted women into a tiny corner of today's sexual world and I suspect most women today would find it too uncomfortable to remain there.

Kaplan's position on this issue illustrates the perennial American "solution" to sexual problems—restricting sexuality as the only solution rather than accepting the reality of sexual behavior and encouraging improved preparation for avoiding disease or pregnancy. Such restrictive approaches simply perpetuate our sexual problems. This is so because anxiety freezes rational thought and blocks our ability to deal effectively with our problems. In my judgment, it is far better to promote condom use in vaginal and anal intercourse than to try to frighten people into restricting their sexuality by exaggerating the chance of picking up the AIDS virus from semen on your leg or from sitting on a toilet seat!

Stretching the Point: The Condom Debates

One of the central issues in controlling the spread of HIV is the question of just how effective the condom is. Most other Western countries have promoted condom use much sooner and far more freely than we have. We need to examine our hesitancy and try to explain the facts of the matter. Clearly some Americans resist even talking of condoms just as CBS radio back in 1934 resisted using the words syphilis and gonorrhea. In 1987 the "Doonesbury" cartoon strip focused for a full week on condom use as a safer sex practice. The *Deseret News* in Salt Lake City, owned by the Mormon Church, pulled the cartoon strip for that entire week. The editor and publisher, James Mortimer, noted:

> Unfortunately the six cartoon strips scheduled for this week contain subject matter that is inappropriate for the *Deseret News*. The sexual and contraceptive material presented does not meet the standards of a family newspaper.[20]

Most Americans would disagree with the editor of the *Deseret News* about what is proper to run in a family newspaper or even on television. In that same year, 1987, some 69 percent of a national sample said that condom commercials should be aired on television in order to prevent sexually transmitted diseases. In 1996 over 60 percent of a national sample favored teaching birth control to fourteen- to sixteen-year-olds even if their parents disapproved.[21] Still the television networks resisted alienating those who might object to condom advertisements. Were the networks concerned about everybody being happy or were they afraid of loss of sponsor income?

Theresa L. Crenshaw, M.D., a past president of the American Association of Sex Educators, Counselors and Therapists (AASECT), and a member of President Reagan's AIDS Commission, has testified: "For the sake of health, casual sex and multiple partners must be abandoned."[22] She called for avoidance of sexual activity with any partner outside of a "committed relationship." On other occasions, Dr. Crenshaw has pointed out the foolishness she sees in "putting a mere balloon between ourselves and a deadly virus." Here, then, was the president of a major national sex therapy and sex education organization discouraging the use of condoms. Her opposition to noncommitted relationships is in line with that of others such as Dr. Michael Osterholm, the Minnesota State epidemiologist, who said: "You can't significantly reduce risk if you have many [sexual] partners."[23] I'm sure you have all heard the "dangerous risk" point of view of condoms expressed by many others.

As noted earlier, Dr. Helen Singer Kaplan believed condoms were far too dangerous. In fact she advised women to discourage *men* from using them: "If he tells you that he's going to use a condom, you know that he doesn't know the facts, and you will have to educate him before you go any further."[24] Masters, Johnson, and Kolodny share Kaplan's distrust of condoms: "It is an illusion that condoms confer an adequate degree of protection against the AIDS virus."[25]

Note that all those who demean the effectiveness of condoms also seem to have little regard for sexual relationships without love. In my opinion they don't want to promote condom use, for that might encourage the very friendship-pleasure-based sex relationships that they feel are harmful and not worth getting involved in. By casting doubt on the safety of condoms they are discouraging couples, whether in love or not, from insisting on condom use, and that increases the risk of HIV infection for everyone.

The majority of experts at the CDC reached conclusions much more favorable to condom use. First, the experts point out that latex condoms are effective against herpes, hepatitis B, chlamydia, gonorrhea, and syphilis, *in addition to* HIV infection. So there are many reasons to use condoms besides the prevention of HIV/AIDS. They comment upon the rate of condom failures:

> Failure of condoms to protect against STDs is probably explained by user failure more often than by product failure. User failure includes failure to: (1) use a condom with each act of sexual intercourse, (2) put the condom on before any genital contact occurs, and (3) completely unroll the condom. Other user behaviors that may contribute to condom breakage include: inadequate lubrication, use of oil-based lubricants that weaken latex, and inadequate space at the tip of the condom.[26]

Estimates are that with consistent and effective condom use the failure rate to prevent pregnancy is about 2 percent. The fact that in actual practice the failure rate can be 10 percent to 14 percent is not due to defects in the condoms. It is due to *user error.*[27] The CDC experts reported that the Food and Drug Administration expanded its inspection of condoms as early as 1987. Now, the failure rate due to water leakage cannot exceed four condoms per one thousand (99.6 percent must be okay) or the entire batch is discarded.

As mentioned, there have been a number of longitudinal studies of couples where only one partner is infected. Comparisons are made in the HIV infection rate for couples who use condoms consistently, inconsistently, and not at all. The results dating back over ten years strongly support the protection afforded by condom use. Margaret Fischl's early work indicated that among couples who did not use condoms there was five times the likelihood of the uninfected partner becoming HIV-infected.[28] And the condom use was not consistent for most couples who did use them. More recent studies show five to ten times the likelihood of infection if condoms are not consistently used. In two recent studies the percent of consistent condom users whose partner became infected was between zero and 2 percent. Condom breakage rates were reported to be 2 percent or less for vaginal or anal intercourse.[29]

William Darrow reports on a study of 568 prostitutes. Sixty-two of them were HIV positive, but none of these cases occurred among those prostitutes who always used condoms. Nancy Padian, an epidemiologist at San Francisco General Hospital, summed up her analysis of studies concerning the effectiveness of condoms in her paper at the Fifth International AIDS Conference in Montreal by saying; "Condom use has been verified as effective in many recent studies."[30] To ignore the reports of all these experts is to allow a personal distaste for the kind of sex that condoms may imply to distort reality. There's far too much at risk to permit that to happen.

Evidently Crenshaw, Kaplan, Masters, Johnson, and Kolodny failed to examine carefully the early research even though they were aware of those studies. In addition, they knew the laboratory studies supported condom effectiveness against HIV infection.[31] Masters, Johnson, and Kolodny even cited those studies in their book:

> The condoms were filled with a fluid containing very high concentrations of the AIDS virus—about 5,000 times greater than the amounts found in semen—and were subjected to pressure, but there was no evidence that the virus leaked out of any of the condoms tested.[32]

It is indeed puzzling! Given all this evidence over the years, how can anyone conclude that condoms are "too dangerous" to recommend? I believe that the low personal value placed on sexuality not based on love is what pressures many people toward such an erroneous conclusion. All these anti-condom writers have indicated their low opinion of friendship/pleasure types of sex and have stressed the importance they place on committed love relationships. No one could object if these writers had said this was their *personal* position. But when they promote engaging only in "committed" sex as "scientific" advice based on "proof" of "unacceptably high" condom failure rates, one begins to see that their scientific judgment may well have been compromised by their personal values.

Fortunately, many people reject the far-fetched advice of the sex therapists we've discussed above. More people are resorting to condoms to protect themselves against AIDS. Sales of condoms have risen considerably since 1985. Women seem to buy over 40 percent of the over one million condoms sold every day. At about the same time the percentage of unmarried women who were currently using condoms as their contraceptive method rose sharply and favorable attitudes toward condoms also have increased.[33]

Another recent study found more dramatic increases in condom use between 1979 and 1988 for teenage youths. In 1988 more than half of fifteen- to nineteen-year-old men reported condom use at last intercourse. The use of condoms had more than doubled for seventeen- to nineteen-year-old young men.[34]

With a large potential market, there is no question that we will see condom companies invest more in the development of improved condoms. Condom machines are now appearing in college dormitories and condoms that females can use are being developed. Our sexual ambivalence is self-destructive, for it opens wide a passageway for the deadly HIV infection. For our own safety we should strongly encourage every effort to increase our protection through condoms.

Once again women are put at the greatest risk. As in virtually every sexually transmitted disease, women run a greater risk than men of contracting HIV. Semen carries the HIV virus and unless condoms are used the infected semen will stay in the area of the vagina and uterus and spread the infection. Roy M. Anderson, an internationally renowned AIDS expert, estimated that "the transmission of the virus from male to female is three times as efficient as from female to male."[35] This helps explain why 40 percent of the condoms in this country are bought by women.

Does Love Mean Never Having to Say You're Infected?

The common advice about condom use says, "*if* you have more than one partner, always use condoms. . . ." Clearly there is no expectation of condom use if you at one point in your life have only one partner. The "good" way to have sex doesn't require that. Bear in mind that most people have more than one lifetime sex partner and thus are "monogamous" several times during their lives. Just how safe is it during these "monogamous" periods to have sex if you're not using condoms? What if your partner goes out and has another partner while going with you? What if your partner never had a blood test, lied about the results of the blood test, or covered up his or her past drug or sex experience? Just how safe is this so-called monogamous, committed sex? How do the risks of monogamy compare to the risks involved in having several partners while carefully using condoms with each partner?

It's true that *one* source of risk comes from having many partners. With each new choice you gamble that the new partner might be infected. But the question is just *how much more* risk each new partner adds versus how much risk you are taking by focusing on one partner and not using condoms. The facts, as I will spell them out, show that failure to use condoms with just one or two partners is far *more* risky than having even twenty partners, *if you carefully and consistently use condoms with these twenty partners.* Focusing your sexual interactions on one partner can be downright dangerous, especially if that person happens to be infected and you're not using condoms.

Together with a colleague of mine at the University of Minnesota, Professor Robert Leik, I set out to test whether reducing the number of sexual partners or using condoms was the more effective strategy for avoiding HIV infection.[36] Of course using both strategies is the safest policy—reduce partners *and* use condoms with every partner you do have. But most people do not use condoms with people they are regularly having sex with and so most people have to choose between reducing partners or using condoms.

Leik and I developed a computer model for measuring the risk of becoming infected. We examined whether the risk of contracting an HIV infection would be lower for people who reduced the number of partners but did not use condoms compared with those who did not reduce the number of partners but did use condoms. Our estimates for the percentage of people infected covered a range of different lifestyle groups, from high-risk groups where one person in four was assumed to be HIV infected to low-risk groups where one person in five thousand was assumed to be infected. In between were American college students, a group in which it is estimated that one student in five hundred has an HIV infection.[37] We also looked at situations where the HIV infection was easily passed on because people were having unprotected anal intercourse or because one partner had a strain of the virus that was exceptionally infectious. In addition, we studied situations where only low-risk sexual behavior was occurring. Condom failure rates were varied from 10 percent to 75 percent. The condom failure rate indicates the percentage of the times one is sexually involved that the condom fails to provide protection from exposure to the HIV virus.

In short, our comparisons included a very wide range of situations so that we could determine whether under all these various conditions using condoms or reducing the number of partners was the safer strategy to adopt to lower one's chances of getting infected. In our model we used a five-year period and assumed that on the average people engage in one hundred sexual acts per year. In this way, we were able to report which strategy produced the least likelihood of HIV infection at the end of that five-year period.

What we found was a remarkably clear answer to our question. Under virtually all the possible conditions *the risk of HIV infection was increased far more by not using condoms than by having multiple partners.* Based on these findings we conclude that it is significantly riskier to focus on just one or two partners and not use condoms than to have twenty or even one hundred partners and use condoms. This holds true under all of the many conditions examined when we assume a condom failure rate of 10 percent, and under almost all conditions even with a condom failure rate of 25 percent. Those failure rates are quite high and effective usage of condoms would likely ensure far greater reductions of risk—closer to 2 percent failure.

Some may question how using condoms with twenty or more partners can be so much safer than not using condoms with only one or two partners. The answer is that when you confine your sexual activity to one partner, if that partner is infected, you have a much higher chance of picking up that infection. This can be compared with the risk of catching a cold virus. If you choose to interact with only one person, you have cut the odds of picking a partner with the cold virus, but if the person you interact with has the cold virus, you are almost certain to become infected with it. If you come in contact with many people, you do increase the risk of interacting with a person that has the cold virus, but you decrease the risk of picking up the virus since you are not interacting with any one person for very long. Now if you take a preventive medicine that reduces the likelihood of being exposed to the cold virus to 10 to 25 percent, even when you come in contact with a person who has the virus, then it is obviously safer to use the preventive medicine and move from person to person than to focus on one person without taking the preventive medicine.

What if you and your partner both test negative for the HIV virus? Is monogamy then safe without using condoms? It would be safe if your partner told you the truth about the test results and if the test was accurately done and if in addition you and your partner remained faithful to each other. In such a case, not using a condom is almost as safe as using one, but you and your partner must be free of the HIV virus and must be 100 percent likely to remain faithful to each other The problem is that most of our young people don't stay with one partner for life and they still don't use condoms when they are having these "monogamous" affairs.

Compounding the problem is the all too common misconception, especially among young people, that the pill protects a woman from disease. In a national study of eighth to tenth graders, 55 percent of the students did not know that birth control pills do *not* prevent sexually transmitted diseases and 35 percent did not know that using condoms was effective in avoiding sexually transmitted diseases![38] That lack of knowledge demonstrates how inadequate most of our sex education programs are. Knowledge is greater today, but far from 100 percent.

The great majority of Americans will have more than one lifetime sexual partner; between five and ten premarital partners is not uncommon, plus more from extramarital sex, divorce, or remarriage. In a 1983 national sample of women in their twenties, an average of five sexual partners was reported. In a 1988 national sample, of the single eighteen- to twenty-four-year-olds, some 40 percent of the men and 15 percent of the women reported having three or more partners in the last twelve months and over 80 percent of these single eighteen- to twenty-four-year-olds had at least one sexual partner in the last year. Two different 1988 national samples reported on the number of partners our sexually active teenagers have had. Thirty percent of the teenage women had four or more partners and the average number of partners for the teenage men was over five.[39] The 1995 survey of ninth to twelfth graders reported that 18 percent of those students already had four or more partners.[40] So it seems ill-advised to put our preventive hopes on expecting people to have only one lifetime partner.

If we set aside any moral feelings about having many sexual partners, it will become clear what advice should be stressed if we want to best protect our young people from infection: Learn early, and learn well, to use condoms! We can't predict at any one point in time how many sexual partners we will have and so we must act to protect ourselves. Instead of trying to convince ourselves that we are selective and "moral," first we have to make ourselves safe. As Karl Malden used to say, "Don't leave home without it!"

One good illustration of the price of focusing only on limiting the number of sexual partners is highlighted when we examine heterosexually HIV-infected women. *The typical HIV-infected woman is not promiscuous. She is in a monogamous relationship with a drug addict.* Most of the male heterosexuals infected with HIV are intravenous drug users and most of the women who pick up the infection heterosexually are their regular sexual partners. A woman takes the highest possible risk of infection if she enters a monogamous relationship with an intravenous drug addict who may well not know he is infected. Staying with an IV drug user and not using condoms is the all too common means of heterosexual infection. Even if he took an HIV blood test before she started having sex with him, the next needle sharing could infect him. Science writer Michael Fumento has put it very cogently:

> Practically all heterosexually transmitted AIDS cases are found in steadily monogamous or virtually monogamous relationships with IV drug users or, much less commonly, with bisexuals, since only such a relationship can expose one frequently to infection.[41]

The medical AIDS research team of Hearst and Hulley sum up their advice on condom use:

> Condoms with spermicide should be used whenever people are uncertain about the risk status of a sexual partner. Even when they have chosen a partner they believe is at low risk, some people may choose to use condoms and/or spermicides to reduce further their risk of becoming infected.[42]

The Institute of Medicine of the National Academy of Sciences is one of the most respected scientific associations in the country. I served on one of their special committees on AIDS and I have high regard for their expertise. Their special AIDS committee made the following statement about condom use and some of the obstacles to its promotion:

> Condoms have been shown under laboratory conditions to obstruct passage of HIV. They should be much more widely available and more consistently used. Young people, early in their sexually active lives and thus less likely to have been infected with HIV, have the most protection to gain from the use of condoms. . . . The committee recognizes that the reluctance of governmental authorities to address issues of sexual behavior reflects a societal reticence regarding open discussions of these matters. . . . If government agencies continue to be unable or unwilling to use direct, explicit terms in the detailed content of educa-

tional programs, contractual arrangements should be established with private organizations that are not subject to the same inhibitions.[43]

Since there is no certain way to identify who is infected and thus to avoid sexual contact with that person, the primary concern must be to reduce the chance of picking up an infection no matter what partner is chosen. The number of partners becomes a major factor only when there is no effective method available to reduce the chance of picking up the infection or there is a very high rate of infection in your group of potential sexual partners. The condom is not foolproof, but a much higher proportion of those who use condoms turn out to be free of HIV infection. If we can set aside our bias against having several lifetime sexual partners, not all of whom will be people we love, then we will be more likely to live until we do meet someone we love.

My conclusion stressing condom usage over partner reduction will not be happily received by some people. When Professor Leik and I submitted an early draft of our paper to a very prestigious journal, a reviewer advised the journal editors against publication, saying: "You wouldn't want to be seen as promoting or approving multiple partners." That speaks volumes about how politics takes precedence over scholarship and concern for public health. Many people are like this anonymous reviewer; they promote the illusion of "morality" because they lack the courage to risk their own reputation even in the interest of saving lives.

Remember—our best judgment today is that most everyone who becomes HIV infected will develop AIDS although it will take ten years for half and perhaps more than fifteen years for most of the other half to show the symptoms of AIDS.[44] The 1996 HIV "cocktail" using protease inhibitors together with other drugs is very promising: it can delay the onset of AIDS and does seem to increase the chances of long-term survival. Eventually we may have a vaccine to prevent HIV infections, but that will not likely happen for at least five or ten years. For now the best we can do is to accept the reality of American sexual behavior and stress the importance of using condoms carefully and effectively.

The Anxious Fantasy of Group Sex

Theresa Crenshaw, the well-known sex therapist and medical doctor to whom I have referred previously in this chapter, has been an advocate of another very widely accepted misconception concerning the spread of AIDS. In a television interview she stated: "When you're having sex with someone today you're having group sex. You're having sex with everyone they've had sex with in the last ten years."[45] This is a popular view even today and it does sound reasonable. After all, if your partner had sex with someone infected with HIV or any other sexually transmissible infection, then you will be exposed. Right? No! It is anxiety and not logic that leads to that conclusion. It is one more sexual myth that we find easy to believe because it attacks pleasure-centered, nonmonogamous sexuality about which we have so many Victorian misgivings.

Let's examine this "group sex" view more carefully. First, if we are dealing with diseases like gonorrhea or syphilis, we have very effective treatments for them. Millions of people who were infected received treatment and are no longer infected. Second, even if one partner is currently infected, there is no certainty that this partner will transmit it to the other. The odds become even more remote when figuring the chances of one partner picking up an infection plus the chances of that partner passing it on to the next partner and so on. To illustrate this, consider that the chances of picking up an HIV infection from one act of unprotected vaginal intercourse with an infected partner are one in five hundred.[46] The chances of your current partner having picked up an HIV infection that way from his or her last partner and then passing it on to you in one act of vaginal intercourse are one in five hundred multiplied by one in five hundred or one in two hundred and fifty thousand. This approaches the odds of being killed in an automobile accident while out on a date with that partner.[47]

The HIV infection is one of the sexually transmitted diseases that is most difficult to contract. Again, I am not minimizing the consequences but rather emphasizing that because it is difficult to contract, it is possible to protect oneself. As I mentioned, there is but one chance in five hundred of being infected from one unprotected act of vaginal intercourse with an infected partner. Now, that is an overall average and there are times when the HIV virus is more infectious. Some evidence indicates that the virus is more infectious in a person who has recently become infected. A second time of high risk is when the symptoms of the disease of AIDS develop, several years later. Another way that risk is increased is by engaging in anal intercourse, particularly for the receptive partner, that is, the person in whom the penis is inserted. The tissues in the intestines bleed easily and are very thin and so infection can spread much more easily there than in vaginal intercourse.

But even with these qualifications the general risk of contracting HIV is small compared to other STDs. Still, an HIV infection is life threatening and so even small risks may well be frightening. Gay males have acted to cut these odds down—a study showed as early as 1987 that almost 80 percent of gay males used condoms when they did engage in anal intercourse.[48] It is doubtful that heterosexual couples practicing anal intercourse are also taking such precautions.

Based on current estimates, it would take a few hundred *unprotected* acts of vaginal intercourse with an infected partner before a person would have a fifty-fifty chance of infection.[49] Therefore, even if a person or his or her sexual partners had been exposed, infection may well not have occurred. So the popular statement made by Crenshaw and repeated by many others that "you are having sex with everyone your partner had sex with" is alarmist, for it implies that sexual contact guarantees infection. Your partner is very unlikely to have every disease that every former partner may have had. Only if there were perfect transmission of the infection to every partner would that make any sense. It is a prejudiced belief that comes from our willingness to believe anything bad about having many sexual partners. Underlying this belief are the vestiges of Victorian prudery.

Our Blindness to the Dangers of Abstinence

Even if condoms do make the sexually active much safer, what about the strategy of abstinence? Isn't that still the safest idea? The promotion of condom use is often drowned out by those who insist that abstinence is the only safe way to prevent an HIV infection, particularly for teenagers. The Surgeon General's 1988 brochure says that abstinence is the safest strategy and millions of parents believe that to be true. How could it be otherwise—if you don't have sex, you won't get infected! But there is a fatal flaw in this logic. *In actuality, abstinence is a much more dangerous path to pursue than condom usage.* Let me explain why.

The blind spot in our vision of abstinence is that a "strategy" alone does not guarantee that people will abide by it. It is an extraordinary fact that virtually no one in our society seems to accurately estimate the risk factor in the abstinence strategy. To evaluate the risk involved in *pursuing* abstinence, one cannot assume that everyone is a perfect adherent and always *achieves* abstinence in his or her behavior. We must calculate in our measure of risk the proportion of people who *fail* in the pursuit of abstinence. Otherwise, we're not facing reality and not making a fair evaluation of the chances that the abstinence strategy will reduce HIV infection.

Consider this: What if we assumed that all condoms and all condom users were perfect? We would then erroneously view the use of condoms as without any risk. Nobody would accept that as a fair estimation. The proper way to judge condom effectiveness is to estimate the *actual failure rate of condoms* in everyday life. By the same token, the fair way to judge the strategy of pursuing abstinence is to estimate what proportion of people *break their vows of abstinence* and what risks of infection they then encounter. We can no more assume that every believer in abstinence invariably abstains from sex any more than we can assume that every condom user will have perfect condoms and be a perfect user.

When one makes an unbiased comparison of promoting abstinence vs. promoting condom use, the results are obvious. *Vows of abstinence break far more easily than do condoms.* Many youngsters start out at age ten believing that abstinence is right for them and most of them are encouraged by their parents to continue that belief until they are out of high school. But before our teenagers are out of their teens over 80 percent of them will be sexually active. Because of the emphasis on abstinence, many of these sexually active young people will not have been prepared to protect themselves from pregnancy, HIV/AIDS, or other sexually transmitted diseases. Promoting only abstinence can be dangerous for our children.

So at some point, usually in their last year or two of high school, most girls will start having intercourse and the stronger the abstinence training the longer the time during which there will be ambivalence about having intercourse. But for most girls, intercourse will occur despite their misgivings. We discussed in chapter 3 that those who are sexually experienced but are conflicted about their sexual behavior are among the poorest at contraception. So the attempt to impose abstinence as the only right sexual standard for all young people means that millions of our teenagers are at high risk of contracting an HIV infection as well as dozens of other serious sexually transmitted diseases and unwanted pregnancies.

The conclusion I reach is that since most young people will engage in intercourse, we only increase their risk of HIV infection by trying to block intercourse instead of emphasizing and legitimizing careful condom use for all acts of sexual intercourse that may occur. I am not saying that we should encourage them to have sexual intercourse; rather we should make it clear to them that *if they do,* they should be certain to use condoms.

I realize that my evaluation is precisely the opposite of that given by many experts and lay people in our country. Nonetheless, it is a rather obvious conclusion if one considers the issue impartially. In a world like ours where the great majority are sexually active, the choice of parents is to deliberately prepare their children for safer sex in case they choose to have sex, or to try to impose abstinence on them, thereby allowing them to drift into sex unprepared to protect themselves or their partners.

A category of people who are at an even higher risk of HIV infection than those trained in abstinence are those who believe in the right to have premarital coitus but who simply do not bother to use condoms. This group is without a doubt taking the highest risks. Unfortunately, young people living in poverty often display this behavior. The fatalism which I discussed in chapter 3 leads some impoverished people to believe it doesn't matter much what they do because their lives have no meaningful direction anyhow. Day-to-day living is problematic, and therefore concern about disease and pregnancy takes a back seat to that basic ongoing life pressure.

Earlier in the book I alluded to the importance of social power in understanding our sexual crises. Nowhere is social power more crucial than in the area of AIDS. Blacks and Hispanics make up only about 22 percent of our population, but they comprised the majority of AIDS cases in 1996.[50] The heavy reliance on IV drugs in our impoverished neighborhoods is one of the major reasons for this high AIDS rate. The same difference in other sexually transmitted diseases is striking.[51] In our own society we are creating an underprivileged, high risk, Third World segment in our major cities. This is not only undemocratic and unfair, but it is a pool from which AIDS is increasingly spreading into the overall heterosexual population. It's about time we stopped promoting abstinence and started to do something to help this impoverished segment of our population.

I know my suggestion that we become more pluralistic and refuse to allow abstinence to be the only moral standard for our children will disturb many readers. Abstinence has been such sacred ground that very few have questioned its worth, at least for teenagers. But we must face reality. The deference to abstinence is an amazing testimony to the paralyzing grip our Victorian past has on our present-day thinking. We need to realize that, in today's world, "old-fashioned" sexual morality may *increase* rather than decrease our risk of infection! To put it bluntly, dogmatic sexual beliefs can actually put the lives of our children at risk! One of the major purposes of this book is to show how we unknowingly promote our sexual crises. It is time to fight back against this hazard just as we would against any other lethal threat to our children.

Special Risks for Gays and Straights

Most researchers report unprotected anal intercourse as the sexual practice most likely to lead to an HIV infection. Warren Winkelstein, a professor of Public Health at the University of California in Berkeley, has been following a sample of men in San Francisco since 1984. He estimates that the risks increase perhaps tenfold with anal intercourse (homosexual or heterosexual) as compared to vaginal intercourse.[52] The highest risks involve "receptive" anal intercourse where semen is deposited and allowed to spread into the bloodstream. The great majority of gay males with AIDS today were infected through anal intercourse.

We often forget that anal intercourse is practiced by both gay and straight couples. Anal intercourse is estimated to be the preferred sexual act for about half of gay men. It is also estimated that about 10 percent of the married couples in America have had anal sex at least once in the last year. This is also true of a significant proportion of couples who are not married.[53] These behaviors would put several million people in both gay and straight groups at special risk. Nevertheless, although anal intercourse affords a dangerous route of infection, condoms with spermicide can significantly lower that risk. Still, condom breakage in anal intercourse is reported to be higher than in vaginal intercourse especially for the inexperienced. There is more need for patience and the use of water-based lubricants to ease entry into the anus. Also, the use of two condoms or the development of stronger condoms would be helpful and research on this is currently underway.[54]

It is important that all people, gay or straight, realize the exceptional risks involved. Gay men do seem well aware of these risks and most are modifying their behaviors, but heterosexuals are much less aware of the risks involved.[55] Perhaps straight males don't wish to recognize the similarity between their acts of anal intercourse and gay male anal intercourse. But the partners of straight men are at risk of infection, and so women must be encouraged to insist on condom use in any sexual act that penetrates the body. Oral sex that transfers semen from the penis or blood from the vagina is a risk, even though researchers feel it is a far lesser risk. Condoms and latex squares are being used by some to reduce the risk of infection in oral sex. It may at first be distracting to think about all these risk situations, but it's much better to be distracted than infected.

Eroticizing Condoms and Making Realistic Choices

But how do we counteract the myriad of negative beliefs about condoms? This negative image has been so effective that not until 1970 was even *Playboy* magazine willing to take advertisements for condoms. If we agree that condom usage is a very efficient strategy for reducing the chance of infection, how do we promote condom usage? Many people think of condoms as "interfering with pleasure" and as a sign that a person doesn't trust his or her partner. To change such attitudes we must create a favorable image of condoms.

Japan is a country that has developed a positive view of the condom by eroticizing it. There the condom is the predominant method of birth control. Since 1967 door-to-door saleswomen transported by minibuses have sold condoms to wives and have given them information on how to make the condom part of sexual arousal. The condom has become a way of expressing concern for the other person and not just a way of protecting your health. It is the method of choice for over two-thirds of the married couples. Because of this tremendous use of condoms, Japan has the lowest rate of AIDS of any industrialized country in the world.

Thinking of the condom as an interruption of lovemaking is a counterproductive attitude. It must become part of lovemaking, perhaps by letting the woman put the condom on the man manually or orally. There are some erotic video tapes (*Behind the Green Door: The Sequel,* 1986) that show males who routinely use condoms in ways that are presented as sexually exciting. Another way to produce positive images of condoms is to stress how condom usage permits one to focus on sexual pleasures and relieves fears of disease and pregnancy. There are books that help people feel comfortable about using condoms and give them specific suggestions for eroticizing condoms.

> Try to include your partner in the act of putting the condom on. If your partner puts it on for you, it can be part of your erotic play. If you'd rather put it on yourself, face your partner and let your partner watch. What may seem clinical or even embarrassing at first can become a sexy part of lovemaking.[56]

Plainly we need to do more than just weaken the negative image of the condom—we need to promote its erotic and positive image. Professionals at family planning agencies and high school clinics know that the condom has a bad reputation. It is associated with disease and prostitution. The condom, they point out, needs to become a sign of concern for the other person and the mark of a thoughtful approach to sexuality.[57]

We certainly have the advertising talents to sell an erotic, caring, and responsible image of condoms to the public. We have the best business minds in the world here and I am convinced that we will eventually do this. The Swedes undertook to do this in the early 1970s with much success. They targeted the opinion leaders and trade and consumer groups to help make condoms respectable. They developed an advertising campaign using humorous drawings about condom usage and, as described in chapter 3, these drawings were then placed on large billboards in major cities. The Swedes also made condoms available in machines on the streets of Stockholm. As a result, they brought their gonorrhea rate down remarkably in just a matter of a few years.[58] Leadership and support in this area belong in our top-priority category.

Part of promoting condoms is to prepare our children to use them. Such preparation involves far more than simply saying to a teenager, "If you can't be good, be careful." That sort of approach doesn't sufficiently endorse responsible selection of partners and conscientious use of condoms. If we want young people who have intercourse to use condoms, then condom use must be enthusiastically and vigorously promoted for those who become sexually active. Such full support for the necessity of responsible condom use is essential to taking control of our sexual lives.

We need social guidelines and support for promoting what I referred to in chapter 3 as the value of pluralistic sexual relationships. To do this we must speed up the HER-compatible changes in our social institutions. Clearly poverty and inequality are key promoters of sexual diseases. We cannot stop our young people from having sex but we can encourage them to avoid exploitation and deception in sexuality and to promote honest, equal, and responsible sexual relationships. We can breathe new life into our pluralistic values and preserve our sexual rights by learning how to choose wisely.

If Not Now, When?

The myths our society has promulgated about HIV infections are very dangerous. From our discussion of condom safety, monogamy, fear of disease transmission from previous partners, and abstinence as a strategy, it should be obvious that the public has been misled by the sexual traditionalists in our society. The consequences can be disastrous for us and our children. This is a powerful illustration of how our residual Victorianism blocks us from seeing the realities of today's sexual world and inhibits us from speaking up even when our own interests are at stake.

The new victims of the AIDS epidemic in the late 1990s are increasingly women and children. The virus has spread to them, particularly among the poor. We need to remember that in Africa and parts of the Caribbean HIV infection is spread predominantly through heterosexual intercourse. We will witness a wider heterosexual spread in this country unless we discard the sexual myths that the fearful Victorians among us promote. We now estimate that almost one million people carry the virus and that we are adding to this total over forty thousand new cases of HIV infection every year.

As of December 1996 we have had over 581,000 cases of AIDS, with over 60 percent of those people having died.

If there ever was a time when the American people needed to remove the traditional sexual blinders, it is now. Pluralism offers us the best hope of dealing with the deadly plague of AIDS with wisdom and compassion. The ethical guidelines of promoting HER in our sexuality are central to containing HIV/AIDS. We cannot afford to miss this opportunity. If we do, we place our lives and those of our children in jeopardy.

6

Clarifying Our Fantasies about Pornography

Mirror, Mirror, on the Wall, Who Is the Dirtiest of Them All?

Have you ever seen a pornographic film? Some readers might respond: "What does he mean by pornographic? Most of us have seen movies like *Dirty Dancing, Dangerous Liaisons, Showgirls, Striptease,* or *The Unbearable Lightness of Being,* but are they pornographic?" If we don't get legalistic or moralistic, it is fairly easy to put forth a clear definition of pornography. The original Greek meaning of the word translates literally into "writings about prostitutes." These writings were intended to sexually arouse the reader and the word pornography became the label for all such writings.[1]

Today, in addition to books, pornography includes films, art work, sculpture, poetry, photos, or any other presentation aimed at sexually arousing the audience. Some of the scenes in the popular movies named above could be called pornographic, for they clearly were aimed at sexually interesting the viewer. X-rated movies are distinct only in that they seek to sexually arouse the audience in almost all their scenes. Those that try to arouse in particular ways, such as focusing on erections and vulvas, are called "hard core." But all movies, books, or other materials that aim to arouse do, to that extent, fit the common broad meaning of the term pornography.

As usual, it is the legal question that causes confusion. What is the difference between legal and illegal pornography? In America all pornography is legal except that which can be shown to be "obscene." To be "obscene," according to the rulings of our Supreme Court, the material must be "prurient" or "improperly arousing," violate "community standards," and have "no serious value" to fields like science, education, or art. These are quite vague requirements and difficult to measure. In 1964, Supreme Court Justice Potter Stewart added to this confusion by admitting that he couldn't define what material is obscene: "But I know it when I see it," he still concluded. Such legal mumbo jumbo opens the door to abuse of our First Amendment rights. If a jury is convinced that a movie, video, or a book fits all of the legal requirements mentioned above, vague as they are, then that material is not protected by our First Amendment rights to free expression and it can be confiscated and banned. It seems that this is the "land of the free" only if a jury doesn't think a form of expression is "obscene."

If we viewed sexuality in a more positive light, would we be so concerned about movies or books that arouse people sexually? It is time for us to get rid of this incoherent legal concept of obscenity. By this time in American history, shouldn't grown-ups be pluralistic enough to accept portrayals of sexuality for others even though they personally do not like them? But many Americans see sexuality as very dangerous, and therefore they think that sexual arousal is likely to lead people to do all kinds of harmful things. Accordingly, we have restricted the First Amendment rights to free speech in the area of sex and virtually nowhere else!

Our reactions to sexually arousing films or books provide insight into our personal sexual attitudes. What we really are reacting to is not the objective material but rather a projection of our own innermost feelings concerning the type of sexuality presented. We may feel that the sexuality being portrayed is too revealing, too embarrassing, too suggestive, or too private. Our fears and misgivings about sexuality are revealed in our negative reactions to explicit materials. What we take pleasure in also speaks to our sexual attitudes. If asked, most people would say that they are not afraid of or against being sexually aroused, but they want it to be in a "morally acceptable" way. But what are the "morally acceptable" ways to be turned on?

In the 1970s some feminist leaders like Robin Morgan and Gloria Steinem began to select those forms of pornography that they favored, which they called "erotica." These feminists did not want to use erotica to cover all types of turn-on materials. Instead they chose to narrow the usual meaning of erotica to include only those sexually explicit portrayals that they felt did not "objectify," "degrade," or "subordinate" women but treated women with affection and as equals. They then redefined pornography to be the label for only the "bad" type of sexually explicit portrayals, which they felt did "objectify, degrade, or subordinate" women.

This new terminology appealed to some feminists, for it reflected their personal view of sexuality—but did it really clarify things? Who is to say what objectifies, degrades, or subordinates women? Is a woman kneeling in front of a man and performing fellatio being "degraded"? How about a man kneeling in front of a woman and performing cunnilingus—is he being "degraded?" As Ellen Willis, a staff writer for the *Village Voice,* has commented: "Attempts to sort out good erotica from bad porn inevitably come down to: What turns me on is erotic; what turns you on is pornographic."[2]

Many feminists reject the Morgan and Steinem classification, for they see it as too limiting to insist that turn-on materials must portray mutual affection and equality between the lovers. Feminist Gayle Rubin gave a devastating description of this narrow view of "erotica":

Sex has to occur in a certain way for it to be good. And the only legitimate sex is very limited. It's not focused on orgasm, it's very gentle and it takes place in the context of a long-term, caring relationship. It's the missionary position of the women's movement.[3]

Ellen Willis further criticizes this attempt to limit acceptable erotica and puts forth an insightful analysis of what's wrong with that tactic:

At present . . . the sexual impulses that pornography appeals to are part of virtually everyone's psychology. For obvious political and cultural reasons nearly all porn is sexist in that it is the product of a male imagination and aimed at a male market; women are less likely to be consciously interested in pornography, or to indulge that interest, or to find porn that turns them on. But anyone who thinks women are simply indifferent to pornography has never watched a bunch of adolescent girls pass around a trashy novel. Over the years I've enjoyed various pieces of pornography—some of them of the sleazy Forty-second Street paperback sort—and so have most women I know. Fantasy, after all, is more flexible than reality, and women have learned, as a matter of survival, to be adept at shaping male fantasies to their own purposes. If feminists define pornography, per se, as the enemy, the result will be to make a lot of women ashamed of their sexual feelings and afraid to be honest about them. And the last thing women need is more sexual shame, guilt, and hypocrisy—this time served up as feminism.[4]

The subjective distinction between erotica and pornography drawn by some feminists is a clear attempt to impose one moral view of sexuality on everyone. This is contrary to the feminist demand often heard for a tolerant, pluralistic approach to sexuality. Morgan and Steinem's definitions express intolerance for those women and men who do not see the more body-centered forms of sexuality as degrading to women. Their view fails to grant to individual women the right to judge for themselves what they personally accept. That is an odd position for anyone to endorse who is striving to "liberate" and "empower" women.

Pornography to many people has a trashy meaning. In the interest of using unbiased words, I will use the term erotica to mean *all* materials aimed at sexually arousing the audience.[5] This is a broader and less biased use of that term than that of Morgan and Steinem and it fits with my pluralistic perspective.

There are some radical feminists like Catherine MacKinnon and Andrea Dworkin who strike out even more harshly than Morgan and Steinem at a great many types of explicit sexuality. They condemn an even broader range of erotica, for they see most of it as the subordination of women. Catherine MacKinnon, an attorney, has put it this way: "Pornography is the central practice of inequality of the sexes. . . . We are treated as pornography depicts us. This is central to why we've been able to do so little for women."[6] In like manner, Andrea Dworkin, a freelance writer, has angrily expressed her condemnation of what she calls pornography:

> Contemporary pornography strictly and literally conforms to the word's root meaning: the graphic depiction of vile whores, or in our language, sluts . . . the word has not changed its meaning and the genre is not misnamed. The word pornography does not have any other meaning than the one cited here, the graphic depiction of the lowest whores.[7]

Of course, if you think that any woman who would consent to act in a role that portrayed her as having sex with men just for physical pleasure is a "slut" or a "vile whore," then *you* will be offended by such a portrayal. But such a view denies other women and men the right to be sexually aroused by these fantasies if they so choose. Some women may view most erotica as too personal for them to enjoy watching or even to read about, but they still would not deny other people the right to their personal feelings. Dworkin's extreme view of erotica is her personal sexual perspective and we cannot deny her that. But we can question her right to impose her judgments upon everyone else and thereby to reject other people's right to their own personal sexual fantasies.

That imposition of one narrow perspective on everyone is the type of straitjacket that blocks us from realistically exploring erotica and understanding its role in our current sexual crisis. Again, let's not lose sight of the fact that Dworkin's position is an unqualified denial of sexual pluralism by a feminist who claims to desire a broader view of sexuality. Her view of sexuality would rule out most erotica today and some of her own previous writings. Chapple and Talbot, in their analysis of erotica, report that much of Dworkin's own writing contains female characters undergoing "the worst kinds of sexual humiliation, which Dworkin describes in exquisite detail."[8]

The prejudice in the debates about sexually explicit materials can be seen in an event that I was involved in St. Paul, Minnesota. In 1988 the St. Paul City Council was seeking a way to restrict bookstores, video rental stores, and movie theaters that dealt in sexually explicit materials. They hit upon the idea of doing a survey of community standards to see what types of pornographic materials were not acceptable. They planned to use the results as the basis for allowing vice officers to make arrests in all sex-oriented businesses. The research organization the City Council hired called me and asked whether I would help them compose the questions to measure "community standards" on sexuality. When it became clear to me that the basic intent was not to discover what people really think about pornography but to find grounds to harass all sex-oriented businesses, I declined to participate. They wanted a weapon with which to close down all erotica businesses, and I was not about to sell it to them.

The research agency persevered without me and did make up a set of questions to measure what types of erotica the citizens of St. Paul found acceptable. They brought the questionnaire to the St. Paul City Council. Then the contradictions and dogmas built into the council position came to the fore. The council found the very questions that were to measure erotica to be themselves obscene and refused to permit the survey![9] What a beautiful example of how narrow, prejudicial thinking can block people from even exploring or understanding what they are dealing with. The council wasn't really interested in measuring erotic preferences. What they wanted was a means for imposing their own view of "sexual truth" on the city of St. Paul. Fortunately, their own rigidity prevented that from happening.

Whether this sort of sexual dogma comes from the St. Paul City Council, Jerry Falwell, or Andrea Dworkin doesn't matter. It is clearly an outgrowth of our sex-negative, Victorian past. It is rather astounding that any feminist who decries the greater restrictions society has placed upon women can at the same time affirm such a restrictive, Victorian view of what is proper sexual fantasy. Women, we are told, even in the fantasy of film, must always be protected from being "used" by men. To accept this position is to support other "protective" restraints like those that the most sexually conservative groups would place upon women's sexuality and their lifestyles. To accept this narrow view of erotica is to endorse the traditional Madonna-Whore view of women. Good women pursue the good type of erotica; whores pursue the other type. As Ellen Willis has said: "This goody-goody concept of eroticism is not feminist but feminine."[10] The roots of the past seem present even in many feminists who say they strive for gender equality.

Philosopher Alan Soble of the University of New Orleans has commented on these contradictions within the antierotica movement. He notes that feminists in other contexts have criticized the notion that women must be "swept away" by mutual affection in order to justify having sex, yet in demanding the union of love and sex in fantasy that rejected notion is being affirmed!

> How coherent can a feminist critique of pornography that presupposes an important connection between sex and love be? A conservative can get away with it, but for a feminist to embrace this bit of conventional wisdom is shocking. The feminist claim that the ideology of love is oppressive to women seems inconsistent with this particular critique of pornography.[11]

To be sure, many feminists do indeed see the inconsistency and do reject the attempt to define "good" and "bad" erotica for all women. For example, the founder of the National Organization of Women (NOW), Betty Friedan, has argued against any restrictive legislation concerning erotica.

> Get off the pornography kick and face the real obscenity of poverty. No matter how repulsive we may find pornography, laws banning books or movies for sexually explicit content could be far more dangerous to women. The pornography issue is dividing the women's movement and giving the impression on college campuses that to be a feminist is to be against sex.[12]

There are widespread feminist organizations like the Feminists Anti-Censorship Taskforce (FACT) that strongly oppose those feminists who join organizations like Women Against Pornography (WAP). As we discussed in chapter 4, men have for millennia restrained women by stressing that they must not have sex without being in love while allowing men a more pleasure-centered approach to sexuality. What the feminists opposed to erotic pluralism are saying supports this ancient restriction on women. It is for this and other reasons that many feminists reject this traditional "feminine" constraint and argue for their right to pursue sexuality as *they* individually see fit.

The Fantasy View of the Subordination of Women

An important issue is whether any forms of erotica are major causes of the subordination of women. We should carefully investigate this possibility, but it must be done fairly to uncover evidence that is not colored by someone's subjective distaste for a particular type of erotica.

Restrictive legislation was proposed by Catherine MacKinnon and Andrea Dworkin in several cities in this country in the mid-1980s because they felt that pornography did subordinate women and lead to unequal treatment of women. In order to increase the opportunity of prosecuting erotica—and they had in mind everything from *Playboy* to hardcore erotica—they proposed legislation making erotica a violation of the civil rights of women and declaring it illegal on that basis. I testified at the hearings in Minneapolis on the question of whether watching erotica of various kinds leads to the subordination of women.[13] The proposal was defeated in Minneapolis.

The MacKinnon/Dworkin pornography censorship law was finally accepted in Indianapolis. But the courts quickly declared it an unconstitutional restraint on free speech. Despite that, in 1992 the Canadian courts, in the *Butler* v. *Regina* decision, adopted the MacKinnon/Dworkin perspective and restricted sexual material "degrading" and/or "demeaning" to women. The results have been harmful, especially to the least powerful groups, such as lesbian and gay bookstores. As the president of the American Civil Liberties Union, Nadine Strossen, has said, "Censorship measures have consistently been used to the particular detriment of the relatively unpopular and powerless."[14] The *Butler* decision in Canada has been used to seize lesbian, gay and feminist material. Strossen reports than in about two years, half of all Canadian feminist bookstores had material confiscated or detained by customs. The vague standard of the *Butler* decision—deciding what is "degrading" or "demeaning"—is the fatal flaw of the legislation. The paternalism in this legal decision is obvious. The law says women need protection by the state from such "degrading" or "demeaning" material. What the law does is empower those in power to censor and those in power are surely not the strongest supporters of feminist, pluralist, or egalitarian causes. Ironically, the law was used to seize two books by Andrea Dworkin herself because they "illegally eroticized pain and bondage."[15] Nadine Strossen and many other feminist writers believe that such censorship laws are the enemy of equal rights for women. Those laws empower the establishment and they can and have been used against groups out of power, such as women.[16]

One of the chief targets of this new law was to be X-rated films. We therefore need to know what X-rated films are actually like. Do they typically aim to portray women as being used and abused by men or do they simply show women eagerly seeking sexual encounters? Author Robert Rimmer studied six hundred and fifty X-rated films to see how many contained "deviational sadistic, violent or victimized sex." He found that only 10 percent of the films were of that type. Other surveys indicate that rape or sadomasochism make up only 3 to 8 percent of commercial erotica.[17] So in the great majority of pornographic films, there is no portrayal of women as being forced to have sex. My own impression of adult videos fits very closely with these findings. Further, the National Coalition on Television Violence reports that PG- and R-rated materials have much *more* murder, general violence, and even many more themes portraying rape than do X-rated films![18]

Most X-rated films consist of a very thin and obvious plot, at best passable acting, and modest film quality, all of which is subordinated to an unyielding focus upon oral, anal, and coital acts. The spotlight in most such films is on genitalia, not on character development. The sexual acts are heterosexual or involve female homosexuality, except in films made for male homosexuals. The story line is aimed at turning on male heterosexuals by portraying women as sexually insatiable and as eagerly pursuing every sexual opportunity. Although this portrayal of female lust may be seen by some as demeaning, that is not the reason it is shown. Rather, the primary goal is to arouse the male viewer by feeding his fantasy of sexually insatiable women. The neglected topic of female erotica will be discussed shortly, but let's look a bit more at erotica aimed at men.

The typical acting demanded of women in X-rated films involves the ability to display an eager, lustful pursuit of their own sexual pleasure. The aim of such films, then, is not to support male dominance or to reject it; rather the purpose is to excite those men who have paid to see the film by picturing the kind of woman about whom men fantasize—a woman who finds them irresistible and who is eager to perform every type of sexual act they may desire. The woman who can best simulate this or actually feel it becomes a star in the erotic industry.

A good example of an erotic film is *The Devil and Miss Jones,* a well-known 1972 film that millions of Americans have seen. The movie opens with Justine Jones, a virgin in her thirties, committing suicide. Before entering Hell she is granted the chance to go back to earth and experience the lustful life that she has missed. The film then shows her eager pursuit of a wide variety of sexual pleasures. The film ends with her trapped in a personal form of Hell—imprisoned with a man who is not sexually interested in her.

How you react to *The Devil and Miss Jones* or any other similar pornographic film depends in good part on your evaluation of male and female sexual desires. If you view the eagerness of the heroine in the movie to have sex with many men as degrading, then you will see such films as "subordinating women." Likewise, if you think of sex outside of deep commitment as a way that men "use" women, then your response will be quite negative. On the other hand, if you are entertained by the plot and see the sexual portrayals as an enactment of some of your own fantasies, then you will enjoy the films. Finally, if you can appreciate the difference between fantasy and reality and enjoy being sexually turned on for its own sake, you will find films like this rewarding. As I noted earlier, your reactions to pornography do indeed reveal your private sexual philosophy. You can reject the portrayal *for yourself* because it is too explicit, condemn it for anyone to see, tolerate it, or enjoy it enthusiastically. Checking your own reactions to different erotica is an excellent way to get to know some interesting things about your personal view of sexuality.

In the 1980s, as we became more egalitarian, more of the X-rated films incorporated scenes of males performing oral sex on females (cunnilingus) instead of focusing only on fellatio. The plots in the 1980s also displayed more gender equality by showing more women in occupations equal to those of the men in the films. Also, there are now turn-on films made by women for women and for couples. Annie Sprinkle, an erotic film star, talks about the change in erotic films.

> In the old days, the sex was already over before they thought about the woman's orgasm. You'd be lying there on the bed. The guy would be toweling himself off, and the director would shout, "OK, take a face." Then the camera would move onto your face for the close-up, and you'd fake the orgasm, like "Ooh! Ahh! Moan! Groan!"[19]

Candida Royal, whose Femme Films makes erotic movies with women in mind, describes her films:

> Very little focus on genitalia in Femme Films. . . . I try to get real-life lovers as often as I can. You get the heat and the love that way. It's wonderful. And if I use real lovers, I don't have to use safe sex.[20]

One of the most famous erotic movie stars is Seka. In an interview with Phil Donahue she pointed out that she doesn't work with anyone she doesn't like. Then she responded to a question as to how she can have sex right in front of a camera:

> I was very turned on physically by the idea of being in X-rated films and the idea that a camera is there is very exciting to me, and knowing that

there are millions and millions of people out there that are eventually going to watch this is more exciting to me, so it makes me perform better in front of a camera.[21]

X-rated films often imitate successful movies. For example, the popular film *Nine to Five* was used as the plot for an X-rated film called *Eight to Four*. The erotic film *Urban Cowgirls* imitated the popular film *Urban Cowboy*. In 1986 the first "safe sex" erotic film was made. It was titled: *Behind the Green Door: The Sequel*—a followup to Marilyn Chambers's (the Ivory Soap girl) famous 1975 porno film *Behind the Green Door*. In this 1986 film all the sex takes place using condoms and latex squares (for oral sex) to avoid transmission of HIV infection. This film was, I believe, the first movie of any type to deliberately attempt to eroticize the safer sex practices. Since that time there have been other porn films showing condom usage in at least some of the scenes. Think about it—the porn industry in this respect has shown more moral responsibility for educating the public about eroticizing and using condoms than our TV networks, mainline movies, or the federal government!

Steve Chapple and David Talbot, two freelance writers, talked to Missy Manners, the star of *Behind the Green Door: The Sequel*. Missy Manners was a former U.S. Senate intern with conservative Republican Senator Orrin Hatch from Utah. Here is the explanation she gave to them as to why she got into erotic movies:

> "I had to get away from my beautiful sisters. I moved to California, and I would go to aerobics every single day, and there would be these pretty blondes again, so skinny, great suntans, perfect teeth. After a while I looked down at myself and realized I had better tits and ass than these women." So Missy, not unlike a few porn actresses, saw adult films as ego-enhancement. Not that lust . . . did not play a considerable part. "I knew I wanted to do *Green Door*. If you really want to know, I get off ten times more than most women do. I'm not one of these people into orgasm retention, like one a year. I could have ten great ones in a day and not feel guilt. The way I look at it, I'm still a good Republican. I worked hard to get Reagan elected, twice. I consider myself the Pat Robertson of porn. This is my fight for individual rights. Once I was a freedom fighter. Now I'm a freedom fucker."[22]

Erotica is a product of our society and as such it reflects our lives just as television and PG-rated films do. Accordingly, women in all these media are not often shown as presidents of corporations, ministers in a church, or generals in the army. But the salient point here is that the aim of X-rated films is to sexually arouse the viewer—not to reinforce any subordinate image of women. The erotic movie makers are not political activists. They stress the erotic turn-on and not the status of women. We are saturated in all the media with the typical view of women and men, and another portrayal in porn films adds little to this image.

I have asked hundreds of men and women who go to X-rated films about their reasons for attending such films. Almost all of them say clearly that they go out of curiosity or to get sexually aroused. Very few of them are going in order to strengthen the second-class role of women in our society and most of them would strongly reject such a role for women.

Given our society in which men, as the more powerful gender, have traditionally been the sexual initiators and are often rejected by unwilling women, it is hardly surprising to find that the most popular erotic theme is of a woman who cannot resist a man's approach. By the same token, since most women are trained to be cautious in their sexual decision making, it is surely not surprising that many women would be disturbed by the portrayal of a woman completely lacking in self-control. The sexually driven woman has lost her negotiating power. And in a society dominated by men in all nonsexual areas, unless a woman is very secure, that is a threatening loss even if it is only a fantasy on the silver screen.

Many single women still view sex as a "service" that a woman performs for a man when she knows and trusts him. It is something she "gives" to him. Surely, she may enjoy doing that, but she believes that it is her key bargaining chip and cannot be used too freely without "cheapening" herself and allowing herself to be "used" by the man. Contrast this with the male view of erotica stressing the sexually driven woman. The interest of men is not as much in the woman's loss of control as in the man's gain of sexual pleasures. Only in a society that treats men and women very differently and unequally could we find such contrasting views of sexuality.

Note that such feelings of being used hardly occur in lesbian sexual relationships. Women having oral sex with other women are not afraid of being used. But a woman performing oral sex on a man may well have this feeling of being used. So it is transparent that the block to women enjoying sex more freely and easily with men is the inequality of the female/male relationship, and not the sex acts. One rarely hears men complain of being "used" sexually by women. Men know they are valued for more than their sexuality. Even in today's more gender-equal world women cannot be sure of that. X-rated films to many women symbolize being used because that is what they think would be the case if they acted like the woman on the screen.

Women's Roles and Women's Erotica

Women, too, have their own types of erotica, but they adorn them with romantic labels. We hardly hear about female erotica because it is not considered a threat to men or any other group. Still, as I shall show, female erotica reflects the problems in sexuality that women typically encounter just as male erotica reflects the typical male sexual problems. Although many women enjoy watching an X-rated video with their boyfriends, many more women seem to get turned on by reading erotic romantic novels. Some of these erotic romances start with a theme of a man who sexually abuses a woman who loves him. Later in the story he falls in love with that same woman and at that point she leaves him.[23] The emphasis throughout is on the power of love to enslave an individual. Romance and the promise of marriage in these novels make the sexuality—which is a key attraction of the novel—more easily digested by a female audience.

These so-called romances typified by the Harlequin series are a form of erotica for people who morally could not allow themselves to read or see the "harder" forms of pornography. Ann Barr Snitow, a Professor of English at Rutgers University, describes these Harlequin romances:

> In these romantic love stories, sex on a woman's terms is romanticized sex. Romantic sexual fantasies are contradictory. They include both the desire to be blindly ravished, to melt, and the desire to be spiritually adored, saved from the humiliation of dependence and sexual passivity through the agency of a protective male who will somehow make reparation to the woman he loves for her powerlessness.[24]

Female romantic erotica cancel out the man's greater negotiating power by picturing him as driven by uncontrollable love feelings for a particular woman. This is analogous to male erotica which cancels out the sexual reservations of the woman by portraying her as driven by lust for her male partner. Female pornography reflects the emphasis upon stable romantic relationships that many women want but can never be sure of obtaining. Women often find they cannot regulate their romantic relations as much as they would like and erotic romantic novels allow for fantasies which grant precisely such control. Similarly, male pornography reflects the search for willing sex partners, which for many men are so difficult to find.

Are men "degraded" or "subordinated" by female romantic sexual fantasies? Very few people would say so because men are not judged in our society predominantly on their romantic involvements. As women have become valued for more than their sexual attractiveness, more of them are speaking out about male-oriented erotica, whether they are turned on by it or detest it. Many women feel less threatened by erotica because they value themselves for more than their bodies. Our erotic fantasies, as I have tried to show, are largely a result of the gender roles we assign to men and women. As those roles change, and allow for more choice, so will our preferences in erotic fantasies and our reactions to them. But if those roles do not change, neither will the fantasies. In this sense, if we want more egalitarian erotica, we shouldn't waste our time trying to do away with what we have, but instead work to promote more equal relationships between women and men. That is what is really important and new erotic themes will follow to reflect the changes that occur.

Erotica: Mirror or Cause of Inequality?

But the question remains: What kind of people see pornographic films and what seems to be the impact on them of those films? In order to get some insight into these questions, I looked at national data concerning viewers of X-rated movies.[25] There are surveys of representative samples of Americans conducted every year by the National Opinion Research Center (NORC) at the University of Chicago. One of the questions asked is whether the respondent has seen an X-rated movie during the past twelve months. I reasoned that if erotic movies develop attitudes that subordinate women, then those who go to such movies should be less supportive of female equality. I examined several NORC surveys to help answer this question.

In the 1980s over 20 percent of the adult population attended an X-rated movie in any one year. Over 15 percent of women and 25 percent of men made up the customers who went each year. About 60 percent of those who did attend were married. But one of the most interesting findings was that college-educated people are *more* likely to go to an X-rated movie. This is interesting because we know that college-educated people in general treat men and women more equally. So how can attending those films be producing attitudes of gender inequality? To examine this more carefully I compared those college-educated people who went to X-rated films to those who did not go to see which group was more in favor of equality for women. Contrary to what the antierotica people say, I found that those who had gone to an X-rated movie were *more* likely to support female equality than those who did not go! It would seem that these women and men perceive such movies more as erotic entertainment than as an attack on female equality. In addition, college-educated women are more likely to be aware of their value beyond the area of sexuality and thus may be less threatened by traditional male erotic films. I rechecked this analysis using 1996 NORC national data and found that it held up quite well. The percentage attending an X-rated movie rose to 26 percent in 1996.

I also examined countries in Europe and found that Sweden and Denmark, where erotica is freely available, are the *most* gender-equal countries in the Western world. Countries like Spain and Ireland, where erotica is much less available, are far *less* gender equal. These findings support the view that accepting men and women as equals promotes a greater willingness to accept erotica. Obviously there are gender equal people who do not go to these films, and there are also men who oppose equal rights for women who do go. But the overall picture based on the NORC data is that people who attend erotic films are the most likely to support equality for men and women. *Most people who oppose erotica are not seeking to promote female equality.* On the contrary, they oppose erotica *and* gender equality because neither is in line with their conservative views of a proper lifestyle.

The supports of inequality are not in erotica. Inequality is rooted in the limited power granted to women in our economic and political institutions. Nan Hunter, an American Civil Liberties Union attorney and a leader of the Feminist Anti-Censorship Taskforce (FACT), testified at the 1985 Meese Commission hearings:

> Pornography is not the cause of oppression in women nor is it even the primary channel in which that supremacy is reflected, validated and glorified. Other much more powerful, established and legitimate institutions contribute far more than does the pornography industry to the second-class status of women. Thus we and many other feminists believe that targeting pornography . . . is a fundamentally misguided attempt to get at the root causes of an ideology which tells us that women are inferior and incompetent.[26]

As a sociologist I would wholeheartedly support these comments. The subordination of women—the treating of women as inferior to men —was even more extreme long before erotic films ever appeared. Gender equality in the economic and political spheres has actually increased since the liberalization of the film industry some twenty-five years ago. That fact alone would discredit any powerful causal relationship between erotica and gender inequality.

If by some magical stroke we could wipe out all forms of "degrading" erotica today, would women become more equal? Would the percentage of women elected to Congress increase? Would the relative amount of pay women earn compared to men change? Would the Catholic Church lift its ban on female priests? Would wives become more powerful in their marriages? Of course not. Nothing would change in terms of the power and prestige of women. In fact, since the key support for banning erotica comes from conservatives, that success could increase their ability to enforce traditional roles on women and men, which could actually *weaken* the power of women. We will not elevate women by banning forms of erotica any more than we will strengthen marriages by banning soap operas about unhappy marriages. Let's face the real issues and stop worrying about other people's sexual fantasies.

A pluralist philosophy endorses choice in erotica even if some forms of erotica are seen as "disgusting" by particular individuals. We should add what we like rather than subtracting what we dislike. We can always choose for ourselves to see none or all of whatever erotica exists. But we do not express our toleration for choice by outlawing everything we personally dislike.

Erotica and Sex Offenses: What Relationship?

Perhaps erotic films do not promote inequality for women, but do they encourage men to commit sexual offenses against women? Susan Brownmiller in her well-known book on rape asserted that erotica "promotes [*sic*] a climate in which acts of sexual hostility directed against women are not only tolerated but ideologically encouraged."[27] Robin Morgan has uttered the most quoted sentiment: ". . . pornography is sexist propaganda, pornography is the theory and rape is the practice."[28]

This condemnatory perspective assumes that all erotica—which they call pornography—displays violence against women and it asserts that fantasy leads to violent behavior. This view ignores the difference between fantasy and reality. This difference between thought and deed is the cornerstone of a democracy that allows free speech. One of the most common fantasies that women report having is of forced sexuality.[29] That type of fantasy may simply be a way for a woman who has been trained to feel guilty about initiating sexuality herself to enjoy a sexual fantasy. These same women would be horrified if that fantasy ever became a reality. Similarly, remember that our "born again" President, Jimmy Carter, admitted that he "lusted in his heart" for other women besides his wife. But that does not mean he carried out that desire into action. Rather it was a cost-free way to enjoy other women and avoid guilt. Fantasy is one thing, behavior is another. Research indicates that it is a mistake to assume that one must lead to the other.

In addition to equating fantasy and reality, the Brownmiller and

Morgan position on sexual violence assumes that most erotica display violence against women. I have already commented that this is not so. Feminist Gayle Rubin supports this conclusion:

> Actually, if you walk into an adult bookstore, ninety per cent of the material you will see is frontal nudity, intercourse, and oral sex, with no hint of violence or coercion ... WAP [Women Against Pornography] show the worst possible porn, and claim it's representative of all of it. ... Their analysis is that the violent images come out of porn and into the culture at large, that sexism comes from porn into the culture. Whereas it seems to me that pornography only reflects as much sexism as is in the culture.[30]

Clearly there is a real controversy over the power of erotica to lead to violence against women. What does the social scientific evidence show?

The research I examined from the 1970s up to 1996 bears directly on this question. In 1970 a presidential commission set up by President Lyndon Johnson examined the possible harmful consequences of erotica. After two years of original research, they concluded there was no connection between erotica and sex offenses:

> If a case is to be made against "pornography" in 1970, it will have to be made on grounds other than demonstrated effects of a damaging personal or social nature. Empirical research designed to clarify the question has found no reliable evidence to date that exposure to explicit sexual materials plays a significant role in the causation of delinquent or criminal sexual behavior among youth or adults.[31]

In 1985 President Ronald Reagan set up the Meese Commission with instructions to see if things had changed since 1970. This commission lacked the scientific rigor and research base of the 1970 commission. They did no original research while the 1970 commission published nine volumes of research done under their auspices. The Meese Commission, headed by then Attorney General Edwin Meese, heard testimony primarily from law enforcement officers who were members of vice squads, politicians and spokespersons for conservative antipornography "decency" groups, and people who identified themselves as victims of pornography.[32]

Much of the evidence that the commission considered was anecdotal and not research supported. People's stories about porn and rape can be horrifying, but the question always remains how common such events are and how fairly and accurately they are being presented. The commission's final report admits the lack of causal evidence but implies that erotica still *may* be productive of violence against women. But as Columbia University anthropologist Carol Vance points out:

> The report's section on harms ... overstates the evidence, leaps to un-supported conclusions about what might be "reasonably assumed" in social science, cites no research to support statements and appears to misunderstand what causality means in social science.[33]

Since almost all sexual scientists agree that the Meese Commission inquiry was very poorly conducted and their conclusions worth very little, let's turn to the findings from recent scientific research, which I analyzed in preparation for my testimony on erotica before the Minneapolis City Council.

If erotica are a cause of sex offenses, then sex offenders should show a heavy involvement with erotica, But consistently, from Kinsey's work to today, research on sex offenders has found that such people didn't grow up with more exposure to erotica than those who are not sex offenders. In fact, much of the research shows that sex offenders often come from very sexually restrictive homes and actually had less exposure to erotica while growing up.[34] You may remember that we discussed this finding when we spoke of child sexual abuse in chapter 2.

The experience of Denmark, Sweden, and the former West Germany is relevant here. Nadine Strossen comments on the evidence from these countries, where restraints on pornography have been eased for several decades:

> Patterns in other countries over time show no correlation between the increased availability of sexual materials and increased violence against women. The 1991 analysis by University of Copenhagen professor Berl Kutchinsky revealed that, while nonsexual violent crime had increased up to 300 percent in Denmark, Sweden, and West Germany from 1964 to 1984, all three countries' rape rates either declined or remained con-stant during this same period, despite their lifting of restrictions on sexual materials.[35]

Kutchinsky, a criminologist, found that the rate of child sexual abuse went *down* significantly. It was possible that the open availability of erotic materials had given a masturbatory outlet that reduced some forms of child sexual abuse. Of course, we can't be sure that there was any causal connection of this sort. But even if we say that sex offenses did not change, we still are forced to conclude that the vast increases in erotica had no effect on sex offenses.

There have also been experimental laboratory studies conducted by psychologists in our country to study the impact of erotica on violence toward women. These studies typically used college men and exposed some of them to various types of erotic films and others to neutral films. The men were then given an opportunity to administer an electric shock to a woman in the experiment. The purpose was to see if those men who saw erotic films would be more likely to give the electric shock to the woman. If that happened, then it was assumed that the erotic films had produced antifemale aggression. Many different results occurred and confusion reigned for several years. Psychologist Edward Donnerstein is probably the best known and most quoted of these erotica researchers. Interestingly, both sides to the controversy over the impact of erotica on violence toward women have cited Donnerstein's findings as supporting their position.

The Minneapolis City Council invited Donnerstein to clarify his views at the same session where I was scheduled to testify. I knew his work and that of others and firmly believed it all indicated that the usual erotic film had no impact on violence against women. Nevertheless, he was being touted by some antierotica groups as saying otherwise and so I wasn't sure how he would testify.

I went to the Minneapolis City Council fully ready to debate the evidence with him in case he argued that erotic films produced violence. But I soon found that Donnerstein and I basically agreed on the interpretation of the research evidence. At the hearing Donnerstein, to the anger of the antierotica right-wing feminist lobby, made it crystal clear that his findings indicated that the erotic content of films did not cause aggressive responses.

> Erotica is not the problem. The problem is violence. What all the research strongly supports is that it is the violent images, not the sexual images, that are important. It is strictly the aggressive content which tends to increase aggressive behavior—not the sexual content or the sexual explicitness.[36]

So Donnerstein's findings indicate that erotic films without clear physical violence showed little evidence of increasing aggression in the viewer. But when physical violence was added, then there was an increase in aggression displayed by the subjects in the experiment—they were more willing to give an electric shock to a woman in the experiment. However, the most important point was that the same aggressive effect could be produced by showing violence alone *without any explicit sexuality!* So the full display of vaginal, oral, and anal sex was not in and of itself productive of aggressive responses.

It follows from this summary that if reducing violence is of concern, there is far more violence against both women and men in nonerotic materials on television and in R- and PG-rated movies. Those displays of violence clearly should be the primary focus of any such protest. But the Meese Commission and, since then, President Bush's attorney general, Dick Thornburgh, have instead promoted ways of harassing erotic businesses. In 1989 Donnerstein aimed his criticism against the Meese Commission for their unjustified conclusions:

> If the commissioners were looking for the most nefarious media threat to public welfare, they missed the boat. The most clear and present danger, well documented by the social science literature, is all violent material in our society, whether sexually explicit or not, that promotes violence against women. Let us hope that the next commission will provide a better example by disentangling sexuality from violence, therefore yielding more useful conclusions.[37]

Thus, after may years of new research the conclusions are very much in line with the 1970 presidential commission. They are also congruent with a 1972 Commission on Television Violence. That commission found experimental evidence that watching violence on television did indeed make it more likely that a child would display aggressive behavior. One of the experiments, for example, showed that children who saw violent films were more likely to punch and attack life-size play dolls. But I hasten to add that conceiving of the viewing of violence as definitely a cause of violent behavior is itself not fully accepted. We do not really know that people who view violence will go out in the real world and commit more violence. We only know that they do show aggression in the laboratory experiments. Nevertheless, if the antierotica groups are motivated by sincere interest in reducing violence, why don't they change the focus of their attacks when the research does not implicate sexuality and does appear to implicate television and nonerotic movie viewing? It does seem that there is a confusion of sexuality with sexism.

I would suggest that the driving force among antierotica people is opposition to body-centered sexual fantasies. The opposition to violence in general does not seem to be as much of a central concern to them. They are opposed to portraying sexually insatiable women no matter what the research evidence on violence indicates. The Victorian slip of the antierotica groups is showing, but their sexual myopia prevents them from seeing it.

Where Do We Go From Here?

Supreme Court Justices William Brennan Jr., Thurgood Marshall, and John Paul Stevens in a 1989 ruling said we should do away with the restrictions on First Amendment rights that our current obscenity ruling imposes. Justice William Brennan Jr. expressed their opinion this way: "I have long been convinced that the exaction of criminal penalties for the distribution of obscene materials to consenting adults is constitutionally intolerable."[38] The state supreme courts of Hawaii and Oregon have invalidated obscenity laws under the free speech guarantees in those states' constitutions. The obscenity ruling is a roadblock in our country's movement toward greater sexual pluralism and the resolution of our sexual crises. It is a remnant of our Victorian approach to sexuality.

About six out of every ten Americans have said they favor making pornographic materials available for people eighteen and older who want them.[39] Studies done in various cities and states also show that the majority of Americans support the right of adults to have books, magazines, films, and videos that display nudity and portray sex acts. Two researchers from the University of Hawaii School of Medicine summarized the research in this area of public opinion:

> As far as we can ascertain, no community of city, county, state or the nation, anonymously surveyed by any reputable agency or government, has yet voted to restrict from adults the availability of sexually explicit material depicting adults in consensual activity. . . . There exists a permissive consensus throughout the United States in regard to adults having access to sexually explicit material.[40]

Note that we are talking of erotica using adult actors. Child erotica is against the law in almost all Western countries.

Pluralism tells us that there is more than one model for good erotica just as there is more than one model for good sex. Our concern should be with how our real sexual *acts* reflect the values of honesty, responsibility, and equality. Those who try to force our sexual turn-ons to conform to their personal tastes are simply abiding by the nineteenth century's dogmatic view of sexuality. The best antidote for a type of erotica that we do not like is to accept its right to exist and then to try to promote the type of erotica we do prefer. Trying to label the type of erotica we do not like with stigmatized words like pornography and then banning it will accomplish nothing.

Be leery of anyone who wants to "protect" women by clothing the Dallas Cheerleaders, or banning college dance lines, or labeling some literary, film, or artistic work as "degrading and obscene." You don't empower by prohibiting choices. You empower by encouraging responsible individual choices. As Justice Brennan has noted, women are treated with "romantic paternalism," which purports to put women on a pedestal but instead puts them in a cage.

No society ever has or ever will be able to stop people from being attracted to the bodies of their fellow humans. Societies do socialize people in regard to what body parts are considered most attractive, but no society rules out the total body. And if any society did succeed in doing that, sexuality would cease to exist and soon that society would also. Erotica basically expresses the attraction that we have been taught to have for one another's bodies expressed in ways that are exciting to a viewing audience. Our social lives as women and men will determine what fantasies turn us on. Some may want love to be present; some may want to be sure that love is not present. What we want and don't get in our real social lives will come out as one major part of our fantasies.

We need to lose our fear of sexual diversity and to open up the realm of possibilities at least for others. The debate we are now going through is symptomatic of a time of adjustment to the greater openness we are developing about sexuality. No one can force a fantasy upon us or take one away from us. Let's stop fighting each other and instead work to eliminate the fear and anxiety we still possess about sexual pluralism. Surely each of us has the right to reject any form of erotica because of personal preference. But when we try to impose our tastes on others we violate our pluralistic values. The battle over erotica is an easy outlet for emotions that would be far better spent in facing up to the really important work that is needed to resolve our urgent sexual crisis. Instead of wasting our time trying to alter the reflection of society in our erotica, let's work to change our society. If we make our basic social institutions more gender equal, we will have produced some really worthwhile changes, and keeping our freedom of expression intact is an essential tool in making such changes.

7

Rape:
The Ultimate Inequality

You Have to Be Taught

Why do men rape women? One rather extreme view of why such rape occurs comes from radical feminist Susan Brownmiller. She asserts that all men are inherently rapists.

> Man's discovery that his genitalia could serve as a weapon to generate fear must rank as one of the most important discoveries of prehistoric times, along with the use of fire and the first crude stone axe. From prehistoric times to the present, I believe, rape has played a critical function. It is nothing more or less than a conscious process of intimidation by which all men keep all women in a state of fear. . . . Female fear of an open season of rape, and not a natural inclination toward monogamy, motherhood or love, was probably the single causative factor in the original subjugation of woman by man. . . . It seems eminently sensible to hypothesize that man's violent capture and rape of the female led first to the establishment of a rudimentary mate-protectorate and then sometime later to the full-blown male solidification of power, the patriarchy.[1]

Brownmiller sees men as having always dominated women by the threat of rape. Now, human creatures have been around for four or five million years and *Homo sapiens* for over 100,000 years, and for all but about the last ten thousand years we lived in small hunting-and-gathering societies. Our best evidence on hunting-and-gathering groups today directly contradicts Brownmiller, for it indicates that such societies have

155

a high degree of equality between women and men.[2] It was the advent of agriculture about ten thousand years ago that brought male dominance into prominence. Property and the accumulation of wealth became far more possible as agriculture developed. Then, male power increased and so did the attempt to control female sexuality by force and persuasion. In the last two hundred years, with the development of modern industrial societies, the pendulum has swung back toward greater equality between men and women. This sort of historical change does not fit Brownmiller's thesis of an original state of male dominance precipitated and perpetuated by man's genital prowess. In short, it does not seem, as Brownmiller asserts, that man's possession of a penis produced male dominance through fear of rape. Rather, as indicated, it was *after* the relatively recent male concentration of power emerged in agricultural societies that men used their increased power to justify rape, and whatever else they wanted to do.

It is men having socially approved power over women that increases the likelihood of rape. The sources of social power lie in economic and political control, not in the ability to rape. By way of illustration, we need only to consider that during slavery in this country white men, because of their greater power, could rape black women with considerable impunity. If a black man raped a white woman, he would not gain power; he would most likely lose his life. Power gives one the ability to obtain whatever is wanted and that includes the body of another person. People who feel equal are not likely to attempt to rape one another. Rape is an act that shows a prior disregard for the personhood of the victim. When men are taught that they are in control and that women are inferior to them, they are more likely to express this feeling of power against women in the form of rape.[3] This doesn't mean that rape is not a sexual act; rather it means that *rape is a sexual way of expressing power.*

Brownmiller's idea that there is a universal, natural basis for rape because of male genitalia and strength would mean that no society would be without significant rape rates. But the anthropologists who study non-industrial societies (hunting, horticultural, pastoral, or agricultural societies) around the world today have found that rape is absent or very uncommon in many of these societies. For example, the research on rape reported by anthropologists Gwen Broude and Peggy Sanday indicates that in about a quarter of the nonindustrial societies rape is absent, and in another quarter of the societies it is rare.[4]

So once again Brownmiller's view of all men using rape to generate fear in women is not supported. It is in societies where men are taught that they are superior to women that we find a high incidence of rape. Rape appears to be a socially learned degradation imposed by men who feel superior to women. Rape may also express the anger some men feel toward women who act in ways that challenge male superiority. Our language reflects the connection of sexuality with dominance and aggression. If we want to say that someone got a raw deal, we say they got "screwed"—the same word that means sexual intercourse.

Brownmiller's book justifiably stresses the harm done by male rape and discusses some valuable historical examples. But she politicizes and oversimplifies the issue by viewing "all men" as rapists. For that reason her point of view is rejected by many other feminists. Criminologist Julia R. Schwendinger, who in 1972 was one of the original founders of the first rape crisis center in the world, disagrees with much of Brownmiller's thesis.[5] Feminist anthropologists like Eleanor B. Leacock, Ruby Rohrlich-Leavitt, Barbara Sykes, and Elizabeth Weatherford as well as feminist sociologists like Janet Chafetz also take exception to many of Susan Brownmiller's points.[6] As I've noted, my own research has made me question much of Brownmiller's perspective. I feel that we do not now need strident, accusatory stereotyping of all men. Instead, we need careful and cool-headed thinking about why there are such immense differences in rape among our Western societies today and why the rate is so much higher in the United States than in most other Western countries.

I can best develop my own view about the importance of power as an explanation of rape by relating an encounter I had with a group of convicted rapists. In order to learn more about the causes of rape I visited the Intensive Treatment Program for Sexual Aggressives at the Minnesota State Security Hospital in St. Peter. This program was established in 1975 and is the premier program in the state. In 1982 I was supervising a doctoral student who was working there and I became interested in talking about my ideas on rape with the sex offenders in her program. So, I contacted the director of the treatment program, psychologist Richard Seely, and arranged to spend time talking with the sex offenders.

Although some of the inmates in Dr. Seely's program were incest perpetrators, most were rapists. Like the majority of sex offenders, rapists have a very narrow and traditional male view of gender roles and of sexuality. The rapist views women predominantly as bodies that can satisfy his sexual desires but who have few other worthwhile characteristics. The treatment program aims to broaden the inmate's view of women. The staff, half of whom are women, try to impress upon the inmates that women offer many characteristics beyond sexuality, such as intelligence, friendship, humor, skills, and other valued traits. The hope is that the inmate will develop a more varied image of women and begin to view women as more than just suppliers of sexual pleasure that men can command by force if need be. In the written description of the program this point is stressed:

> Women staff are seen as essential to the . . . goal of socially rehabilitating men who almost universally have a history of difficulty relating to women. Including women in virtually all aspects of the treatment program, and ensuring that the legitimacy of their power is supported by male staff, is the backbone of the program's effort to break stereotypic notions of women as filling limited roles, always subservient to men.[7]

The program also aimed at expanding the range of acceptable sexual behaviors of the inmates to encourage them to see the possibility of other sexual outlets besides just male-centered intercourse. In short, they were trying to pluralize the inmate's view of sexuality. The staff pointed out a wide range of sexual practices that are possible, such as masturbation, combining affection rather than force with sexuality, extended foreplay, allowing women to initiate sex more, learning to take pleasure in the woman's pleasure, and the like. I was impressed with the wisdom of the treatment program. By teaching the inmates to be more pluralistic in their view of women and in their practice of sexuality, they were encouraging greater acceptance of equality between men and women. Experience has shown that equality will help reduce the likelihood of any future rape. The record of the program continues to give strong support to this belief.

After describing the program, Seely led me into a large room where all the offenders had been asked to gather. As I walked into that room, Seely said: "See you in an hour or two," and closed the door. There I was surrounded by forty-eight men, all of whom had been convicted of sexual assaults. I must admit that I felt a bit uneasy being there alone, even though I knew that very few of these inmates had committed offenses against adult males. I had the feeling of being surrounded by a wall of violent emotions.

I distracted myself from my concerns by focusing on my purpose for being there—to get these inmates to talk to me about why they had committed rape. I knew that they would never believe any of my ideas about rape. After all, in their mind, I was a university professor who didn't know much about the "real world" of hard knocks. My plan was to present my ideas knowing that they would reject them. When they started to correct my ideas about rape, they would do so by telling me about their own ideas concerning rape, and that was the information I wanted.

My view of the causes of rape, as I've noted, is that the inequality between men and women makes it easy to vent on women any hostile feelings a man may have. A second factor, also related to male power, that supports rape is our promotion of macho male roles stressing physical aggression and sexual conquest. Such macho roles help men to feel that it is proper to let out their feelings by using physical force. When those two factors are combined in a society like ours, which permits many opportunities for men and women to be alone, the setting for high rape rates is created. I put forth this viewpoint to these sex offenders. As expected, they did not buy my ideas. They were far more concerned with their own individual situations and had little interest in any abstract societal perspective. But, as I had hoped, their annoyance with me did start them talking about rape as they saw it, in order to straighten out my thinking.

"Hank" began by telling me that his life was in a shambles. He had been out of work, had broken up with his girlfriend, had no friends, and didn't get along with his family. As he put it: "I just didn't give a shit what I did." He said he wanted to let out his frustration some way and so one night as he was leaving a bar he sexually attacked the first woman who came near his car. I asked him why he chose that way of venting his frustration—why didn't he get drunk, or pick a fight with a man, or put his fist through a wall? He looked at me like I was missing his point. He said: "Look man, with a broad I know that if she fights back I can beat the hell out of her and put her in her place by screwing her. With a man, I may get the shit beat out of me. Why the hell would I risk that?"

Then "Billy," a large, dark-haired, muscular individual, broke in and noted that he committed rape for very different reasons than "Hank." "Billy" spoke in a subdued voice but one that occasionally trembled in its effort to cover the powerful emotions lurking underneath. "I always liked to hunt—rabbits, deer, anything. I liked the challenge. With a woman as the game, it's even more exciting. I would hide in the shadows, choose my prey as she passed by, and then stalk her, slowly and methodically. When I grabbed her, I earned getting whatever I wanted from her, and if she knew what was good for her, she would give me what I wanted!"

I felt a chill just listening to his description. It was disturbing to hear someone talk of another human as "prey" to be stalked. Surely you don't treat your equals as "prey" to be hunted. Both these men clearly had a strong belief in the traditional double-standard view of men and women. They saw women as subservient to men and they saw men as having the right to use violence against women in many situations. It was as if women owed them sexual pleasure and had better not deny it to them. Some of them believed that women actually enjoyed the rape experience —they thought women liked being forced into sex. In fact, two of the inmates told me they had been caught because they came back to see their victims the day after the rape, convinced that their victims would welcome another sexual encounter with them!

I thought to myself that all these men had unknowingly given support to my ideas concerning two key causes of rape: gender inequality and macho male roles. They had told me indirectly that women are less valued than men and so were their first choice for a victim. Also, they embraced the macho male role that stresses physical aggression as appropriate for men. There were many other stories besides those I've noted but they all, in one way or another, pointed to the strong belief on the part of most of the rapists in female inferiority and macho male roles. The attempt in this program to broaden the narrow and degrading views the rapists held about women was surely well justified.

We shouldn't be surprised to find that rapists think of women they rape as lower in status and power than themselves. Throughout our own history we have seen how violence has occurred more easily against low prestige groups such as the poor and ethnic minorities like blacks and American Indians. We need only to remember the imprisonment of over one hundred thousand Japanese Americans in special detention camps during World War Il. At the time, they were the group lowest on the prestige totem pole.

This is but one of many examples of how people abuse groups lacking in power and prestige. The preponderance of blacks among those who have been the victims of lynchings and among those who have been executed under our death-penalty laws also fits with this same line of thinking. A look at Scandinavian countries like Sweden, Denmark, and Norway with their very high degree of equality between men and women and their very low incidence of rape certainly lends further support to social power being one very important factor in rape.

It's possible to check whether societies outside the Western world show this connection between low social power for women, macho roles for men, and high incidence of rape. Anthropologists have put together extensive data files on 186 nonindustrial societies around the world. I spent a considerable amount of time looking over the information on these societies to find out if my thinking held up there. Without burdening the reader with the details, let me say that it did.[8] It was not true in every instance, but in general those societies that treat men and women more equally and do not stress macho male roles are the same societies that have the lowest incidences of rape. It seems likely that rape will have to be added to the list of costs that come with the low power of women and macho roles for men. In regard to the latter, there is still much evidence of machismo in our male roles today. The male role is often portrayed as emphasizing danger as exciting, physical aggression as manly, and sex as a conquest. This is best seen in sports and in the military, and there is still much admiration for the John Wayne or Rambo method of settling differences.[9] One rather mundane example concerned my own Minnesota Twins, world champions in 1987 and 1991. Two of our players, Dan Gladden and Steve Lombardozzi, had some arguments. After flying home from a loss to Boston, Lombardozzi went out to Dan Gladden's home to continue their disagreement. That led to a fist fight. Gladden suffered a broken bone on a finger and Lombardozzi got a black eye. Tom Kelley, manager of the Twins, put his machismo endorsement of the fight this way:

> Two men had a disagreement and they settled it like men. . . . It's probably better it happened. . . . It's something they had to get done and it probably had to get done in a particular way. Maybe it's for the best that this is the way they took care of it.[10]

Most of the inmates' comments I received concerned rape by strangers. However, the majority of the estimated one million rapes that occur in America every year are perpetrated by men known to the victim—either acquaintances or dates.[11] Therefore, if we want to understand rape, we must explore how these key forces of inequality and machismo influence our dating system to cause rape. There must be something in the way women and men relate to each other that helps explain why rape occurs.

Adversarial Dating: A Blueprint for Rape

Only about 10 percent of all the rapes that occur are reported to the police.[12] Of the rapes that are reported, a high proportion are committed by a stranger rather than by an acquaintance or a date. Accordingly, the public is led to believe that rape by a stranger is the most common form of rape. In reality, probably over 80 percent of all rapes involve people who know each other! A large proportion of rapes occur among young women under eighteen. We need to understand why acquaintance and date rape is so common and yet so unlikely to be reported to the police. Let's start by looking at an important study of rape among college students.

In 1985 the feminist magazine *Ms.* sponsored a study of rape which produced some interesting results. The study was a survey of almost sixty-two hundred college students at thirty-two different schools chosen to represent colleges throughout the country. It is one of the most representative samples of rape among college students. Psychologist Mary P. Koss from Kent State University reported in depth on this major study.[13] Professor Koss found that 15 percent of these college women had experienced rape at some time in their lives. Rape was defined as forced intercourse, and intercourse included vaginal, anal, or oral sex.[14] In addition to the 15 percent who had been raped, 12 percent of these college women had experienced an attempted rape. In the male sample of college students, only 4 percent of the men admitted raping a woman and 3 percent said they attempted to rape a woman. What do these findings imply about how men and women relate sexually to each other and how they define rape?

In the *Ms.* magazine study the researchers asked questions that sought to ascertain whether force or threat of force was used to have vaginal, oral, or anal sex. Then if the answers indicated that force in some way had been used, it was clear from a legal point of view that a rape had occurred. But the researchers still needed to ask whether the *participants* thought a rape had occurred, There was quite a surprise in their findings: *An astonishing 73 percent of the women who had met the legal definition of rape did not label themselves as rape victims!* Similarly, the great majority of men (88 percent) who were classified as having committed a rape said that what they did was certainly not rape. Only 5 percent of the women who were raped reported the incident to the police. Both men and women admitted that force or the threat of force had been used to penetrate the woman and that such use of force meets the legal definition of rape. Why then did both the men and women in the great majority of cases deny that a rape had occurred?

The answer becomes a bit clearer when we note that the women who had been raped revealed that 84 percent of the rapists were known to them and that 57 percent of the rapists were their dates! These women thought that what had happened was part of a relationship and therefore somewhat their fault. As a result they would not call it rape and preferred to personally deal with the offender. In fact, 42 percent of the women who were raped said they later had sex again with the offender! The men reported that they later had sex with 55 percent of the women whom they had legally assaulted. This is not the first study to report this sort of reaction to sexual assault among acquaintances.[15] The key conclusion is that a great many forced sexual encounters that meet the legal definition of rape are not thought of as "really" rape by either participant. This is so despite the fact that many women feel very damaged by these experiences.

But no matter how it is labeled, we need to know why there is so much forced sexuality among dates and acquaintances. It certainly sounds like there must be some very serious lack of clear communication for so much unwanted behavior to be happening. When asked, these women said they had made their objections to having sex clear to their partners. But the offenders stated that the women they pressured into sex were ambivalent and didn't really know what they wanted or were just pretending not to want sex.

I am convinced that a major cause of this miscommunication is our traditional dating system with its adversarial script, which portrays the woman as the sexually reluctant person and the man as the persuader. That script is the poison pill in any formulae designed to control rape. The fact that this system still operates at all is powerful testimony to the lack of equality between women and men. It further shows that even in the late 1990s this inequality makes it difficult for young people to clearly communicate their sexual feelings to one another.

The adversarial system allows little open discussion concerning willingness or desire to have sex. Clues, not clear language, have to be used to solve the mystery of sexual intentions. This is particularly the case the first time a couple is together and especially so for younger couples. For clues a man will look at his date to see if she took another drink, if she came to his apartment, if she let him touch her breast, if she laughed at a dirty joke. A woman will check to see if her date smiled in a friendly way at her, if he laughed at her jokes, listened to her opinions, and kissed her tenderly. Then both the man and the woman guess what are the intentions of the other person. Clear communication is not a likely outcome of such a telepathic system of dating.

Open and honest discussion is blocked by the roles men and women are supposed to play in the adversarial system, and so manipulation to achieve goals becomes the technique of choice. A date may come to a man's apartment to show him that if he keeps seeing her something sexual might happen. A man may show affection to his date to make her think that if she has sex with him he might get serious with her. How can one tell, without open discussion, whether these acts are honest expressions of feelings or manipulative poses? The man might interpret her visit to his apartment as a sign she's ready right then for sex and she may view his attention to her as indicating lasting interest—and they both may well be mistaken. Of course, some young people are starting to grow beyond such primitive and misleading games, but most still seem to play by these cat-and-mouse roles and then end up in a trap they themselves helped produce.

The *Ms.* magazine study affords us insight into how this situation of mutual confusion operates:

> Although the "deafness" of some males involved in acquaintance rapes may, in part, be due to not being told in a decisive way what the woman wants, many men simply discount what a woman is saying or reinterpret it to fit what they want to hear. They have been raised to believe that women will always resist sex to avoid the appearance of being promiscuous (and indeed, some do), will always say "no" when they really mean "yes," and always want men to dominate them and show that they are in control.[16]

This study and others found that the men with the most traditional attitudes toward women were most likely to hold these views. Traditional attitudes toward the "proper" roles of men and women are a basis for this play acting in sexual and romantic communication. Psychologist Charlene Muelenhard of the University of Kansas has undertaken research on college couples. She reports that some 39 percent of women said they did offer token resistance even when they wanted sex. Muelenhard found that when a woman thinks a man is traditional and therefore expects her to show resistance, then she is most likely to feign token resistance.[17] More recent evidence from Susan Sprecher and her colleagues in the United States, Russia, and Japan also supports Muelenhard's findings.[18] Let us not forget that these same men whose traditional beliefs put pressure on women to keep up this pretense are the most likely to accept some force as part of their end of the adversarial script. Just like the imprisoned rapist "Billy," they set up their prey and then they pounce.

The adversarial system of sexual encounters is a no-win situation for both women and men. The man's role is to convince the woman to enter a sexual relationship. Little wonder, then, that many women think of men as only interested in sex and as "using" women. Empowering women to initiate sexuality as freely as men do, when they wish to, would make the seduction role of men unnecessary and that would reduce the sexual pressures on women as well as on men. Likewise, if men were more honest and open about their sexual feelings, they would give women a clearer basis upon which to decide if they wanted to proceed with a relationship.

Both men and women would gain a broader perspective on each other if they spoke their minds more honestly. But honesty requires willingness to risk and that requires an equality between men and women in society. As things stand, women have more to risk in a relationship, for they are judged more harshly and they are pressured more to get married than men are. Again, the traditional inequality between men and women comes back to haunt us.

We can hardly expect most young people to be able to define a rape situation clearly when they hardly understand their own or the other person's real motives. When pressure by the male for sexual "favors" is part of the system, how can this pressure not be expected? When women are taught not to express their sexual interests freely, then men will have an excuse for not believing women who say no. The system is a mine field waiting to explode in the faces of all participants.

A key reason for our paralysis in regard to openly declaring our sexual interest is the fear of being thought immoral by showing "too much" interest in sexuality. Given these conditions, how can we expect people to use contraception reasonably and to think of other outcomes?

They are too busy saying to themselves: "Let's not be crude and talk openly about sex but instead let's guess what the other person thinks and then see who is better able to get what they want out of the relationship." I think it's time for all of us to give a different message to people who are dating. My message would be: "For everyone's sake, sit down and tell each other how you feel about your relationship and about having sex with each other."

It is not an easy situation to resolve. *Both women and men* must stop playing this dangerous sexual guessing game. For if just the women stop, then the men who are trained to get as much sex as they can will still abuse them. Likewise, if just the men stop, then the women who are trained to attract men but not to initiate sex will feel there is something wrong if men are expecting them to initiate sexuality equally. Both men and women must change their attitudes toward sexual honesty for there to be a significant change. There has to be a moratorium on sexual game playing and we need a great deal of help from parents, schools, friends, and professionals so we can learn together how to be honest about sexual feelings. Fundamentally, we need to promote gender equality in our basic economic, political, religious, educational, and family institutions. There are moves in this direction in some school programs and in group therapeutic sessions run by social workers and others. Also, we do find more women today rejecting the adversarial system and defining a situation as rape that earlier they might have tolerated as the price of dating.[19] But we still have a long way to go and very little leadership is forthcoming.

There are many other social scientists who agree with my perspective on the major causes of acquaintance rape. For example, sociologist Allan Johnson of Wesleyan University states a similar position about rape:

> It is difficult to believe that such widespread violence is the responsibility of a small lunatic fringe of psychopathic men. That sexual violence is so pervasive supports the view that the locus of violence against women rests squarely in the middle of what our culture defines as "normal" interaction between men and women. The numbers reiterate a reality that American women have lived with for years: Sexual violence against women is part of the everyday fabric of American life.[20]

Bear in mind that when we talk about college couples we are dealing in most cases with people who accept premarital intercourse under some conditions. Between 80 percent and 90 percent of college men and women are sexually experienced. If there were no traditional roles dictating that women must pretend sexual restraint and men must pretend romantic interest, women and men could talk more honestly to each other.

Wouldn't it be far better to have pluralism in the scripts we allow? Isn't choice better than the single battlefield script to which we now adhere? With a more pluralistic view, women who felt more sexually interested than their date could reveal that fact. Men then would feel less compelled always to be ready for sex. A couple could discuss what they really believed about sex and romance, and this openness would afford each of them insight into discovering what type of person and what type of relationship they really wanted. Most importantly, the honesty and equality promoted by pluralism would minimize the miscommunication that is related to date rape.

But many people now think such honesty could ruin a blossoming relationship, for it violates the traditional adversarial dating system that young people are trained to abide by. Maybe the man will feel threatened by female sexual initiation? Maybe the woman will be afraid to take the sexual initiative equally with the man? Surely it takes time and some pain to build and accept a new pluralistic system of dating. But the alternative is to keep women in an inferior position, to risk miscommunication from both women and men, and to have a great deal of unwanted sexuality. The adversarial system is a blueprint for perpetuating interpersonal disasters like date rape. We just cannot accept it!

But why has the way men and women sexually interact changed so slowly? The major reason is the difficulty of changing the two factors we spoke of earlier—the lesser power of women and macho roles for men. As long as women have less power than men in society, they will be leery of risking their future by boldly declaring their sexual interests. Also, as long as we encourage men to think of themselves as dominant and to legitimize their physical aggression, they will be more likely to use force when someone in the less powerful group denies them what they want. The only way to change all this is to do whatever it takes to achieve a more pluralistic system of dating. Let me turn to that now.

The Pluralistic Model of Dating

The adversarial mode of dating protects the woman from force only as long as she presents herself as without a doubt unwilling to have sex. To the degree that she expresses any interest in sex she becomes fair game. This issue was the subject of the award-winning 1988 movie with Jodie Foster and Kelly McGillis titled *The Accused.* To the men who raped her the behavior that "justified" the rape was Jodie Foster's seductive actions in the bar. She wore a short, tight dress, she danced suggestively, and she openly showed her sexual interest in one of the men by kissing him while dancing with him. Under the adversarial system, by doing that she had given up her protection from physical force. In the adversarial system the woman is not supposed to make direct statements affirming her readiness for intercourse. That means a man can take any hint of sexual interest as indicating her readiness to have intercourse. The bolder her actions the more likely the man will conclude she's ready for anything. This system of female silence places all women at risk of rape if the man interprets their actions to mean they are ready. It means that a woman cannot show any of her sexual feelings without the risk of being misunderstood. It is, therefore, clearly a system that restricts women's freedom of expression and treats women as inferior to men.

It is surely not just or fair but it is true that as long as women do not have the right to say yes to sex and to say it openly and without recrimination, many men will not grant women the right to say no. When there are no honest, direct words for a woman to show her interest in sex, then her denials will not be believed. That opens the door wide to the sexual abuse of women.

If we accept a pluralistic system in which both women and men are allowed to say both no and yes, then words are taken more seriously. This has important consequences for men as well as women. The adversarial system tells men to be always ready to pick up the indirect clue showing that a woman wants sex. Because she is not empowered to speak, he must always be ready to act. It is high time to give men and women a pluralistic system that allows them both to start with a two-word vocabulary. Both women and men must be granted the right clearly to say yes and clearly to say no. What a difference that would make! How that would clear the air!

Some people with good intentions stress that the man must search for and abide by any hint of sexual rejection by the woman in order to protect her from being forced into sex. What is not realized is that by taking that stance one is focusing on the woman's role in rejecting sex and the man's responsibility as the initiator of sex. In effect that means one is supporting the adversarial system, and that surely is not helpful to women. Women must be treated as having an equal right to assert sexual interest and men an equal right to deny interest. We must equalize these rights if we are to have honest, equal, and responsible sexual negotiation. When a woman is pictured as someone who has to be persuaded, who cannot make the first move, and who better not be too forward about sex, she is forced into the role of a person who is unable to speak her mind. This is surely not the image of someone who is equal in rights with a man. To support such an image is to support a system that promotes rape of inferior creatures who cannot speak for themselves.

This view of women as rejectors of sex, in need of protection by men, is similar to an approach to erotica that we discussed in the last chapter. Some people argue that we must censor erotica because only then will women be safe from overly aroused men. That position also supports the view of women as sexually restrictive and men as sexually uncontrollable. Such a perspective supports traditional male/female roles and does more harm than good in any attempt to equalize the rights of men and women.

Let us be aware of the contradictory view of men that is presented by right-wing feminists on pornography as compared to rape. Catherine MacKinnon has portrayed men who see pornography as responding with forced sexuality because pornography is, in her words, "comparable to saying 'kill' to a trained guard dog."[21] But how can we square that bestial view of men in response to porn with the demand that men stop when they are with a woman who attracts them but doesn't want to go further? Once again the answer seems to be not to demonize all men as uncontrollable beasts, or expect the current adversarial system to produce answers. Rather, we need to work to create greater equality in society between men and women so they can both openly and equally negotiate their sexual encounters.

The best protection for any human being is empowerment to act independently—not the assignment of a "protected" role that restricts speaking on one's own behalf. As Katie Roiphe has said, that childlike view infantilizes women and blocks the path to equality.[22] Of course, we all need help sometimes. But if we need it all the time, we are more like children than adults. How many readers believe that a woman would freely choose to be seen as an innocent always in need of help rather than as an autonomous person who makes up her own mind? The answer to this question is a good indicator of just where each individual stands in terms of promoting an egalitarian and pluralistic sexual script.

We need to accept the reality that both men and women have sexual desires and thus they both will seek some type of sexual relationship. Therefore, both must be equally empowered to make free choices in the area of sexuality. Surely there are differences among people in regard to what conditions must be met before a sexual relationship occurs. Some people require marriage, some require just a smile. But we must first admit that both genders desire sexual relationships. Affirm that in a straightforward and frank fashion and you open the door to honest, equal, and responsible negotiation. Deny that and you promote the good girl/bad girl view of women and the mutual manipulation inherent in the adversarial system.

To enjoy a pluralistic system we must create enough equality among people so that we all feel free to make honest choices. Sexual pluralism requires that women and men learn to negotiate with each other about sexual relationships much the same way as we usually negotiate about other relationships, like friendships. We indicate to others if we are interested in a type of friendship that allows deep sharing of intimacies or in a casual type of pleasure-sharing friendship. We can do precisely the same with sex and thereby find those who are like-minded and who will share what is expected. As we move in this direction, pleasure and affection will increasingly replace force and violence.

The bottom line is that in order to build a pluralistic system and lessen rape we must work to create greater equality between women and men.[23] Under our present system many women are having sex but having it under conditions that leave them confused and hurt. Most men too are perplexed and frustrated. We desperately need to make some changes. A pluralistic system would extricate us from the sexual quicksand in which we are mired today.

Getting from Here to There

There is broad agreement among experts throughout the world that Western societies with repressive sexual attitudes and traditional male/female roles are more likely to have high rates of all forms of sex crimes. This position was clearly stated by the key participants in the International Conference on the Treatment of Sex Offenders held in Minneapolis starting in 1989.[24] The United States is the prime example of the truth of this assertion. Compared to Scandinavian countries, West Germany, France, and even England we are sexually repressive, and though we are changing, we do retain strong support for traditional gender roles in our sexual relationships. Sociologist Gilbert Geis and psychologists Paul Abramson and Haruo Hayashi have estimated that the incidence of rape in the United States is several times as high as that in most other Western countries![25] Can anyone doubt that there are things we must change in our gender system?

On the personal level we need to learn how to express the fine nuances of what we think and feel about sexuality and to listen to how the other person feels and thinks. We have to do this to get our own thoughts and feelings clear to ourselves. Then we can level with one another, for we will really know what our sexual views are and we will therefore be able to express ourselves and to understand one another with more clarity. Under these new conditions we will be more capable of negotiating a relationship that has a much better chance of being mutually rewarding instead of mutually threatening. Some of this type of change is occurring right now but clearly at too slow a pace. Despite the last sexual revolution, many women still feel that most men continue to judge them only in terms of their physical attractiveness. Also, men report that women continue to look at men predominantly in terms of their success potential.[26] The cost in violence against women in our country is too high to allow these old behavior patterns to continue. Equality in the economic and political spheres is the essential ingredient needed to free ourselves further from the traditional gender role trap. Then we can better negotiate the kinds of relationship we want in terms of love as well as sex.

As noted in chapter 4, gender power changes are occurring. Steven McLaughlin, a sociologist at the Batelle Memorial Institute, led a team of researchers to examine the evidence of changes in women's roles in this century.[27] McLaughlin and his coauthors concluded that there has been a long-range trend toward greater power and independence on the part of women throughout this century. The parents of the baby boomers, born in the late 1920s and 1930s, were the generation who temporarily moved away from that trend, at least in their traditional family attitudes, during the 1950s. But their children, the baby boomers, renewed with vigor the quest for equality between men and women. There is no doubt that we are on a long-term path toward greater gender equality and we are pluralizing our concepts of gender roles. But in order to speed up this movement we must encourage this pluralistic view of sexuality and afford some relief from our very high incidence of rape.

My purpose in this chapter was not to cover all types of rape. I have said nothing about homosexual rape, female rape of men, statutory rape, or sadistic rape. I have focused on acquaintance/date rape, for it is the most prevalent form of rape and is most directly relevant to the dominant culture in this country.

But there is one other type of rape—marital rape—that throws additional light on my pluralistic thesis and which I must briefly mention. Marital rape illustrates that our traditional gender roles have consequences for long-term love relationships as well as for short-term dating relationships. The first prosecution in this country of a husband for rape by his wife occurred in 1978 in Oregon (*Stave* v. *Rideout*). So enamored are we of our Victorian past that the very idea that a husband could rape his wife did not make sense to most people. Even today many of our states do not have laws against rape in marriage. Such rape does occur even though, like date rape, the victim often does not define it as rape. Nevertheless, studies indicate that about one in every eight wives are forced to have intercourse in ways that meet the legal definition of rape.[28]

Clearly marital rape is a further outcome of male dominance.

Accepting such an act as legal denies a married woman the right to make a sexual choice. According to the male-dominant view, when she married she gave up her right to say no. Before marriage the traditionalists expect the "good girl" to always say no and after marriage to always say yes. Greater gender equality has made most married couples open to more sexual negotiation, but this will not be successful until the general economic and political power of wives in this society is closer to that of their husbands. Directly in line with my views are the suggestions from two sociologists who have carefully studied marital rape:

> Marital rape will not be eliminated until the status of women in society is fundamentally changed. In particular, this involves the empowerment of women through improved economic, political and social opportunities so that they are no longer the dependent and vulnerable partners in marriage.[29]

Clearly my ethical standard of accepting those sexual acts that are honest, equal, and responsible should motivate us to pursue this equality in all our institutions. I will deal more specifically in the last chapter of this book with how such egalitarian changes can be encouraged. But it is clear that a breakthrough in gender equality will not occur without greater conscious awareness of the tragic outcomes, like rape, of the traditional way men and women still relate to each other in today's society. We need to recognize that power differences between women and men in the overall society are the roots of much of the violence between the sexes.

Our present-day society benefits by the increased empowerment of women to share in all walks of life. When we see at what price, for women and men, the subjugation of women is purchased, can we hesitate to promote this change in our own lives and in that of others? The future incidence of rape will reflect the way we answer this all-important question.

8

Sex Therapy:
Conforming to a Troubled Society

Americans: Experts in Creating Sexual Distress

The American approach to sexuality guarantees that sex therapy will be a growth business. America is exceptional at producing sexual anorexics who constantly worry about whether they are engaging in too much sex, sexual gluttons who constantly seek ways to stuff themselves, and more than a few sexual bulemics who both purge and binge. It's as hard to find a sexual gourmet in America as it is to find a beggar at Tiffany's.

Do sex therapists help us to understand and resolve the many causes of our sexual distress? Let's begin to answer this question by remembering that the sex therapists who attempt to assist us in our distress are themselves a product of our society. They, too, have grown up in our sexually ambivalent culture. So it is very important that sex therapists overcome the biases and myths that we have discussed in this book and that block so many Americans from a clear understanding of their own sexuality. Unless therapists have a clear understanding of our society, they will simply end up teaching clients how to conform to our sexually troubled and confused society. And that helps no one, for it simply perpetuates our sexual problems on both the personal and social levels.

Most therapists would agree that therapy is supposed to empower clients so they can become better able to make their own problem-solving choices. To accomplish that the therapist must present the client with a broader range of choices than those traditionally offered by our society. As I will illustrate, it is the narrow choices offered by society that produce much of the distress we experience. Today many more therapists do indeed learn to become aware of the sexual biases and blind spots in our society and are able to share their expansive views with their clientele. But many sex therapists do not have that social perspective and rather than empowering their clients to greater awareness of the causes of their distresses, they simply promote conformity to popular ideas about sexuality. Sex therapists surely want to contribute to our sexual well-being, but all too often they are taken in by some of the same sexual beliefs that are distressing their clients.

Let me illustrate my position by discussing the specific ways a large number of sex therapists treat three of the most common sexual problems that people bring to them:

1. Difficulties experienced by women in reaching orgasm in coitus.
2. Problems of men who reach orgasm "too quickly."
3. Fears of people who believe they are "addicted" to sexuality.

Look Ma—No Hands!

In the medical jargon of sex therapy, a woman who is unable to achieve orgasm during intercourse without her clitoris being touched "suffers" from what is called "coital anorgasmia." The late sex therapist Helen Singer Kaplan estimated that this inability holds true for the majority of women and that it is the most common sexual complaint of women.[1] She left open somewhat the question as to whether all of these women suffer from a sexual "dysfunction," but William Masters and Virginia Johnson, who in 1970 introduced sex therapy to the world, feel that this is definitely a sexual dysfunction. Masters and Johnson reject the idea of telling women that it is normal to have this limitation, saying: "Since many women who have coital anorgasmia are distressed by their situation, what is gained by telling them that everything is normal and no cause for concern?"[2]

I have an answer for that question. What is gained is the woman's sense of relief and her realization that she can choose to live with the fact that her clitoris must be touched to have an orgasm. It sounds to me like a very reasonable conclusion to reach. But in our society women who cannot have an orgasm in coitus without clitoral contact are often made to feel personally inadequate. *What is gained by that?* As I shall show, there is no objective basis for calling this a dysfunction. The therapist who negatively labels coital anorgasmia as a sexual "dysfunction" is thus increasing the anxiety of the client instead of decreasing it. Is that a sound therapeutic stance?

A century ago women who did not achieve coital orgasm would not have been so pressured as they are today. The historian Carl Degler relates the story of a nineteenth-century English mother who was asked by her daughter how she should behave on her wedding night. The mother advised her daughter: "Lie still and think of the Empire."[3] But times have changed, and now such women would be violating the newer cultural norm which says that the sexually "functional" female is "fully" sexually responsive and can have orgasms in a very wide variety of sexual ways, and certainly in that most socially favored act of vaginal intercourse. But when the smoke of this modern-day hype has cleared, those who bother to look can see the real difficulty felt by most women in achieving a "hands-off" orgasm. Here is a quote from one of Masters and Johnson's cases:

> I've always been able to have orgasms when I masturbate, but it's never happened with my husband. After eight years of marriage this has really become a strain on our relationship—for him, because he feels he's inadequate; for me, because I'm missing a special kind of sharing.[4]

Women who do have coital orgasm without clitoral contact by themselves or their partner often manipulate their sexual positions to ensure pressure on the clitoral area. They do this commonly by getting on top of the man so they can produce clitoral pressure from the man's pubic area. Others lie on their stomachs and have the man enter them from behind while they get clitoral pressure from the bed or a pillow below them.

Therapists have their own techniques of trying to help women achieve hands-off orgasms in intercourse. The treatment that Masters and Johnson and others recommend is the "bridge technique." This involves having coitus in a position, such as facing each other side by side, so that one of the partners can easily manually stimulate the clitoris during coitus. Over time the manual stimulation is gradually reduced and coital thrusting alone carries one into orgasm. The technique is called the "bridge" because it affords a means of traveling from needing manual clitoral contact to not needing it. Helen Singer Kaplan has said that this technique works for less than half of her clients, but a variety of other therapies helps some of the others.

The problem I have with the therapeutic approach to coital anorgasmia does not concern the "bridge technique." My objection is that therapists define coitally anorgasmic women as having a "sexual dysfunction." I see no scientific ground for labeling the vast majority of women "dysfunctional" and thereby raising their anxiety levels and pressuring them into therapy. To me that is not empowering the client because it is not giving insight or choice to the client. Instead, it is instructing the client to conform to the prevailing custom of pursuing hands-off coital orgasms. After all, is there really anything wrong with a woman playing with her clitoris or having her partner do that during intercourse? That can be very exciting to her partner as well as to herself. Why not promote that as one perfectly acceptable choice and that way stop stigmatizing such women as "dysfunctional"?

I've used the word "dysfunctional" several times. It's a term from physiology referring to the disruptive operations of our bodily organs and it was borrowed by the sex therapists from medicine. Why are sex therapists using this term and what do they mean by it? Here's how Masters and Johnson answer that question: "Sexual dysfunctions [are] conditions in which the ordinary physical responses of sexual function are impaired."[5] That definition is not very helpful for it simply substitutes one unknown term for another. We aren't told what the "ordinary physical responses" are supposed to be and so we can hardly tell if they are "impaired." Further, since the majority of women respond mainly to direct clitoral stimulation, isn't that an "ordinary physical response"? When only a minority of women can experience coital orgasm without clitoral contact, can that be called "ordinary"? Are we sure there is something broken that we are trying to fix or do we just like the impressive medical sound of the word "dysfunction"?

A woman who decides to have her breasts enlarged does not get labeled as having a "breast dysfunction." From a medical standpoint such a woman is normal. The changes that she chooses to make are not at all essential to the normal functioning of her breasts. Rather, she is conforming to a society that prefers a larger breast size. Similarly, the woman whose only complaint is that she's coitally anorgasmic is not thereby indicating any disturbance of sexual functioning. She, like the woman undergoing breast enlargement, is merely choosing to conform to societal expectations. As I see it, the coitally anorgasmic woman may well be distressed; but she has no physical dysfunction. Why not offer her the choice of nonconformity rather than teaching her how to conform?

Most of you will recall that around 1980 the possibility of women having a "G-spot orgasm" was publicized.[6] A G-spot orgasm occurs by massaging the anterior wall of the vagina at a depth of about two inches, the location of the G-spot. Now that we know that a G-spot orgasm is possible, should we add G-spot orgasms to what is considered necessary for a "fully functional" female and create a new dysfunction called "G-spot anorgasmia"? I see both coital orgasms and G-spot orgasms as potentialities that some women can develop. But that is very different from saying that if you do not learn to develop these potentials, then your "ordinary physical responses are impaired."

Those sex therapists who call coital anorgasmia a dysfunction are being taken in by today's popular customs pressuring women to be more and more sexually responsive. Therapists can personally favor this orgasmic expansiveness, but that does not justify pressuring their clients into therapy by placing stigmatized labels on them. As mentioned earlier, therapy is supposed to be about empowerment of clients, and not about pressuring people to conform to popular customs.

Let me relate a little story that will show you just how far some people will go to conform to social expectations about "no-hands orgasms." At a convention of the prestigious International Academy of Sex Research, a gynecologist from Dayton, Ohio, James C. Burt, described a surgical solution for coital anorgasmia.[7] He had devised an operation that would realign the angle of the vagina so that, in the man-on-top position, the entering penis would directly contact the clitoris and thus would help ensure female orgasm. He said hundreds of women came to him asking for that operation because they could not achieve coital orgasm in their husbands' favorite position. The surgical procedure is rather drastic. It involves cutting into the major muscle that runs from the pelvic bone to the tail bone, the pubococcygeal (PC) muscle. It is a very delicate procedure. If the PC muscle is too severely damaged, it could well make it more difficult to reach orgasm, not to mention other difficulties that might occur in giving birth.

When this "love surgery" was reported at our International Convention, I suggested to Dr. Burt a simpler solution for women who wanted to be coitally orgasmic in the man-on-top position. Some adult sex stores sell a "sex toy" that is a two-inch-long hump shaped of soft material and is attached atop the base of the erect penis by elastic straps. Then when the penis enters the vagina, the soft cushion attachment on top of the penis easily makes contact with the clitoris and aids in female orgasm. I suggested that this was a far easier solution than surgery for those women who insisted on hands-off coital orgasms. Dr. Burt seemed surprised by my suggestion, but after a moment of silence he responded: "Well, that might work, but you and I both know that most men would never bother to wear such a contraption." A most revealing commentary on our culture! Women will undergo major surgery but men will not wear a simple sex gadget.

Dr. Burt called his operation "love surgery" and performed it on hundreds of women who wanted to achieve orgasm in the man-on-top position without manual contact with the clitoris. These wives were willing to undergo surgery to conform to their husbands' wishes and become "functional." This is an extreme example of how inappropriate terms like "functional" and "dysfunctional" can help convince women to undergo dangerous surgery.

A final footnote to this story: Many women found this operation to be unsuccessful and physically damaging, and Dr. Burt was sued for harm done to the bodies and sexual lives of these women. Because of these lawsuits, his "love surgery" practice has ceased. Some women alleged that Dr. Burt performed the operation without their permission because he felt it was in their best interest to be "fully functional."[8]

One other way to look for an answer to the "naturalness and ordinariness" of the hands-off coital orgasm is to examine how women masturbate. Women are not typically instructed how to masturbate. Do many women masturbate without touching their clitoris? Hardly any women do! The vast majority of women rub the clitoral area. They do not rely on vaginal insertion to produce their orgasm. So women know what feels like an "ordinary physical response" to them. Isn't it time for all sex therapists to accept this?

Masters and Johnson and others have argued that there is some indirect pressure on the clitoral area which is the result of vaginal intercourse and which can produce orgasm. In a public response, Dr. Sanford Copley has compared this argument by Masters and Johnson to expecting men to reach orgasm by pulling on the scrotum—the skin covering the testes. This scrotal skin is, after all, connected to the penis, and so pulling on it will create some sensation in the penis. It is conceivable that a man could reach an orgasm if such stretching of the scrotal skin occurred long enough and he could be induced to wait around for that to happen. But surely it would be more efficient simply to rub the penis directly, just as men do when they masturbate.

No one has yet invented the term "scrotal skin dysfunction" for men who require direct penile contact to reach orgasm, and not very many men would seek treatment for that "dysfunction." But women do accept the label of "coital anorgasmia" and hope to "cure" themselves by therapeutic and surgical treatment. So the "dysfunctional" label sticks. You tell me who benefits the most from all this unscientific labeling.

Society's Clock: Just How Fast Is Too Fast?

My criticism of unnecessary therapeutic labeling also applies to the way in which sex therapists handle a very common sexual complaint of men. Many men feel distressed because they reach orgasm "too quickly." Sex therapists are rarely at a loss for developing additional stigmatized labels. They see this quick orgasmic ability as a "dysfunction" and call it "premature ejaculation." In a typical case of premature ejaculation, a couple comes in for therapy and both report that the man "comes too quickly."

Now think about that statement for a moment. Orgasm is pleasurable.

Consider: would a young boy who was participating in a "circle jerk" with other young boys to see who could come first think he "came too quickly" if he won the contest? Of course not; he'd be admired as the champ by the other boys who couldn't get that sought-after orgasmic pleasure so speedily. But adult customs indicate that men must be able to prolong their orgasms. When men say they come too quickly, they usually mean that they feel bad about not conforming to some social expectation regarding the speed of orgasm. In "circle jerks" and intercourse the proper timing is based on quite different social expectations. Let's see just what those expectations are in sexual intercourse.

Think back to the time before the 1960s when we had a more male-dominated society. There was less concern then for the female partner and many men desired to reach orgasm quickly because of the fear of discovery or doubts about how long the interest of their female partner would last. In those days, men often bragged about the speed with which they could reach orgasm. A man would relate with pride how quickly "he had come." To reach orgasm quickly was to fulfill the male social demands of that day. Today when men think they "came too quickly," they are responding to a new set of social demands. Plainly, the desired orgasmic speed varies far more by custom than by any measure of "ordinary physical response" of one's body.

As our sexual standards became more egalitarian, we began to insist that more attention be paid to the orgasmic satisfaction of women. So today when we say "too quick" we mean that there was not enough time for the woman to reach orgasm. If a man has been taught to believe in this egalitarian sexual standard, then he will feel something is wrong if he reaches his orgasm long before his partner has time to reach hers. But let's be clear—endorsement of this notion doesn't necessarily mean that a man is egalitarian. He may get a sense of power and control from feeling that he can help produce his sexual partner's orgasm.

In today's more sexually egalitarian society, both men and women may really feel that something important is missing in their lovemaking if the man has an orgasm too quickly for the woman. But there is no obvious physical or psychological dysfunction in any sense except that the man's orgasmic speed is out of sync with the egalitarian expectations of our day. Women today do want more sexual satisfaction in intercourse—remember therapists are promoting that search by defining coital anorgasmia as a "dysfunction." If women are to alter the "dysfunction" of coital anorgasmia and to learn to achieve hands-off orgasms, men will need to learn to prolong their orgasmic time. Those men who don't do this will see themselves as "premature ejaculators." Those men who do learn to delay ejaculation will accordingly expect their partner to be better able to achieve orgasm in intercourse. So here we truly have two "dysfunctions," each of which promotes therapy for the other. Not bad for the therapist.

Just because a premature ejaculator and a coitally anorgasmic woman may wish to change doesn't mean they deserve to be labeled as "dysfunctional" by a sex therapist. These people are *distressed* because they don't quite measure up to the current fashion in how to have orgasms. Such fashions won't be the same a decade or two down the road. Sexual customs like these are written in sand. The tide of social change will come in and wash one custom away and some other custom will then be etched in the same wet sand, until the next social tide washes it away.

One basic technique that is used to "correct" premature ejaculation is called the squeeze technique, developed by Masters and Johnson. The woman stimulates the man's penis until he tells her he is close to orgasm and then she squeezes just under the crown of the penis to stop the orgasm. Then they resume stimulation and she stops his orgasm the same way again. Eventually the man learns how to control his orgasm himself. This technique is successful with most men although occasionally men in therapy become unable to achieve orgasm when they do want it. But by and large the squeeze technique and similar methods are very successful in enabling most men to gain more control over their orgasms. Helen Singer Kaplan claimed that 90 percent of her clients were "cured" after fourteen weeks of treatment.[9] Others point out that changes do not last.[10]

If sex therapists can reduce a couple's distress due to premature ejaculation, why then am I criticizing those therapists? Surely it is proper to offer people the option of prolonging their copulatory time—many men and women do appreciate that. But my point is that this can be done without demeaning the premature ejaculator by labeling him as dysfunctional. Medical sex therapist Helen Singer Kaplan has called premature ejaculation "ejaculatory incontinence."[11] That makes premature ejaculation comparable to lacking control of urination and defecation. Is that a nice, thoughtful label for a therapist to use?

Bear in mind that when sex therapists make these harsh judgments, they believe they are promoting "healing" of the "dysfunction" and thus greater sexual satisfaction for everyone. Most sex therapists would vigorously assert that they are not ordering people to come in to see them. Only those who want to change and are distressed sufficiently will come for therapy. Despite such denials, labeling something as a "dysfunction" spreads the word to all with that condition that they *should* be unhappy and that they really do *need* therapeutic services, whether they know it or not.

Accordingly, I believe it would be fairer and more scientific simply to point out that such speedy ejaculation doesn't conform to today's sexual expectations. Also, the therapist could offer a couple the possibility of accepting the situation as it is and increasing manual or oral orgasms. By calling premature ejaculation a dysfunction, choice is removed. Who would choose to remain "dysfunctional"?

What does the American Psychiatric Association (APA) say about premature ejaculation? The APA represents the high-prestige medical therapists (psychiatrists) in all fields who have a strong influence on the terminology and therapeutic ideas used by sex therapists. The third edition of the APA's *Diagnostic and Statistical Manual of Mental Disorders* (DSM-III, 1980) defines premature ejaculation as the "absence of reasonable control."[12] But that definition is not much help because we aren't told how to recognize "reasonable" control. Instead, the APA tells us that the clinician will make that judgment. But that simply gives free rein to whatever sexual norms that clinician happens to endorse as "reasonable." Just how scientific is a set of labels that is applied at the whim of the therapist you happen to be seeing?

The fourth edition, DSM-IV, defines premature ejaculation as orgasm with "minimal stimulation and before the person wants it."[13] Again, who defines "minimal"? The concept can always be filled by using societal norms and not by scientific measures of a carefully defined concept. The social influence is seen in how differently we view the woman who has quick orgasmic abilities. If a woman reaches orgasm within seconds after intromission, no sex therapist would call that a sexual "dysfunction." No one says she lacks "reasonable control." In fact, such a woman is praised for being sexually "responsive." Most women would call such a woman lucky and not label her as dysfunctional. Why such unequal treatment of the male and female by sex therapists? Why isn't such a female called a "prematurely orgasmic woman"? The difference between "too quick" and "responsive" seems to depend on whether you're male or female.

You may be thinking that we don't label fast orgasmic women as "dysfunctional" because we trust that such women will not turn over and go to sleep after their orgasm. But we do wonder whether men after orgasm will fulfill their partner's desire for orgasm and so we encourage men to learn to hold back their orgasms. Of course, it is true that most men require a rest period before they can regain their erection after orgasm and therefore, unlike women, they would have to wait to resume vaginal intercourse.

But even after orgasm a man's hands and tongue are still functional. He is fully capable of oral and manual stimulation of the woman to orgasm. Indeed, he could use those capabilities and help the woman have several orgasms before he even enters her, or he could masturbate before trying intercourse and thereby delay his next ejaculation. What's wrong with these options? Why are they not more routinely recommended by therapists? Again, I believe the answer is that some therapists just don't trust the dominant male to do any of those things for the woman.

We should not lose sight of the fact that we expect a woman who has reached orgasm to remain active until the man reaches his orgasm. So we are *obligating* the woman, no matter how she feels, to continue having intercourse until the man reaches orgasm. We don't even question whether she will do this. Many people think of this sexual service as showing a woman's nurturance. But it also demonstrates her inferior power to that of the man and sometimes makes her feel "used." Our therapeutic labeling of quick orgasms only for men reflects the inequality in our gender roles. And so, even when we encourage men to be concerned about women's orgasms, we do it in a way that reveals the man is still in control.

One question remains: Why has vaginal intercourse occupied center stage in our sexual scripts for so long? We would not be going to sex therapists if "premature ejaculation" occurred only in oral, anal, or manual sex. One reason is that vaginal intercourse is an act which is connected to reproduction and so in a society that has a long history of placing importance on the Biblical command "Be fruitful and multiply," intercourse will be valued. That emphasis upon reproductive sex may also indicate our discomfort with having sex only for pleasure and our need to justify sexuality.

The emphasis on vaginal intercourse is not really to the woman's orgasmic advantage. For as we have seen, such intercourse without clitoral contact is probably the poorest condition for guaranteeing her orgasm but it does virtually guarantee the male orgasm. So in the name of egalitarianism we promote an act that has poor orgasmic possibilities for most women. I must add that even though orgasm is less certain, vaginal intercourse is sought by many women for the physical pleasure involved.

But if we are striving to become an egalitarian society, and are aware of overpopulation, shouldn't we consider giving more equal emphasis to other ways of achieving orgasm for *both* men and women? We can at least make people more conscious of why they don't give other acts more equal rank. The aim is not to push for change as much as to get the couple to see that other choices are possible. Isn't that a better approach than scheduling an intake interview and then setting up fourteen weeks of sessions to learn the squeeze technique?

The real narrowness of much of our therapeutic view of premature ejaculation is apparent when we look at non-Western cultures like East Bay in Melanesia (located just northeast of Australia). In this culture men are expected to reach orgasm within fifteen to thirty seconds after vaginal entry.[14] If a man took longer, people would see him as having a sexual problem. If there were native sex therapists in East Bay, they would label all these nonconforming men as dysfunctional, retarded ejaculators, while our American sex therapists would see them as the only men in East Bay with "reasonable control." As I've noted, the speed of ejaculation seems far more rooted in social customs than in any physical or psychological problems.

A brief look at our evolutionary cousins, the nonhuman primates such as apes and monkeys, might also change the ease with which we throw out labels of "dysfunction." There is abundant evidence of very quick ejaculation by males in many of our closest relatives on this planet—the nonhuman primate species. For example, the average male chimpanzee, gibbon, or lemur reaches orgasm seven to fifteen seconds after vaginal entry.[15] Kinsey felt that such quick orgasm was a sign of biological competence. Others too have argued that there was an evolutionary advantage in being speedy. It lessened the time that the animal could be attacked while it was preoccupied. In any case, it should not be surprising that rapid ejaculation, which is so common in nonhuman primates, would also be an "ordinary physical response" among many human primates.

Instead of stigmatized labels let's give our clients choices to make and help empower them to decide their own futures. We know from many years of research that those people who have a sense of control over their futures and who are flexible in their thinking have the lowest amount of felt distress.[16] So if the function of therapy is to reduce distress, therapists would do well to be more flexible and reduce their negative labeling.

Sexual Addiction: Victorianism in Modern Dress

Sex therapists in general are a sex-positive group who want to expand the frontier of sexual satisfaction. Despite their use of terms like "dysfunction," they generally are very tolerant of sexual behaviors of many kinds. Still, there is also a minority of sex therapists who are rather conservative in their values and who feel that our society's more restrictive sexual values should be encouraged. It is predominantly this small group of conservative sex therapists, plus those who unthinkingly follow them, that have introduced a new stigmatized "medical disease" label to add to the many already imposed on our sexual behaviors.

The new "disease" or "dysfunction" is called "sexual addiction." The sexual addiction label is a product of the fearful and dangerous view of sexuality that is characteristic of traditional Victorian attitudes. Although the last sexual revolution developed a more positive, pleasureful view of sex, which did partially replace the fearful Victorian view, this more positive view has only shallow roots among many people.

Patrick Carnes, a former prison psychologist, is one of the pioneers in the development of the idea of "sexual addiction." Carnes organized one of the nation's first programs for treating what he called "sexual addiction." It consisted of a four-week inpatient treatment modeled after the twelve-step program of Alcoholics Anonymous (AA). By the late 1980s Carnes's twelve-step approach had become the model for "sexual addiction" programs across the nation. In line with this model, Sex Addicts Anonymous (SAA) groups were founded as early as 1978 in Minneapolis. Such groups have today spread to most of our nation's major cities.

Carnes's definition of addiction is another example of the vague definitions that plague sex therapy. He defines sexual addiction as a "pathological relationship to a mood-altering experience."[17] But "pathological" is like "lack of ordinary physical response" or "not reasonable." Who defines what is pathological? Carnes simply substitutes one undefined word (pathological) for another (addiction). Such circularity adds little meaning and thereby leaves the final clinical judgment about addiction up to the subjective feelings of the therapist. This clears the way to accept any therapist's subjective views of what is "not good enough" sexual control.

The very concept of addiction is borrowed from physiology where there are scientific models of the *chemical* addiction experienced by our bodies. The notion of sexual addiction, however, has little to do with the medical concept of addiction to substances such as heroin or crack cocaine. I think you'll understand my rejection of the sexual addiction concept more clearly if we look at one of the case studies that Carnes uses to explain sexual addiction.

Carnes talks at length of Carrie, an elementary school music teacher who aspired to become a professional singer. She took a job in a hotel with a piano bar and gradually got involved in one-night stands with out-of-town men who were staying at the hotel. She would select the most interesting patron and end up in his room after her work ended. Then in the morning she would teach her music classes. Carnes notes: "Looking at the trusting faces of the children, she would feel the profound incongruity of where she had been a few hours before."[18] Carrie did want to marry eventually but began to feel that no man would want her if he knew about her life.

Carnes believes that Carrie fits his definition of a person having a "pathological relationship to a mood altering experience." There is no dispute that Carrie was *distressed* over how her sexual behavior fit into her current lifestyle. The question I am raising is whether there is any scientific basis to call her a "sexual addict" and put her through a twelve-step program.

The twelve steps of the sexual addiction program Carnes uses involve admitting you are powerless over your sexual addiction and that you need a greater power to restore you to "sanity." You must decide to turn your will and life over to God, confess all your "wrong doings," and ask God to remove your "defects of character." The twelve steps are identical to the steps of the Alcoholics Anonymous program except that they refer to a sexual addiction rather than an alcohol addiction.

1. We admitted we were powerless over our sexual addiction—that our lives had become unmanageable.
2. Came to believe that a Power greater than ourselves could restore us to sanity.
3. Made a decision to turn our will and our lives over to the care of God as we understood Him.
4. Made a searching and fearless moral inventory of ourselves.
5. Admitted to God, to ourselves, and to another human being the exact nature of our wrongs.
6. Were entirely ready to have God remove all these defects of character.
7. Humbly asked Him to remove our shortcomings.
8. Made a list of all persons we had harmed, and became willing to make amends to them all.
9. Made direct amends to such people wherever possible, except when to do so would injure them or others.
10. Continued to take personal inventory and when we were wrong promptly admitted it.
11. Sought through prayer and meditation to improve our conscious contact with God as we understood Him, praying only for knowledge of His will for us and the power to carry that out.
12. Having had a spiritual awakening as the result of these steps, we tried to carry this message to others and to practice these principles in all our affairs.[19]

Now, just stop and think what accepting these so-called therapeutic steps implies for Carrie. Carrie must give up responsibility for her actions and must admit that she is powerless over her sexual addiction. That certainly does not sound like a step toward developing greater insight or building a sense of control or responsibility in one's life. In addition, Carrie has to admit that she is lacking in "sanity" but that God will restore her sanity and enable her to give up her "wrongful" sexual behavior.

Far from encouraging any empowerment of Carrie or any awareness of choice, the first two steps define Carrie as lacking in sanity and being helpless to do anything about it. What accepting these steps does is to reinforce the reasons for the guilt she already feels about her past lifestyle. That quick guilt response may well be a major reason that sexuality is so hard for her to handle. These steps also assume a strong belief in a personal God and that may or may not fit Carrie. Now, this strategy may work with some people who are already very traditional and religious, but it does not sound to me like a helpful strategy for most young Americans today.

Social psychologist Stanton Peele has written insightfully on the harm done when these twelve-step approaches tell the client that he or she is helpless and addicted for life:

> The myth of addiction as a "lifelong disease" does more than excuse addicts and alcoholics for their past, present and future irresponsibility. It actually sets them up for relapse and retards personal growth.[20]

Peele believes, and I agree, that the movement in our country aimed at calling everything an addiction is itself out of control.[21]

Besides accepting herself as a lifelong sexual addict, Carrie must also abide by the other eleven steps that demand that she admit to God the nature of her "wrongs" and ask God to remove those "defects of character." Here again, Carrie has no chance to entertain the possibility that perhaps her behavior was not so much "wrong" as it was conflicted. After all, it is possible that one way to help Carrie is to encourage greater acceptance of some of her sexual acts rather than to ask her to confess that she has a defect in character. But in Carnes's treatment approach, Carrie must admit to a negative view of herself as a sexual "sinner."

Such use of the twelve-step Alcoholics Anonymous type of therapy, as it was presented by Carnes in his book, sounds more like religion than therapy. It puts forth condemnation joined with the hope of redemption through confession of sin. In point of fact, Alcoholics Anonymous was founded in 1935 right after prohibition ended and was supported by the Oxford Movement, a religious organization. That movement reflected much of the orthodox religious guilt and opposition to drinking. Such orthodox religious thinking also supports the view that the eager pursuit of sexual pleasure is a sign of addiction. Many professionals working in the field of chemical addiction have suggested that the twelve-step program substitutes an addiction to religious dogma and dependence on a higher power for the addiction to alcohol or drugs.[22]

But let's briefly explore the specific moral assumptions that Carnes is making about Carrie's lifestyle. First he has defined her one-night stands as wrong because he sees them as conflicting with her role as a music teacher and her desire for a husband. He evaluates these other goals as obviously the more important goals and as incompatible with her one-night stands. Of course, it would be difficult for any woman raised in our society not to feel some qualms about purely pleasure-centered sexuality. Those men raised with strong religious traditions might well feel the same. But despite these social pressures, some women do come to accept occasional pleasure-centered sex. There are sexually liberated women who manage their lives quite well and aren't guilt-ridden about their sexual pleasures. Why doesn't Carnes entertain the possibility that Carrie could move in the direction of such women and increase her acceptance of pleasure-centered sex? Is sex really so unmanageable that one taste of it and Carrie would be back to flings every night? Has Carnes really tested or examined that possibility?

Carnes simply and without question accepts the sex-negative dogma that casual sex cannot be managed "properly" and should be totally eliminated. Stopping casual sex is a general recommendation by Carnes to all "addicts." He explicitly states: "The addict runs a great risk by being sexual outside of a committed relationship."[23] Carnes's conservative view of all parts of social life permeates his analysis of Carrie. Recall his comment emphasizing the "trusting faces of the children"—another traditional stereotype. Such a "trusting faces" view of children is part of the old image of children as innocent—an image that we strongly disputed back in chapter 2. Children, just like adults, have a variety of feelings toward those in authority over them, and surely not all of these feelings involve trust. Some children are bored or annoyed by their teachers, or even, perish the thought, dislike them. Carnes may be unaware of this reality, but more likely he simply prefers, based on his own sense of morality, to view children as innocent and trusting and to favor actions that assume that view.

Further, if Carnes had wanted to examine more openly Carrie's situation, he could have asked what business it is of the children what Carrie did the night before. They really don't know what she did and even if they did, why should the possible reactions of these children determine her future life anyway? Is being a music teacher and also being in tune with sexual pleasure really so incompatible? Should we go back to the days just a generation or two ago when only single women could teach, or when married teachers who became pregnant had to quit teaching because seeing them might encourage sexual behavior?

It seems obvious that Carrie was in serious conflict about her professional, sexual, and marital interests. Her conflict affords an opportunity for reexamination of these life interests and their relative importance. The problem is not in her behavior as much as it is in her difficulty in deciding priorities and learning to fit all the pieces of her life together in a way that is meaningful *to her.* But Carnes's conservative values led him to conclude that marriage was the best goal to pursue and no exploration of other possible rankings of her interests was even mentioned. He is seeking to relieve her distress by directing her behavior to what *he* feels is the highest priority—marriage.

The other examples that Carnes gives of sexual addiction are also cases where the "addict" violates conservative values for "unacceptable" sexual reasons, such as a salesman visiting prostitutes when on the road. At the heart of Carnes's notion of an addict is an image of a person who has feelings favoring conservative lifestyles but who has strayed from them by pursuing a less socially acceptable lifestyle. It seems that to Carnes it is the failure to give priority to the conservative life style that is the main symptom of addiction. The possibility of rethinking society's dominant values and rejecting them is hardly even entertained. Accordingly, the twelve-step treatment reinforces belief in a conservative lifestyle and thereby keeps the patient permanently in what is called "recovery." This approach takes therapy out of the realm of the helping professions and into the realm of indoctrination.[24]

California therapist Marty Klein sees the sexual addiction approach as destructive and contrasts it with other forms of therapy:

> At the end of competent sex therapy or psychotherapy treatment, the patient is a grown-up, able to make conscious sexual choices. Sex addiction treatment offers a patient the chance to be a recovering sex addict. Which would you rather be?[25]

No doubt, there are some people with problems of sexual control who would benefit from the twelve-step approach. In particular, I am sure that the support given by fellow "addicts" at group meetings would be valuable to people even if they didn't endorse the twelve-step beliefs. Just to have a support group consisting of other people suffering from the same distress is valuable to many people. But support groups can go with any number of approaches. The twelve-step approach has its own very specific philosophy of therapy and that is what I am criticizing. Most people who have problems of sexual control require much more than the twelve steps or support groups. For a lasting change they must rearrange their life priorities in a fashion that is meaningful to them. They must examine their conflicting sexual attitudes and behaviors and find how to put them back together. Confession and indoctrination won't cut it for most people.

Carnes and others who have dealt with those who are distressed about problems of sexual control report that in the great majority of cases the "sexual addict" was raised with very restrictive family and sexual values

—in short, with a strong sex-negative upbringing. It seems to me that such a person may well be harmed further by reinforcing those sex-negative values in the narrow, moralistic, twelve-step approach that Carnes proposes. Isn't it much more useful for people who have problems with controlling their sexuality to gain a *broader* perspective on sexual values rather than simply to reinforce the narrow sex-negative values with which they were raised and which very likely helped produce their conflict?

Given the much more sexually open type of society that we have had since the sexual revolution of the late 1960s, it is natural to expect that a number of people who were raised with older restrictive standards would be in severe conflict. Such traditional people are not prepared to make sexual choices, for they have been taught that there is but one true choice which supposedly applies to everyone and that is the *only* way to act. The major problem then, in cases like this, is to *reduce,* not strengthen, this sexual rigidity. It is precisely that rigidity about sexuality and the resulting strong guilt and anxiety that is the cause of the problem. Despite that fact, the twelve-step approach attempts to make that rigidity the solution to the problem!

People with problems of sexual control can be helped to see that they can gain control over their behavior if they become more pluralistic and flexible in their view of sexuality. Pluralism, as I have pointed out, has its own limits that require honesty, equality, and responsibility (HER), but this is much broader in acceptance than the sex-negative views of people with sexual control problems. A person is less likely to become obsessed with a sexual act that is seen as at least acceptable for others. But clients can't evaluate choices when they are encouraged to confess their errors and keep their dogmas rather than examine them.

Adopting a pluralistic approach and carefully thinking through your priorities may not lead to your changing your preferences. But it will make you more accepting of the sexual behavior of others. We all change our sexual beliefs and behavior as we go through life, and so ten years down the road you are unlikely to be the same sexual person you are now. If you are pluralistic and in the future you do become more permissive, you won't be as likely to panic and start a vicious cycle of guilt, anxiety, and inability to think calmly about sex. If you accept a broader range of behavior than you currently practice, you leave room for yourself to change your mind and choose differently without a flood of guilt to wash away your ability to evaluate. Tolerance of others can make you more tolerant of yourself.

Prescribing a Cure for Dysfunctional Sex Therapy

Why have so many sex therapists applied their labels of sexual "dysfunction" and sexual "addiction" so freely? I think the answer to this question is that sex therapists have been influenced by the medical people who dominate this field. For example, William Masters, the leader of the former Masters and Johnson therapy team, is a medical doctor. Another very influential sex therapist in our country, Helen Singer Kaplan, was also a medical doctor. The basic concepts of sex therapy have been written largely by these therapists and their followers. Their influence on sex therapy today is still very strong. Without a doubt they have contributed a great deal to the field and I do not want to detract from that. We can accept many of their therapeutic ideas while rejecting their imposition of stigmatized medical labels like "dysfunction," "addiction," and "illness."[26] These types of medical concepts are appropriate for physical *diseases*—sexual or otherwise. One might argue they are appropriate also for severe psychological states like psychoses or neuroses although this has been vigorously disputed by many.[27] But sex therapists agree that most of their clients do not fit any of the above categories. Therefore, for explaining the sexual distresses I am discussing in this chapter, medical concepts are most often *inappropriate*.

The medical concepts of "dysfunction" and "addiction" make sense when we speak of medical conditions such as a viral infection or a chemical dependency. In such an instance the viral infection or the chemical addiction disturbs a known healthy state of the physiology of the body. It is clear that viruses and chemicals can "impair the ordinary physical responses" of the body and create what may be called a "dysfunction" of our physical system. We can say that because we have an accepted scientific model of the proper "ordinary" ways that the body physiologically operates.

However, the very important point here is that for sexuality we have no comparable scientific model of the proper ways in which sexuality should operate. For physiology the interrelationships of our bodily organs define the system. The human physiological system operates pretty much the same way in all human societies. Our society doesn't define the specific way our heart and lungs affect each other or the way our kidneys and bladder interrelate. It is different for sexuality. It is the current preferences of a group, whether those are broad or narrow, that determine what is thought to be sexually acceptable. The medical model pressures us to find the *one way* the sexual system *should* function and to label all else as "dysfunctional." But unlike our physiology, our sexual customs vary tremendously according to the group in which we live. To use the medical model we would have to impose one view of "functional" sexuality on our society and other societies. That is just what has happened in our use of the concept of "dysfunction." That is not an acceptable procedure in a democratic, pluralistic society.

The pluralistic model is far more appropriate for understanding our sexual systems than is the medical model. Think about the vast array of possible ways there are to act sexually. No society activates all of the potentialities of our sexuality. There are societies where women are told that they cannot have orgasms, where men are told that they need not bother with sexuality after middle age, or where oral sex is promoted for eight-year-old children. There are societies where marriage is accepted between brother and sister, where men are advised to have many mistresses, or where sexually interested women tackle a man to indicate their sexual desire. In some societies homosexuality is highly valued while in others it is forbidden. The variety goes on and on and is immense.[28] All those sexual systems function in the sense that they operate over a period of time without destroying the society. No one system can be found that is the best or the true functional sexual system. So we have no one sexual model by which to judge "dysfunctions." Rather than pursue the futile search for the one right sexual system, we should each try to find what combination of sexual customs best fits our personal values and our goals. The more pluralistic a society is, the more likely we are to empower people to successfully carry out that search.

A society's choice of sexual customs reflects the basic values it has in other areas of social life. For example, if your group sees women as passive creatures who accept male domination, then your group will most likely try to keep women sexually inactive and would view female sexual response as "bad" or "dysfunctional." That was precisely the approach of some medical people during the Victorian era. In the nineteenth and even in this century, some medical doctors removed the clitorises of women in order to better control their "excessive" sexuality.

Dr. Burt's love surgery was aimed at doing the reverse—promoting orgasmic possibilities for women because that goal fit today's society. In the course of the last one hundred years, we in the Western world have changed our social mind about sex quite a bit. Accordingly, our uses of medical labels like "dysfunctional," "disturbed," or "deranged" have changed.[29] No one set of sexual customs can be scientifically established as the one right and moral way to behave. The wisdom of the pluralistic approach is to acknowledge that reality and to ask us to be tolerant of others just as we desire their tolerance of us.

The pluralistic approach, as I have mentioned earlier, accepts all forms of sexuality that involve honesty, equality, and responsibility. Each of us has our own preferences and feelings about what type of sexuality is better for ourselves. We don't have to see our choices as the right choices for everyone. We can accept the free choices of others that we would never personally make for ourselves. For example, Havelock Ellis, the famous British sexual scientist, was reputed to have been a urophiliac, that is, a person who sexually enjoys watching people urinate or being urinated upon.[30] You don't have to try that if you don't want to. You don't even have to like it. But why object to someone else enjoying that freely chosen behavior?

All cultures have expressions to indicate that in matters of taste there is no dispute. If we can move all sex that is honestly, equally, and responsibly chosen into the realm of taste and out of the realm of dogma, we will defuse our tendency to condemn and label those who disagree with us. We will also see sexuality as an area where we can each make important choices. The pluralistic approach increases the possibility of clearer thinking by reducing the dogmatic, emotional element in sexual decision making.

A pluralistic view, by accepting all freely chosen HER sexual behavior, affords the best philosophy to undergird a therapeutic treatment that empowers clients to examine their sexual choices. The focus in sex therapy then can be taken away from the bridge technique, the squeeze technique, or the twelve-step program and placed squarely on thinking through what are the alternative ways to reduce the felt distress. There is no effort to make the client conform to some model of "healthy" or "functional" sexuality popular in society at the moment. *The focus is on reducing distress and building a sense of well-being by empowering the client to choose among a wide range of choices.*[31]

The terms "sexually healthy" and "sexually unhealthy" are other medically inspired concepts that are very widely used. Those terms are used interchangeably with the concepts of "functional" and "dysfunctional." Like those other concepts, "sexual health" is so vaguely defined that people can't really tell if they are "healthy" or not. For example, here is the definition of sexual health offered by the World Health Organization:

> Sexual health is the integration of the somatic, emotional, intellectual, and social aspects of sexual being in ways that are positively enriching and that enhance personality, communication and love.[32]

About the only thing missing from this definition is God and motherhood! There is no guide as to how you decide what "enriches and enhances." Does coitus without orgasm "enrich and enhance"? Does intercourse with quick orgasm "enrich and enhance"? Does casual sex "enrich and enhance"? There is no scientific way to decide. Further, if you use the term "healthy" sexuality, then you must also accept the idea of "unhealthy" sexuality. In legal cases today *"unhealthy* sexual interest" has become part of the vague definition of obscenity. From a pluralistic point of view, all sexuality that is honest, equal, and responsible is acceptable.[33] To assert a belief in "unhealthy" sexuality beyond this promotes bigotry and is dangerous to all our sexual freedoms. If the act is freely chosen and meets our pluralistic HER values, why should we stigmatize it?

As I have been suggesting, a good first reform would be to substitute the term *distress* for the term dysfunction. Distress is a subjective state which no one can argue with. If a person feels distressed, that is a feeling which no one can challenge. But "dysfunction" is a judgment imposed from outside on a particular behavior. That can be challenged—just as I have done in this chapter. Let's use the concept of felt *distress* and envision the goal of therapy as the creation of a sense of *well-being*. Those terms focus on the person, not on the "dysfunctions" and "functions" of some abstract sexual system imposed by the therapist.

We need to remember that not too long ago therapists offered "cures,' to homosexuals. There, too, we allowed our personal preferences to create a medical label of "illness" and of "unhealthy" sexuality. In 1952 the American Psychiatric Association (APA) listed sixty mental disorders. Included among those "illnesses" then were behaviors and lifestyles that the APA now regards as normal such as masturbation, fellatio, cunnilingus, homosexuality, and promiscuous sexuality.[34] But today there are new listings that include forms of coital anorgasmia and premature ejaculation. One ray of hope is that the APA, in its fourth edition of the DSM in 1994, did reject adding a dysfunction category for sexual addiction. But until the inappropriate use of medical terminology in sex therapy ceases, we are all in danger of being stigmatized by some new label.

It's Not Just Doing What's Natural

A generation ago Harry Harlow, a primate psychologist at the University of Wisconsin, studied the sexuality of Rhesus monkeys.[35] He raised some infant monkeys in isolation and kept them from the playful interaction of peers and the nurturance of their mothers. He found that after just six months of such isolated rearing the monkeys were sexually damaged for life. Upon reaching adulthood those monkeys were unable to engage in sexual relations with other monkeys.

Harlow introduced his most popular male monkey to the females raised in isolation and found that there was no way they would mate with him. When some of these females were artificially inseminated, they had to be separated from their offspring because the mothers injured them instead of nurturing them. Now if monkeys display such significant changes due to the environment in which they are raised, it is reasonable to expect an even larger role for social learning when dealing with humans, for we have a much greater capacity for learning.

Of course, there are physiological bases for sexual behavior in our hormones, nerve endings, and genitalia. Human infants do exhibit sexual responses of lubrication and erection. But those responses have no social meaning to them. The social meaning of sexual behavior has to be learned in social groups as we grow up. That will determine whether we will be taught to masturbate as has been the case with many men in our society or have to learn it on our own as has been the case with most women in our society. The meaning of masturbation and the amount of guilt varies by how or if one is taught that behavior.

Without such social learning we would be like Harry Harlow's monkeys—unable to perform sexually with each other. Some sexual problems may be rooted in physiological defects limiting our hormonal or our organ structures. But the majority of sexual distresses that are brought to the therapist, like the three problems of coital anorgasmia, premature ejaculation, and sexual addiction discussed in this chapter, seem to be simply a result of our type of social life. And it is in that social life that such problems must be remedied.

The same therapists that misapply dysfunctional labels still recognize in some way the importance of social learning. Masters and Johnson's therapeutic experience with thousands of patients has led them to conclude that many of the most serious sexual distresses, such as the inability to ever experience orgasm, come from being raised with a belief that sex is dangerous, dirty, and degrading.

> A rigid religious background during childhood seemed to be associated with many sexual dysfunctions. What was striking about these cases was not the specific set of religious teachings (since these did not always condemn sexuality) but that sex was strongly regarded as evil and dirty in these rigidly religious families.[36]

Helen Singer Kaplan in her explanation of premature ejaculation also comments about the harm done by a restrictive sexual upbringing:

> Among the most common emotional problems we see in people with sexual disorders is guilt or shame about sexual pleasure. These are leftovers from old "messages" that sex is disgusting, sinful, and harmful

which are transmitted to children by some puritanical families, schools, and churches. Such early antisexual "programming" tends to remain with a person into his adult life.[37]

But the solution to personal sexual problems is *not,* as Masters and Johnson would have us believe, simply a matter of undergoing therapy to remove the so-called dysfunctions so that sex will be free to function "naturally." Once you overcome the rigid, negative training, you must *substitute* a positive, more pluralistic view of sexuality. We must be socialized for less distress in sex just as we were socialized in ways that produced that distress. In computer terms: we are born with the "hardware," but society gives us the needed "software."

Sex is not like defecating or urinating; it is more akin to learning how to relate to other people in all kinds of social situations. The specific ways we think and act sexually are socialized ways of thinking and acting much more than they are innate, natural functions.[38] The tremendous variety of sexual behaviors and beliefs in societies around the world is testimony to that fact.

When women try to learn how to have coital orgasms, they are not returning to some natural biological way of functioning. They are simply seeking to get rid of one learned way of responding and substituting another learned way of responding. Neither way is more natural, healthy, or universally preferable.[39] There is no reason to expect that we should develop all the possible ways we can behave sexually. It is far more important that we know what choices there are and that we be encouraged to decide, without pressure from negative labels, what directions we personally want to pursue. The "minimalist" sexual ethic of HER seems to be a standard that can guide our choices into the proper ethical arena. Then we can each choose what we feel is best for ourselves at a particular point in our lives. But to accomplish this we must have a society that encourages such choices by promoting honesty, equality, and responsibility in its basic institutions.

9

The Role of Religion in Our Sexual Crises

Fatal Attraction: Sex and Sin

In the year 313 C.E. Emperor Constantine converted to Christianity. The persecuted Christian sect had become the religion of the Roman Empire and Christian beliefs began to change and adjust to this newfound legitimization. By the end of that century one of the most famous saints of all time, Augustine (354–430), began to convert people to his innovative interpretation of the biblical story of Adam and Eve. Augustine tied the Gordian knot that links sexuality to sin and thereby influenced the Catholic Church right down to the present day. His conception of the story of Adam and Eve became a key part of the orthodox Church's approach to sexuality.

St. Augustine's view of original sin was strongly opposed by many powerful contemporary figures in the church such as St. John Chrysostom, the bishop of Constantinople, Pelagius, a Catholic ascetic from Britain, and Julian, a bishop from southern Italy. To understand the newness of Augustine's idea, it is necessary to realize that prior to the fourth century, most Christians read the message of Adam and Eve in Genesis quite differently from the way Augustine did.

Early Christians read the story of Adam and Eve as symbolizing the importance of human freedom and the power of human choice. They felt Christ had said the same thing in his Sermon on the Mount by demanding that his followers exercise their will and learn to master anger and to control sexual desire. The exercise of one's free will to achieve moral ends was seen as the fundamental message of the story of Adam and Eve for the first four hundred years of Christianity. Most Christians today are not aware of this.

Princeton University historian Elaine Pagels, who carefully studied this time period, comments on this early Christian perspective:

> Adam's sin was not sexual indulgence but disobedience: thus . . . the real theme of the story of Adam and Eve is moral freedom and moral responsibility. Its point is to show that we are responsible for the choices we freely make—good or evil—just as Adam was. . . . [F]or nearly the first four hundred years of our era, Christians regarded freedom as the primary message of Genesis 1–3—freedom in its many forms, including free will, freedom from demonic powers, freedom from social and sexual obligations, freedom from tyrannical government and from fate; and self-mastery as the source of such freedom.[1]

Early Christians believed God had created human beings in His image and thus all humans were equal and responsible for their actions. Parts of this early belief have survived and have formed one key basis for our Western ideas today of human freedom and democracy. But St. Augustine promoted a radically different interpretation of the story of Adam and Eve. Before his conversion to Christianity, Augustine had been a member of the Manichaean sect. This group espoused a religious philosophy that denied the goodness of creation and the freedom of the will which Christians believed in. Although in 386 he converted to Christianity, traces of his past convictions were to remain.

What others saw in the story of Adam and Eve as human freedom, Augustine saw as human bondage. Augustine's message was that the human will was impotent against sexual desire. To control such desire humans needed external government consisting of a Christian state and an imperially supported church. He challenged the view held for four hundred years that slaves and freemen, men and women, even children were equal and all had the right and the ability freely to choose what they believed in and what they did. Thousands of Christians during those early centuries had risked their lives and many had died for those beliefs.

It is true that the ascetic idea of renouncing the world and its temptations and choosing a life of celibacy was appealing to many early Christians. But that was a choice that one made and not something imposed. To Augustine all humanity was "fallen" and human will corrupt and even the ascetic person was incapable of self-mastery. Augustine believed that we were all damned by the original sin of Adam and Eve. When they ate from the tree of knowledge, they had freed their uncontrollable sexual desires and marked all humankind with that original sin. From then on, Augustine believed, all humans would carry that original sin from the very moment of conception. Augustine had joined sexuality with sin in a way that up to the present influences our thinking and feelings about sexuality.

Many churchmen argued with Augustine against this new doctrine, for they saw the nature of human beings as good. Since God had created mankind, He would not visit "original sin" upon all humanity just because of the actions of Adam and Eve. Julian, an influential bishop from Eclanum in the south of Italy, argued most strongly against Augustine. For over twelve years Augustine and Julian debated and argued their very different views.

Julian saw the story of Adam and Eve as symbolizing the subjective experience of sin through Adam and Eve's disobedience to God when they ate from the tree of knowledge. Julian read this message not as one of resignation to original sexual sin but as saying that we are capable by an act of will to commit or to avoid sin, and since we have this power of choice, we must strive to make the right moral choices in our lives.

Augustine saw the disobedience by Adam and Eve, when they ate of the tree of knowledge, as releasing forever the power of sexual disobedience in all human beings. In Genesis, he thought, God was telling us that human sexuality would now be uncontrollable. Because of Adam and Eve's sin, we all would be cursed with "original sin"—it would be present in the sexual conception of every human being. As a result sex was too dangerous and uncontrollable for men and women to engage in except under very special circumstances. Augustine therefore believed sex should be allowed only for procreation and never for pleasure—never, not even in marriage.

The late Yale University historian John Boswell, in his award-winning book on Christianity, explains that erotic love even between husband and wife was rejected by Augustine and his followers due to their radical antierotic doctrines.[2] As I noted above, every sexual act had to be a marital act aimed at reproduction or it was evil. Saint Jerome went so far as to say that "A man who loves his wife very much is an adulterer. . . . The upright man should love his wife with his judgment, not his affections."[3]

Augustine had suffered during his life from his own inability to control his sexual desires and he felt that the same must be true for all people. He was a man with two very powerful passions—one for religion and the other for sexuality—and they conflicted and tormented him for much of his life. In his *Confessions* Augustine notes the immense conflict he felt between these two passions.

> But I in my great worthlessness . . . had begged You for chastity, saying: "Grant me chastity and continence, *but not yet.*" For I was afraid that You would hear my prayer too soon, and too soon would heal me from the disease of lust which I wanted satisfied rather than extinguished.[4]

Augustine feared sexual desire so much that he felt it should be severely restricted, for if one ignited the flame of sexual desire, one would never be able to extinguish it. The Victorian view of sexuality I commented on in chapter 1 clearly is a recent version of this very same fearful view of sexuality.

Bishop Julian argued vehemently with Augustine saying that God has given us free will to choose the good and that we have no "original sin" from Adam. Julian did not see all people as having the same problems of sexual control that plagued Augustine. Pagels sums up the different perspectives of Augustine and Julian:

> Augustine was, by his own admission, insatiable, a man who never married and whose experience of sexual pleasure was illicit and guilt-provoking. Augustine assumes that frustrated desire is universal, infinite, and all-consuming. Julian, who had once . . . been married to the daughter of a bishop . . . obviously wrote from a different kind of experience. For Julian, sexual desire is innocent, divinely blessed, and, once satisfied, entirely finite. Sexual desire, as Julian sees it, offers us the opportunity to exercise our capacity for moral choice.[5]

Augustine's views asserting that human beings cannot govern themselves justified the power of the church and of the state. His notion of the corruptedness of all humanity and the need for control fit perfectly with the new alliance of the Christian Church and the imperial power of Rome. It was a way of uniting the church with the state and it therefore had strong backing and appeal. After all, Christians were now the emperor's coreligionists. The original sin of Adam and Eve was now seen as a sexual sin that illustrated the human inability to control one's own nature. Pagels affirms the political appeal of Augustine's doctrines:

> . . . what Augustine says, in simplest terms, is this: human beings cannot be trusted to govern themselves, because our very nature—indeed all of nature—has become corrupt as the result of Adam's sin. In the late fourth century and the fifth century, Christianity was no longer a suspect and persecuted movement; now it was the religion of emperors obligated to govern a vast and diffuse population. Under these circumstances . . . Augustine's theory of human depravity and correspondingly, the political means to control it—replaced the previous ideology of human freedom.[6]

Nevertheless, Pagels believes that there was another powerful reason why Augustine's views triumphed. Original sin justified why we suffer in life. If some unexplainable bad event occurred, such as the death of an infant, we could blame it on the fact that all of us, even infants, are cursed with the original sexual sin in which each of us is conceived. Therefore, the death of an infant is more understandable. That belief might induce some guilt in us for our own sexuality, but guilt was preferable to admitting that we have no explanation for the bad things that happen to us. The view of Julian and his followers, on the other hand, made human mishaps simply a natural part of living and was therefore not as satisfying to a people who knew so little about controlling the physical world. Julian's views were rejected and he was eventually denounced by the Church as a heretic.

Augustine's view of sexuality has had an extraordinary impact on Western civilization. The foundation of a negative, fearful view of sexuality is clearly visible in Augustine's perspective. The impact of these views on us even today is born out by Pagels:

> From the fifth century on, Augustine's pessimistic views of sexuality, politics, and human nature would become the dominant influence on western Christianity, both Catholic and Protestant, and color all western culture, Christian or not, ever since.[7]

In my discussion of sexual addiction in the last chapter, I noted that many people are still very much bothered by problems of sexual control. Many of these individuals have been raised with the strict doctrines of sexual control that emanate from Augustine's perspective. The notion of original sin makes sex something that is to be feared and so it informs one that there is great difficulty in controlling this dangerous force. The advice of Augustine that sex for pleasure must be avoided sounds very much like the advice of Patrick Carnes and other sex-addiction therapists. This danger-soaked view of sex, in my opinion, helps produce the very outcome it fears. With so much forbidden, so little tolerated, and a philosophy of helplessness promoted, is it any wonder then that even today many people are unable to think clearly and plan rationally for their sexual behaviors?

The Western world was not always so antierotic in its views of sexuality. The Greeks and Romans had a far more ambivalent but acceptant view of sexuality for a thousand years before Augustine. John Boswell points out that these civilizations accepted, and in many ways, valued homosexual relationships. Greeks and Romans had in fact no special name for persons who engaged in sex with someone of the same gender. It was simply thought to be a natural part of the sexual repertoire of human beings and so no special name was given to those who practiced same gender sexuality. But by the time of Augustine, as the Roman empire was collapsing, intolerance had developed and homosexuals were disparaged.

By the end of the sixth century this sexual intolerance subsided. But it was to reappear at the end of the twelfth century. Here is how Boswell describes that rejuvenation of this antieroticism:

> Beginning roughly in the latter half of the twelfth century, however, a more virulent hostility appeared in popular literature and eventually spread to theological and legal writings as well. The causes of this change cannot be adequately explained, but they were probably closely related to the general increase in intolerance of minority groups apparent in the ecclesiastical and secular institutions throughout the thirteenth and fourteenth centuries. Crusades against non-Christians and heretics, the expulsion of Jews from many areas of Europe, the rise of the Inquisition, efforts to stamp out sorcery and witchcraft, all testify to increasing intolerance of deviation from the standards of the majority, enforceable for the first time in the newly emerging corporate states of the High Middle Ages.[8]

During this time of growing intolerance in the thirteenth century, St. Thomas Aquinas (1225–1274) expanded upon the antierotic views put forth centuries earlier by St. Augustine. St. Thomas's views, too, have prevailed until the present day in the Catholic Church. Aquinas emphasized a "natural" view of sexuality which stressed that sex was to be engaged in only for purposes of producing children.

Semen, he believed, was intended by "nature" to produce children and any other use of it was "contrary to nature" and therefore against the will of God. This meant that any acts that "impeded the natural propagation of the human species" must be condemned as "unnatural." Masturbation, oral sex, anal sex, homosexual relations, and nonprocreative heterosexual intercourse all failed to produce progeny and thus were "unnatural" and evil. In this perspective, rape became more acceptable than masturbation or sodomy because rape could cause pregnancy! To modern ears that ranking sounds unbelievable, but it was incorporated into Christian codes of the Middle Ages.[9] Thomas's thinking was not accepted without controversy, but like Augustine his perspective eventually became Church dogma. Undoubtedly one major reason for the eventual victory of Thomas's ideas was their conformity with the growing sexual and religious intolerance in thirteenth and fourteenth century Europe.

Augustine's view of original sin and Thomas Aquinas's conception of "unnatural" sexuality have both contributed greatly to the sex-negative dogmas that still impede our ability to cope with today's sexual crisis. With our increased egalitarian ideas and our ability to control the consequences of sexuality, our view of sexuality has become more positive. Many modern-day theologians have challenged and rejected the views of

Thomas and Augustine, but consciously or not, those views still influence our emotions about human sexuality.

The Unique Mixture of Religion and Secularism in America

When the French historian Alexis de Tocqueville came to America in the 1830s, he was amazed by what he saw. He found a country composed of people far more religious and yet also far more secular and pragmatic than any in Europe. Our very unusual blending of religiosity and worldliness has remained to this day.

Americans have been able to produce this unusual cultural mixture because we have viewed our religion in a very individualistic fashion. We never had only one established church as so many European countries have. Rather, we have been the haven for refugees fleeing the persecution of established churches. Because of that, America has developed its own unique form of religious organizations. We have literally hundreds of different denominations and we stress the right of the individual to choose which church or synagogue, if any, he or she wishes to identify with.

In short, we take a pluralistic approach to religion. We are taught to accept all types of freely chosen religion. Even though we may prefer our own, we are taught not to deny or to restrain the acceptability of the religious preferences of others. That is precisely the same kind of pluralistic attitude that I am promoting in this book as the way to remedy our sexual crisis. An essential part of any pluralistic approach is an affirmation of the individual's right and ability to make a free choice. Democracy encourages such freedom of choice. Pollster George Gallup and reporter Jim Castelli arrived at this same point in their conclusions about religion in America:

> Americans do ... take a very independent approach to religion. Their faith must make sense to them, and it must reflect the values of freedom that they assume in their daily social and political lives.[10]

But despite this individualism, we Americans share an unusually powerful set of religious beliefs. We often don't realize it, but we are far more devout in our religious beliefs than most other modern Western nations. We would have to look at countries like Ireland or perhaps Spain to find a nation with as devoutly held beliefs.

The Gallup people have been asking questions on religion to representative samples of Americans for over sixty years. They note that in response to the question "Are your religious beliefs very import to you?" 58 percent of the adult American population said they are very important. In Western Europe the percent saying religion is very important averaged only about 25 percent. The Gallup surveys also found that over 95 percent of Americans believe in God and almost three in every four pray to God at least once a day. About two-thirds of our population belong to churches or synagogues and over 40 percent attended services in the past week. These figures are very high compared to Western European countries. In addition, over 40 percent of our adult population say they have had a "born again" religious experience.[11]

Still, even in America, the "highly spiritually committed" amount to only about 10 percent of the adult population.[12] But to be called highly spiritually committed in Gallup's reckoning, you had to answer "completely true" to statements about the divinity of Christ, belief in the Bible, religion as of first importance in your life, seeking God's will in your prayers, and several more questions about your religious faith. Women and people with less than a college education were more likely to be in this "highly spiritually committed" group. About 13 percent of Protestants fit that label, but only 8 percent of Catholics did. Taking all these indices together, religious beliefs are very widespread and common in America despite our many modern social changes.

Nonetheless, since the mid-1960s there have been secular trends showing some weakening of parts of this powerful emphasis upon religion. Ironically, the baby boomers who were destined to break so many of the conservative religious norms about sexuality were born during the high point of religious growth in this century. From the late 1940s until the early 1960s—exactly the time when our seventy-six million baby boomers were born—church attendance, prayer, and the general importance of religion was cresting.

This religious emphasis and the baby boom were both part of the post-World War II prosperity and the renewed emphasis on the family and religion that accompanied that prosperity. Divorce rates were low—not much higher than they were in the 1920s, young people were marrying at earlier ages than at any time in this century, and there was a strong emphasis upon traditional religion and the family. But all this was to change. The long-range twentieth-century trends in this country were away from stability and in the direction of less traditionalism in the family and religion. Those long-range trends were to reassert themselves starting in the mid-1960s.

Elaine May, a Professor of American Studies at the University of Minnesota, argues that this postwar emphasis on the family and religion in the baby-boom years occurred because Americans emerged from the stresses and uncertainties of World War II yearning for peace and prosperity and temporarily sought security in family and religion.

> With depression and war behind them, and with political and economic institutions fostering the upward mobility of men, the domesticity of women, and suburban home ownership, they were homeward bound. But as the years went by, they also found themselves bound to the home. This ambiguous legacy of domestic containment was not lost on their children. When the baby boom children came of age, they would have different priorities and make different choices.[13]

In the 1950s the percentage of Americans who felt religion was very important in their lives was 75 percent![14] By the early 1960s, as the first wave of the baby boomers entered their late teens, things began to change dramatically. I noted above that only 58 percent of Americans in the mid-1990s said that religion was very important in their lives. The percentage of people who saw religion as capable of "answering today's problems" also dropped sharply from the 1950s to the 1980s (81 percent to 61 percent). In those same years church membership also decreased, and among Catholics, church attendance dropped from about three in four attending church weekly to only one in two attending church weekly.[15]

The Sounds of Religious Conflict

Surprisingly, Catholics today practice abortion and birth control in about the same proportion as Protestants.[16] In fact, one study found that Catholics had a higher abortion rate than Protestants or Jews. The Guttmacher Institute conducted that study and they felt that Catholics may not be using birth control as effectively as other groups because they are ambivalent about it and so their abortion rates are higher.[17] I fully expect that Catholics will become less ambivalent about birth control and their abortion rates should decline accordingly.

A major change in Catholic sexual and gender-role attitudes occurred right after the 1968 encyclical *Humanae Vitae* which maintained the Vatican's ban against birth control by insisting that "every conjugal act must be open to the transmission of life." Since the Commission of the Second Vatican Council in 1963 had supported removing the ban on birth control, many Catholics had expected that the 1968 decree would take the same stand. But a new Pope was reigning and in his 1968 edict he saw sexuality in accordance with St. Thomas Aquinas's views—solely as a reproductive act. The great majority of Catholics in America have rejected that stance. The Second Vatican Council had shown American Catholics that the church could be more pluralistic and Catholics liked that position too much to retreat from it even after the 1968 encyclical. Recent surveys indicate only about 15 percent of Catholics accept the official church doctrine on birth control.

There are other debates about sexual and family values within the Catholic faith.[18] Catholics today support the following changes in considerable numbers: women as priests (65 percent); priests being allowed to marry (72 percent); acceptance of birth control (84 percent); Catholics being allowed to remarry (78 percent); and the ability of homosexuals to be good Catholics (47 percent).[19]

The issue about condoms was one of the most contentious. A position was put forth in December of 1987 by a fifty-member administrative board of the U.S. Catholic Conference that represents the nation's three hundred Catholic bishops. The board was formulating a Catholic AIDS program and felt that discussion of condoms would have to be included in order to make sexuality safer for those who did not abide by the official teaching of abstinence. The conference board explained their stance:

> We are saying that we don't like [condom use] at all, but we know that ignorance about this matter could cause death. Our position is a toleration of a lesser evil to prevent a greater evil.[20]

When the matter was taken up by the full complement of bishops in November of 1989, this position was rejected and the discussion of condoms was removed from the educational recommendations. The ancient dogmas of Augustine and Aquinas still prevail—at least in the church hierarchy.

Catholic theologians around the world have questioned the official stance of their church. Some of them, like Stephen Pfürtner in Switzerland, Ambrogio Valsecchi in Italy, and Anthony Kosnick and Charles Curran in the United States, have been dismissed from their teaching positions because of their writings on sexuality.[21] Charles Curran, the former theology professor at Catholic University of America, is perhaps best known. In 1987 he was fired for his unorthodox views and in 1989 he sued his university for violating his rights of academic freedom. The judge in the case ruled that the university, being a religious institution, had the right to show its loyalty to Pope John Paul II instead of to academic freedom. Curran had criticized his church for its patriarchal nature, its stance against homosexuality and abortion, and other matters of sexual ethics. He predicts much more dissent from many other Catholic theologians in the future.

The clashes within the Catholic Church are not unique. Protestants and Jews find similar divisiveness within their denominations. Sociologist Wade Roof and Seminarian William McKinney examined value differences among and within religious groups. They compared responses to questions on sex, race, women's rights, and civil rights to see if there was any difference between those who were very active in a particular church and those who were not. Those who were the most active members of a church were significantly *less* tolerant on all questions regarding values. Then they compared the different religious denominations on these same value questions. There were very large differences among the religions. For example, on almost all the issues Jews came out as more tolerant than Catholics and Catholics came out as more tolerant than Protestants.

Within the Protestant group the Religious Right represented by conservative Protestant denominations like Southern Baptists, Church of Christ, Assemblies of God, Mormons, and other Evangelical groups had by far the least tolerant values. The most tolerant attitudes among Protestants were found among Episcopalians, United Church of Christ members, and Presbyterians—the old mainline Protestant religions. In between the liberals and conservatives were the Methodists, Northern Baptists, and Lutherans.

To make what I am saying more concrete, let's look at the attitudes toward homosexuality examined by Roof and McKinney. Their question asked whether homosexuality was or was not "always wrong." The percentage of people affirming that "homosexuality was *not* always wrong" was 60–94 percent for Jews and for Unitarian-Universalists, 31 percent for Catholics, 36 percent for liberal Protestants, and 11 percent for conservative Protestants.[22] The range of differences, then, was vast and reflected the degree of pluralism or tolerance of each particular religious group.

Liberal and conservative religious groups can be distinguished by many social characteristics. One of the most important is educational level. The higher the education of the congregants, the more liberal the congregation on most value questions. For example, only 11 percent of college graduates believe that the Bible is the actual word of God, whereas 34 percent of high school graduates and 45 percent of those with less than a high school education believe that.[23] As one's education and income change, there may be a tendency to switch denominational affiliation. A great deal of such switching does occur in America. About 40 percent of Protestant adults say they are no longer in the denomination in which they were raised.[24]

Most of our major denominations have a liberal/conservative or what is often called a moderate/fundamentalist split within their congregation that causes a great deal of strife. These two religious subdivisions do not think highly of each other. Princeton sociologist Robert Wuthnow sums up their impressions of each other:

> People who identified themselves as religious liberals were prone to stereotype their conservative brethren as intolerant, morally rigid, fanatical, unsophisticated, closed-minded, and simplistic. The animosity recorded from the other side was equally blatant. Self-identified religious conservatives thought religious liberals were morally loose, were too hung up on social concerns rather than truly knowing what Christianity was all about, had only a shallow knowledge of the Bible, and were deeply compromised by secular humanism.[25]

Religious liberals and conservatives have been battling each other for a long time. I wouldn't look for a final victory for either side in the near future. Rather, I would predict an intensification of the battle during the late 1990s as pluralism increases in all areas of social life. One of the major reasons that fundamentalist groups became so well organized was their feeling that religion had become too pluralistic, too secular, and too individualistic. Those trends will continue and therefore so will the battle. After the Scopes trial on evolution in 1925, people thought fundamentalism was finished, but by the 1970s it had returned to take up the fight once more.

Analysis of the membership trends of the last forty years indicates that mainline religions like Episcopalians, United Church of Christ, and Presbyterians have lost ground. The Evangelical religions such as Southern Baptists did not lose ground. Catholics, despite the rejection of official beliefs among parishioners, did not decline in membership—in fact they grew due to the immigration of Hispanics and somewhat higher birthrates. Overall, however, there has been a rise in the percentage of people who do not belong to any church. That now stands at about 33 percent. Many Americans are expressing their religion in their own personal ways rather than by joining or believing in organized religion. But among those who do belong, the largest gains have been in the Evangelical/fundamentalist denominations.

In terms of the religion people identify with (*whether they join a church or not*), Protestantism is named by just 58 percent of our population—the lowest percentage ever. Catholics have grown to 25 percent and Jews have fallen to just over 2 percent of the population. Of the remaining people, a record 8 percent have no religious preference and a few percent identify with a wide variety of other small and/or Eastern religious groups.

What all this indicates is that both ends of the religious continuum are now more fully occupied. We have a sizable minority who are conservative or Evangelical/fundamentalist and another sizable minority who have no preferences or who do not join the denomination of their preference.[26] In between are the majority in the mainline religions, but they seem to be losing members to both ends of the religious continuum. The gains by the Religious Right in the last twenty years have important implications concerning how Americans think about sexuality, and so we should take a closer look at that segment of our religious spectrum.

The Agenda of the Religious Right: Televangelism and the Family

Although televangelists are but one segment of the Religious Right, they are worth some attention because of their views on sexuality. One of the most discussed televangelists was Jim Bakker. He is of some interest to us because it was his sexual activities that got him into trouble with the Assemblies of God Church. Bakker was a personal friend of Oral Roberts and had worked for several years for 1988 presidential candidate Pat Robertson at his Christian Broadcasting Network. He had become a top star of the televangelists when the sex scandal broke in 1987. Bakker espoused a kind of "prosperity theology."[27] He felt that those who believed in the Bible should be materially rewarded. The trouble began when sex became part of the reward system.

The Bakker scandal was triggered in 1987 by the revelation of his 1980 sexual encounter with Jessica Hahn, a Pentecostal Church secretary. The resulting investigation also revealed a great deal of questionable handling of many millions of dollars of his church's money by Bakker and an eventual conviction and sentence of forty-five years.* But most relevant to our interests in this book, that investigation showed the ways in which a fearful, dangerous, sex-negative view flourishes in the Evangelical Christian tradition. In 1983, after his encounter with Jessica Hahn but before that had become public, Bakker made some revealing comments about sexuality. See if you recognize the Victorian and Augustinian thinking in these comments by Bakker:

> And in the heat of lust, who thinks of the awful price being paid for a moment of passion? No one expects to feel so guilty, so ashamed . . . so dirty. No one intends for those he really loves to be hurt. No one expects to end up diseased—permanently marked with an insidious infection like herpes for which medical science can find no cure.[28]

---

*Bakker is now out of prison and is seeking to rebuild his life.

Note the stress on the inability to control this dangerous force and his horror of a sexually transmitted disease. Of course, there are problems in handling any strong feeling, but why picture sexuality as so unique? Herpes is no fun, but over one quarter of the adult population in America has the genital herpes virus and most of them manage to live a normal life. It is the association with sex that makes what otherwise would most often be seen as a tolerable disease seem so disastrous. The stress is on anxiety and fear and not on preparation and decision making. When sex does occur, it is handled very badly. No one illustrated that better than Jim Bakker.

The Bakker scandal greatly raised the visibility of Evangelicals. It made Americans more aware of the immensity of the Evangelical communication network in America. There are over sixteen hundred televangelist ministers who operate over three major religious networks, with about two hundred television stations and over a thousand radio stations carrying their message. During Reagan's eight years in the White House, this conservative religious grouping was able to develop strong ties with the Republican party.[29] One indication of this was the fact that in 1988, Pat Robertson, a former televangelist minister and a founder of one of the three religious networks, was able to get enough support to run for the Republican nomination for President.

As I have indicated, the Religious Right takes a conservative stance on abortion, sex outside of marriage, homosexuality, gender roles, and husband/wife family roles. Their views are often based on a conception of America as a religious nation with a divine destiny.[30] In 1989 the Republican Party in Arizona even passed a resolution, with support from Pat Robertson's backers, stating that "the United States is a Christian nation" and that the U.S. Constitution created "a republic based upon the absolute laws of the Bible, not a democracy."[31]

The passage of that resolution in Arizona is not a major threat in itself but it does demonstrate the reason for our constitutional principle of separation of church and state. Without that principle, one church, or a coalition of churches, could seek to dominate our government and promote a theocracy instead of a democracy. Our earliest settlers were fleeing from just such a tyrannical rule by religious organizations. The principle of separation of church and state was our founding fathers' attempt to make certain that would never happen here.

That separation principle has been increasingly violated by religious conservatives over the past twenty-five years. Religious conservatives were incensed by the liberal changes in abortion, premarital sexuality, divorce, and other areas of social life. As a consequence, many of the Evangelical/fundamentalist religious groups in America have striven, particularly since Reagan's presidency, to gain increased influence in our political system. Back in 1987, Bill Moyers, the Public Broadcasting System's well-known special reporter and himself a Southern Baptist, commented upon the political action taken by fundamentalist Southern Baptists against political candidates with "anti-Biblical" views. In a reference to the fact that Baptists in the nineteenth century had fought for their own freedom from oppression by dominant religious groups, Moyers commented: "Of all people, Baptists must know that making biblical doctrine the test of political opinion is democratic heresy."

Baptists are surely not the only religious group moving into politically aimed activities. For example, some bishops of the Catholic Church have denied communion to Catholic politicians who come out on the "wrong" side of issues such as abortion. This "punishment" was meted out to Lucy Killea who in 1989 ran for a California State Senate seat in San Diego. The tactic boomeranged. Killea won the election and credited her victory to the public's negative reaction to the communion ban.[32]

In 1990 Mario Cuomo, the governor of New York, was criticized by Cardinal John O'Connor of New York and by one of his auxiliary bishops, Austin Vaughan. They speculated that Cuomo might be spending eternal life in Hell because of his abortion stance. Governor Cuomo responded by asking:

> Must I, having heard the Pope renew the Church's ban on birth-control devices, veto the funding of contraceptive programs for non-Catholics or dissenting Catholics in my state? I accept the Church's teaching on abortion. Must I insist you do? By law? By denying you Medicaid funding? By a constitutional amendment?[33]

Many of these battles between religious liberals and conservatives center on family and gender role conceptions. This is a point I emphasized in the opening chapter of this book. Conservatives often criticize today's family and cite the family of the 1950s and earlier generations as the model to pursue. But remember what those "good old days" were like—married women denied equal access to jobs, contraceptive information legally banned, abortion illegal, male dominance much greater than today in all walks of life. Women were viewed as gullible and in need of male protection, preparation for sex was almost totally absent, and very high *rates* of disease and pregnancy existed for those who did venture forth into "Satan's playground."

Perhaps what is really being proposed by the Evangelical fundamentalists is a return not to the 1950s family but to the family of biblical days. What sort of family was that? The Old Testament is clear that this was a strong patriarchal family. Men were permitted several wives and concubines. Children were legitimately conceived by these concubines outside of marriage. In fact, four of the twelve sons of Jacob were born to two women, Bilhah and Zilpah, who were the maids of Jacob's two wives, Leah and Rachel.[34] Is this the Evangelical's idea of an ideal family?

If we look at the traditional relationship of husband and wife as pictured in the New Testament, we also find severe restrictions on the rights of women:

> Wives, submit yourselves unto your own husbands, as unto the Lord. For the husband is the head of the wife, even as Christ is the head of the church; and he is the savior of the body. Therefore, as the church is subject unto Christ, so let the wives be to their own husbands in everything. Husbands, love your wives, even as Christ also loved the church, and gave himself for it.[35]

The Victorian family of a hundred years ago does not fare much better in terms of gender equality when you examine it. It was simply a nineteenth century innovation on male-dominant family forms. It was in fact common mostly on the East Coast and not elsewhere in the country. In part the Victorian family form was a result of the desire of nineteenth-century middle-class men to show that they could earn enough so that their wives did not need to work. Middle-class men in the nineteenth century took great pride in providing a private home for their wives and their children.

The increased emphasis upon care of children was another nineteenth-century innovation. Prior to that time children were not the center of attention they were to become. The Victorian bourgeois family was popular in England and parts of Europe as well as in America.[36] In time the working classes, too, came to strive to achieve that new type of family. As a result, the remnants of opposition to a wife working outside the home is most noticeable today among the working classes.

The trends of the last thirty years are toward a more pluralistic view of married and family life. We have older ages at first marriage, longer delays in having children, fewer children per family, and more people who choose not to marry.[37] All of these trends indicate that although marriage and the family are still very important institutions, increased choices are being allowed. People can with greater ease design a lifestyle inside or outside of marriage to fit their personal needs. One can choose a traditional family lifestyle or a nontraditional one. We no longer have one Procrustean family bed that all people must be stretched or cut to fit into. These modern changes make it easier for women to choose, if they wish, to work outside the home and to gain equal status with men in our society.

All such changes have costs as well as benefits. But if there were a magic button that would return one to the family of the 1950s, or the biblical family, or the Victorian family, not very many people would press that button. Still it is anyone's right to choose to live in a traditional family form. Pluralism simply rejects the position that this is the *only* acceptable form that everyone must strive to live up to.

Nevertheless, some of my fellow sociologists do believe we are underestimating the power of the Religious Right. They think we are moving back to those "good old days" in more ways than we realize.[38] Let's take a closer look at changes today in the Religious Right so we can learn more about these possible future trends.

Coming Down to Earth

Just how unified is the Religious Right in its beliefs and what trends are visible? In reality the Religious Right is quite a diverse group. "Evangelicals" is a general term used by some to include fundamentalist, Charismatic, and Holiness groups even though these groups are by no means identical. Professor James Hunter, a sociologist at the University of Virginia, studied the Religious Right to find out just what they do believe and what trends have been occurring.[39] He uses the term "Evangelical" to include the full range of those in the Religious Right. In the 1980s Professor Hunter surveyed a few thousand Evangelical college students, Evangelical seminary students, and faculty at sixteen institutions committed to the Evangelical worldview.

Evangelical leaders claim that they want to maintain "the purity and integrity of theology." They profess that the Bible is faultless and inerrant and that it is to be literally interpreted as the precise word of God. Despite this official policy, only 40 percent of Hunter's Evangelical collegians and seminarians maintained this traditional orthodox position on the Bible. Another 50 percent qualified this official position by saying that "The Bible is the inspired Word of God, not mistaken in its teachings, *but* is not always to be taken literally in its statements concerning matters of science, historical reporting, etc."[40] In addition, the Evangelical students said they felt that spiritual concerns take precedence over social and political justice. In that sense they were distinct from most mainline religions where social justice takes first place. So purity of belief is more important to the Religious Right than are efforts to correct social problems. This is an old distinction between conservative and liberal religions and it still makes some sense today.

Nevertheless, over the last decades there has been a tendency for

Evangelicals to become less orthodox in their religious beliefs. The social changes in the broader society have had an impact on them, too. For example, Hunter compared findings from previous studies on Evangelical students in 1951 and 1961 with his data from the 1980s. He found a clear trend toward greater acceptance of activities like card playing, social dancing, movies, and drinking.

But does this mean that Evangelical students are no different than any other group of students? Hardly—they are quite distinct. Hunter compared his Evangelical students with students taking classes in religion at a public university in California in order to get a rough measure of difference. The differences found were vast. About 90 percent of the Evangelical students believed that premarital intercourse was always wrong, whereas only 15 percent of the public university students believed that. Over 95 percent of the Evangelical students believed that homosexual relations were always wrong compared to only 30 percent at the public university. Sixty-five percent of the Evangelical students felt that watching X-rated movies was always wrong compared to 13 percent at the public university. So, despite the trend toward more permissive attitudes, large differences remain between Evangelical and public university students.

Hunter came up with some interesting findings in the area of beliefs about the family. As we've discussed, religion and the family have always been intimately related. As Hunter puts it:

> It is difficult . . . to exaggerate the significance of the "traditional family" to Evangelicals. It is viewed as the bedrock of the American way of life—its social, cultural, and political institutions . . . its defense has become an Evangelical passion. It is its cause célèbre.[41]

Evangelicals picture the nineteenth-century middle-class Victorian family as the ideal traditional family. The husband is responsible for providing materially and spiritually for the family. He must see that his children are raised in traditional religion and that they will follow the Lord. A wife is expected to devote herself to her husband and her children. Children are to be shaped and directed. They are never to talk back to their parents. But social pressures against this family type are increasing today and changes can be seen even among Evangelicals.

Hunter asked the Evangelical students about their degree of acceptance of this nineteenth-century version of the family. He found that about two-thirds supported the view that the husband had the final say in the family's decision making and that he should be primarily responsible for the spiritual well-being of the family. Just 12 percent of the public university students agreed with that statement. However, my key point here is not that difference but the fact that over a third of the Evangelical students did *not* endorse that traditional view of husbands. Furthermore, women at these Evangelical schools were even less likely to endorse this dominant husband view. There seems to be a "liberal" minority even within the Evangelical group of students.

Even more variance from tradition is found in the case of child rearing: only about a third of the Evangelical students say that strict, old-fashioned upbringing is the best way to raise children, and less than half of them think it is best if a wife stays home and the husband supports the family. Other research on Evangelicals by the National Opinion Research Center (NORC) indicates that Evangelicals under age thirty-five are far more likely to reject traditional views of the family than are those over age thirty-five.[42] So the younger Evangelicals do seem to be moving away from the traditional family view promoted by their religious leaders. In answer to the question as to what proportion of the Evangelical students endorse the nineteenth-century model of the middle-class family, Hunter states:

> On average only about one in ten of the collegians and seminarians would be likely to endorse, enthusiastically, the model of the family advocated by Evangelical spokesmen. Another one-fourth to one-third would be sympathetic with that model, but this still leaves less than half of the coming generation holding to the ideal of traditional bourgeois familism.[43]

This divergence from the traditional family model is even more striking when one asks about the female role rather than the male role. Both men and women are even less likely to accept the traditional female role than they are to accept the traditional male role. So there is a faint echo of feminist influence here, too.

The faculty at Evangelical colleges rejects even more so the older dogmatic views of religion and the family. Here are the words of one faculty member:

> Who wants to preserve [religious] dogmatism and [moral] parochialism? Not me—and not most of my colleagues. We want salient evangelical faith, but since when must this type of religious commitment also include a firm commitment to male-centered households and all the rest of that nasty stuff? What [some] may call "contamination" or "erosion" I call a "success." Maybe Jerry Falwell thinks what we're doing is "counterproductive" but most of us who teach here . . . do not.[44]

Hunter also reports that the majority of Evangelicals have serious reservations about some of the extreme rhetoric of their more abrasive and radical leaders. Among Evangelical members there is a tradition of civility plus a hesitancy to be confrontive that keeps a number of Evangelicals from joining political movements. Fundamentalists like Falwell are commonly viewed as too abrasive and combative. When one adds to this the modernizing changes that are occurring in the beliefs of many of the Evangelicals, the prediction that America will be increasingly dominated by a Christian theocracy professing fundamentalist religious beliefs is rather difficult to sustain. It is much more likely that the fundamentalists will change with America rather than the other way around.

A fascinating insight into the liberalization of Evangelical views comes from the work of two sociologists, Lionel Lewis and Dennis Brissett,[45] on Evangelical attitudes toward marital sexuality. They studied thirteen sex manuals written by Evangelical clergy, published by sectarian publishers, and sold in stores selling religious materials. (Many readers may well be surprised to find that there were thirteen sex manuals written by Evangelical clergy! It shows an openness toward sexual discussion that you might not expect from Evangelicals.) Lewis and Brissett found that while sex outside of marriage was condemned, sex within marriage was celebrated as a spiritual act in these manuals. For married couples, sexual play was encouraged. In addition, the authors of these sex manuals seemed to be saying that good Christians are better lovers. Lewis and Brissett comment on this point by quoting from one manual:

> A Christian's relationship with God produces a greater capacity for expressing and receiving love than is possible for a non-Christian. The fruit of the Spirit (love, joy, peace, kindness, etc. . . .) removes the specter of resentment and bitterness that devastates an exciting bedroom life.[46]

The theme often presented in these manuals is of marital sex as a confirmation of God and as an act that can and should be pursued for its own pleasure. Traditional views of male dominance are present in these manuals but so is marital sex as fun and pleasure. The old uncontrollable view of sexuality has clearly been abandoned by these Evangelical sex manuals. This is a significant change, for if sexual pleasure is seen as manageable and good in marriage, then the children of these people may well raise the question as to whether they can also learn to control the unwanted outcomes of premarital sexuality.

I expect that many of the younger Evangelicals are in increasingly serious conflict over these modernizing changes. There is little support for such new ways of thinking from their older leadership. So the burden falls upon the younger generation. Some of the loud complaints about the evils of society from the leaders of the Religious Right may be in part an anxiety response to their increasing awareness that the old ways are "a-changin'" and new more moderate traditions are being formed.

The New Religious Left and Sexuality

The religious emphasis in America on the importance of a personal relationship with God is a major support for a liberal interpretation of religion. Most Americans believe in what the Baptists call the "priesthood of the individual." Each person interprets God's meaning through his or her own conscience. In several recent Gallup Polls, about 80 percent of all Americans agreed that "one should arrive at his or her religious beliefs independent of any church or synagogue." In addition, 76 percent said that they believe that a person can be a good Christian or Jew without attending church or synagogue.[47] These beliefs prevail despite the fact that about 84 percent of Americans believe in Christ and two-thirds have made a "commitment" to Christ.

Thus, while we do indeed have a very religious nation, the style of religion reflects the pluralism and individualism upon which this country was founded. Most Americans take a rather private view of their relationship to God. There is thus resistance to bend to any dogma that demands that one believe there is only one way to honor God. This means that if your conscience is so inclined, even if you are a member of an Evangelical group, you can personally accept liberal notions of sexuality, family, and gender. As Hunter's research shows, some Evangelicals have done precisely that. *The doctrine of freedom of conscience opens the door to a more pluralistic view of sexuality even for members of orthodox religions.*

There is a liberal element in all three major religious groups about which I should at least briefly comment. The Reform and Conservative Jewish groups, but not the Orthodox, score very high on liberal beliefs on sexuality, gender equality, and family roles. As Catholics have risen to a position of equality in economic and educational areas, they too have become more liberal religiously. As I have noted, on the average, Catholics are more liberal than Protestants on most issues. However, that difference would disappear if only mainline Protestant denominations were compared to Catholics because 40 percent of the Protestant group is composed of Evangelical/fundamentalist churches.

Bishop John Shelby Spong of the Episcopal Church in New Jersey is one representative of the liberal religious thinking. Bishop Spong's views concern new ways of conceptualizing human sexuality. He accepts homosexuality as a part of life, not a curse, and he does not accept any biblical condemnation of homosexuality. He notes that the same Bible that condemns homosexuality says many other things that even members of orthodox religions would never support today:

> I have yet to meet a conservative Christian who would advocate execu-tion for cursing (Lev. 24:14), blasphemy (Lev. 24:16), being a false prophet (Deut. 13:5), worshipping a false god (Deut. 17:1-8), or cursing or dishonoring one's parents (Lev. 20:9). Though we have discarded these Torah injunctions, some still continue to presume that the Torah's condemnation of homosexuality is valid, that it is not based upon igno-rance, and that it is still binding on the church today. That point of view simply will not hold.[48]

Bishop Spong argues further for the acceptance by the Church of the full range of caring, loving relationships whether they be homosexual or het-erosexual: "My assumption is that sexual activity is designed by the Cre-ator not just for procreation but also for the enhancement of human life."[49]

At the heart of the liberal religious view of sexuality is the rejection of the orthodox Augustinian notion that pleasure leads inevitably to loss of control. Fear of loss of control is a key part of the sex-is-dangerous view that came to dominate Victorianism and is still influential in so much of Christianity.

Another liberal theologian is James B. Nelson, professor of Christian ethics at the United Theological Seminary of the Twin Cities in Min-nesota. Professor Nelson belongs to the United Church of Christ and he believes that we can teach restraint and responsibility even in areas of pleasurable sexual acts. We can make moral judgments on the basis of whether a sexual act promotes love. He believes that what we need:

> . . . is an ethics that finds its center and direction in love rather than in a series of specific, absolute injunctions . . . love is the central (albeit not the only) norm for Christian ethics, it is the central meaning of human sexuality and the measuring standard and justification for any particular sex act. . . . An ethics centered in . . . love . . . will not guarantee freedom from mistakes in the sexual life. It will place considerable responsibility upon the individual. . . . It will be more concerned about the authentic fulfillment of persons than the stringencies of unyielding laws or the neat cataloguing of types of sexual acts.[50]

There are even televangelists ministers with similar liberal views. Dr. Robert H. Schuller from the Crystal Cathedral in California has said:

> We have not given human beings the teaching that they should be leaders—and a leader is a person who is aware of his personhood, meaning his freedom to make choices. But basically, the dominant

influence of Christianity, that is, Roman Catholicism and Protestantism, resulted in a tendency which was not to train believers to be persons or leaders or individual thinkers—hence truly moral creatures—but rather to be followers. The church would make the decisions as to what ought to be done, and the believers would be expected to learn what ought to be done, and then they were supposed to obey.[51]

So there have been for the past few decades new ideas coming out of conservative as well as liberal groups and they may ultimately change sexuality in the conservative as well as the mainline churches in America. Favoring greater freedom of choice for everyone implies support for pluralism and acceptance of those who choose sexual standards other than abstinence, and backing for gender conceptions other than male dominance.

Those who leave the liberal churches most often become the nonaffiliated people, and that group is growing at a rapid pace. The disenchanted member of a liberal church does not usually become a member of a conservative religion. The liberal church is searching, with the leadership of people like Spong and Nelson, to add new vigor and boldness to their religions and thereby increase the commitment of their congregants. The Catholic and Jewish groups have their own liberal leaders too. What they all are constructing is a more pluralistic ethical view. Here, for example, is a statement of hope by James Nelson that the church will recognize a far broader range of sexual events:

> Is it too bold to suggest that we consider ways of naming and celebrating the onset of a girl's menstruation? Or a boy's coming of age— in the face of the currently destructive secular rituals of naming and achieving "manhood"? Or the affirming of one's sexual orientation? Or the commitment to a new relationship of intimacy other than marriage? Or rites of abortion which convey faith's healing resources after agonized choice? The church is losing countless teenagers and young adults, not to mention older persons, because it continues to be silent, timid and negative about sexuality.[52]

I know that some readers will feel that Professor Nelson's suggestions are pretty far out. But brace yourself, I want to go a step further. I praise what the Religious Left is doing, but I do feel it is not pluralistic enough. They have released sexual pleasure from the solitary confinement imposed by St. Augustine and St. Thomas, but they have released it only in the custody of love. If we examine ourselves, we are aware that sexual pleasure has a value to each of us—without being joined to love or anything else. Most of us masturbate for reasons other than love and many people have had sexual relations with people they were not in love with.

A pluralistic approach has to recognize that there are circumstances in which people can benefit from freely chosen sexual relations that are pleasure- and friendship-centered. As long as the basic pluralistic values of honesty, equality, and responsibility are present, then the respectful treatment of each person is present, even though lasting affection and love may not be there. Sometimes love may develop, but more often than not, it won't. Most Americans view love relationships as ideal, but we are not always in ideal circumstances in our lives. My point here is that we ought not to back away from endorsing pleasure- and friendship- centered sexual choices as legitimate options for single people at some times in their lives. The key check should be: Is the sexual relationship HER-oriented? If it is, then it meets the ethical test of pluralism.

Enhancing Religious Pluralism

All generations transform religion to make it meaningful for themselves. Rodney Stark and William Bainbridge, two university sociologists, have presented strong evidence that when an established religion does not fulfill the needs of its members, new religious sects are formed which, over time, will become new established denominations.[53] Some of the new Evangelical religions were formed because some people found the mainline religions lacking. Religion is an essential and a dynamic element in society. No one religious view—whether it be mainline or Evangelical—can fulfill the needs of everyone. From a pluralistic perspective all the religious views of sexuality are acceptable as long as they do not claim to be the one right way. There are those who would say that God is behind their position and so they must condemn all others. I would simply reply that the God of a democratic society would surely be seen as a pluralist.

We need the flexibility afforded by our traditional pluralistic approach to religion. Our country was founded on a belief in religious pluralism. We cannot allow any one specific religious view—liberal or conservative—to monopolize our country, our conception of sexuality, or our understanding of God. Pluralism permits persons to choose for themselves among a wide variety of perspectives; that freedom to search is vital. Religion can supply the motivation for us to help one another resolve the multiple sexual crises we face. It is the place of religion to make us believe in a better world. And it is the responsibility of those who believe in a better world to use religion in ways that make it an ally rather than an enemy in our search for how to restructure our society so as to make it a more honest, equal, and responsible place in which to live.

10

Shaping Today's Sexual Revolution

Public Judgment and the Right to Sexual Privacy

Americans today clearly see sexuality in a more tolerant, pluralistic light. They twice elected Bill Clinton as president despite a series of charges regarding affairs from Gennifer Flowers to Paula Jones. The polls indicate that Americans generally do not see sexual behavior as a sound basis for predicting political competency. Further, Americans see sexual behavior as private, although they will often read the tabloids about such events. We are still a prurient nation, but we are becoming much less judgmental regarding private sexual behavior. The media present these events because they sell and the public knows this and doesn't buy into the justifications given by the press. As conservative news analyst George Will has said, "It is easy to dress up voyeurism as 'the public's right to know.' "[1]

The 1997 Lt. Kelly Flinn case was a clear indication of America's more private and less judgmental view of sexuality. Lt. Flinn was the first female B-52 bomber pilot and well respected for her skills. But she was to be court-martialed for carrying on an affair with a civilian who was a married man and for disobeying orders by her military superiors to stop that affair. Through her lawyer she made her situation public. The basic public reaction was that the military had no business butting into her private life and that the military conception of sexuality was outdated and unnecessarily intrusive.[2] Perhaps the most unexpected bit of evidence of political support for this more pluralistic view of sexuality came from Senate Majority Leader Trent Lott, a Republican from Mississippi. Senator Lott spoke in defense of Lt. Flinn: he explicitly said that she was being unfairly treated and that the military code regarding sexuality was unrealistic. Many other politicians also took that position.

Americans still opposed the forced sexuality that the Navy exhibited in the 1991 Tailhook scandal and the use of power between male drill sergeants and female trainees in the Army's Aberdeen scandal. But the Air Force case was different—it involved clearly consensual sex between two adults. Even though most Americans condemn extramarital sexuality, polls have indicated that they feel that adultery is a private matter and one that the people involved should deal with. Lt. Flinn was given a general discharge, "under honorable conditions." This is a step below an honorable discharge, but it avoided the court-martial trial and both the Air Force and Lt. Flinn seemed content with this compromise. To be sure, Lt. Flinn did disobey her superior's orders and that is a serious charge. But if there had been no regulations against private consensual affairs, that order would never have been given. I feel confident that all branches of the military will soon reexamine their sexual codes and they will become more in line with the new pluralism of the public. But knowing the military, I am sure that they will still endorse a sexual code that falls short of HER sexual pluralism.

Pluralizing Our Moral Choices

The traditional approach does not encourage us to think for ourselves; it basically asks us to do what we're told. In contrast, the pluralistic philosophy affords us the chance of exercising and developing our own moral judgment. That isn't always easy. It does take careful self-examination and patience to work out one's own preferred sexual lifestyle. To exercise the right to choose you must work to learn what it is you want in the area of sexuality. Morality does not consist of simply following other people's orders about how we should behave. Morality is based on our concern for the welfare of others as well as our regard for ourselves. Choice lies at the heart of morality. To program a robot to help old people cross the street does not make the robot a moral actor. We hesitate to assign blame or praise for actions not freely chosen.[3] Blind obedience does not qualify as a choice. Moral acts require the freedom to make choices. A nation that seeks to make robots of its people in their sexual lives is one that will be lost when its social life changes. A nation of people who are capable of reasoning and thinking clearly about sexuality is far better able to cope with crises than is a nation filled with guilty and conflict-ridden people who are encouraged to "just say no." *It is time for Americans to have their long overdue rendezvous with sexual reality.*

Let me emphasize what I've said earlier in this book. To oppose sexual dogmatism is not to favor an "anything goes," libertine philosophy. If we oppose the prohibition of alcohol, that does not mean we favor drunkenness. A person can be sexually tolerant and still be discriminating. To favor a rational, thinking, and caring approach to sexual choices is the way to bring control into our sexual lives. The pluralistic position explicitly requires moral restraint by its insistence that we seek to be honest, equal, and responsible (HER) in *all* our sexual relationships. Pluralism is surely not saying "just say yes." If there were a slogan for pluralism, it would be: "Choose wisely."

There is nothing uniquely modern in the right to search our own conscience to decide what we believe is right for ourselves. The Puritans who came to this country in the early 1600s believed in a "privatized" religion. Their religion was a personal matter between an individual and God. Only the individual could say what beliefs and behaviors were in line with God's desires.[4] God was seen as instructing each person's conscience about right and wrong. This position allows for those with strong religious convictions to seek their own views on sexuality, rather than to follow an official view as to what is sexually right and wrong.

Pluralism asks that instead of arbitrarily condemning or approving a specific sexual act, we attempt to determine whether that sexual act fits into the basic values of pluralism—honesty, equality, and responsibility. *All sexual encounters should be negotiated with an honest statement of your feelings, an equal treatment of the other person's feelings, and a responsibility for taking measures to avoid unwanted outcomes like pregnancy or disease.* In doing this pluralism is ruling out the use of force or exploitation. So pluralism does offer objective bases for judging your own or other people's sexual behaviors. It does not accept doing whatever you want if that violates these basic values. But within the above limits pluralism does grant each person the right and the responsibility to make his or her own subjective choices. Each of us must also decide how well a particular sexual act fits with our personal values and what impact it may have on those close to us. These personal values can involve the importance of intimacy, pleasure, new experience, privacy, modesty, commitment, love, security, permanence, personal growth, and whatever else an individual finds worthwhile in a relationship.

People can make mistakes but that doesn't mean that they should be denied the right to choose. Of course, a person can give up the right to make this sort of choice and try to abide by someone else's rules, but mistakes can be made that way too. Pluralism encourages us to exercise carefully our own choices since we are the ones who will have to live with the outcomes of our actions.

Lifestyles: The Key to the Sexuality Debates

As I have tried to indicate throughout this book, the sexuality debates in America are embedded in the clash of two major philosophies of life: (1) a traditional restrictive philosophy that directs the individual to a relatively narrow view of the right way to live and (2) a pluralistic philosophy that asks each of us to choose from a broad range of lifestyles what fits us best at a given point in our lives. We can see from the religious ideas discussed in the last chapter that the traditional philosophy is more in line with St. Augustine's view that human nature is corrupt and needs strict controls. The pluralistic philosophy is more in line with Julian's view, which sees human nature as capable of self-governance to a much greater extent.

The pluralistic philosophy is broader and more accepting of changes in the individual's set of values and life goals. You may decide not to have sexual intercourse at one point in your life and later on you may revise this judgment and decide to have intercourse under some conditions. We *all* have to judge what *now* fits best into our lives, and what consequences are likely to ensue for us and those close to us if we make a certain choice. Those consequences have to be judged by our individual values as well as by HER values.

Intercourse and all other freely chosen sexual behaviors can be helpful or harmful for a person depending on how these behaviors fit into that person's values. But freely chosen sexual acts that are in accord with the pluralistic values of honesty, equality, and responsibility are all legitimate choices for people to contemplate. On the other hand, the traditional position would view sexual intercourse and many other sexual behaviors occurring when not married as wrong no matter what a person's values or situation might be.

The pluralist lives in a world that sees *freely chosen sexuality* as potentially good. If it is honest, equal, and responsible sexuality, it contains a treasure of riches from which to choose. The traditionalist lives in a world that sees most sexuality as potentially bad. The fear of sexuality as something degrading, subordinating, and obscene is stressed. This contrasting perspective on sexuality is the most basic difference between a pluralistic and a traditional view. Your choice between these two perspectives will determine the sexual world in which you will psychologically live. Which choice do you feel would best allow you to grow and learn?

The pluralistic lifestyle, as I've noted, presents us with a very broad range of choices, and for some people that may create a feeling of insecurity. But pluralism has the advantage of giving us the chance to find what way of living best suits each of us at any one point in our lives. If we think about it, pluralism is the way most of us orient ourselves to religion. As we've discussed, we feel we have the right to choose whether to join and, if so, what religion to join. The same is true in politics. We feel we have the right to choose whether to join a political party and, if so, which one.

This same pluralism is employed in choosing a job or a place to live as well as in many other areas of our lives. It is a basic element in a democratic society such as ours. This freedom to choose is precisely the type of freedom that the former Eastern Bloc countries are so eagerly trying to promote today. They have known what it is to be without that freedom in all areas of life and they now realize, perhaps better than we do, how valuable it is.

But in the realm of sexuality millions of Americans feel they have no choice but to follow whatever is conventional. That conventional view may come from a fundamentalist religion, but it may also be imposed by a peer group. Our friends can tell us not to bother with thinking about choices—"If it feels good, do it." That is a libertine position and, as I've explained, it is not a pluralistic position. It says nothing about honesty, equality, and responsibility and, equally important, it says nothing about examining what fits best into our other values and life situations. Doing what feels good is an impulsive approach to sexuality that ignores thoughtful choices just as much as does a fundamentalist approach.

We are praised for being thoughtful when we carefully choose our religion, our political party, our job, or our home. But in sexuality we are so frightened of choice that we praise "just say no" or "just say yes." When we accept either of those positions, we are giving up our right to choose. The pluralist agrees with the ancient Greek philosopher Socrates who stressed the value of the examined life. We are capable of so much more than blind conformity.

The choice between pluralism and traditionalism applies to all areas of life in our society. Each ethical position leads to different conclusions regarding the basic life issues involved in female-male relationships, social class differences, race equality, the choices of family forms, religious beliefs, and questions of political, economic, and educational decisions.

The position we take on any of these other issues will be reflected in the decision we make regarding a specific sexual issue. Therefore, the strong emotions expressed in a particular sexual debate on abortion, homosexuality, or teenage sexuality are there because those choices reflect our basic stand on gender equality, social class, politics, and other key parts of our lifestyle. The choice between pluralism and traditionalism reflects, whether we know it or not, an overall lifestyle and ethical choice, not simply a position on one sexual issue.

We know, for example, from our discussion in chapter 1 that those who are abortion-rights opponents are also more likely to oppose egalitarian roles in marriage and equal rights for gays and lesbians, and to believe that the Bible is the literal word of God. So any one sexual issue under debate can be felt as a questioning of a person's positions on all these other public issues. Because all these positions are most often tied together, every specific sexual issue represents a serious challenge to our pluralistic or traditional way of life.

Equality: Foundation for Pluralism

If we as a nation are to continue to become more pluralistic in the realm of sexuality, we must increase the equality of sexual choices available to men and women. As long as women are not seen as the equals of men in all our basic institutions—family, religion, politics, economics, and education—then men will feel justified in seeking to control women's sexual lives.[5] *So we must make changes in our fundamental institutions if HER sexual choice is to flourish for women as well as for men.*

Certainly, there is a trend in our country and the entire Western world toward gender equality.[6] The percentage of men's wages that women in America earned has risen from 59 percent in 1981 to 74 percent in 1996. Women now represent over 30 percent of almost all the major professionals in training in our graduate schools of medicine, law, and business. The vast majority of married women in their twenties are now employed. Both women and men are increasingly supporting these changes toward gender equality.

Using national samples from 1977 and 1985, two sociologists from the University of Michigan, Karen Oppenheim Mason and Yu-Hsia Lu, reported significant increases in profeminist views on wife and mother roles among both men and women.[7] Several other social scientists have commented on the remarkable rise in America of the values of autonomy and tolerance, and the decline in the emphasis upon obedience and conformity.[8] These trends are obvious in our sexual, family, religious, and civic behaviors. The path to equality is being forged in all major parts of our social life and it is very likely to continue to go forward. Women in Congress were 5 percent in 1990 and in 1996 they were 11 percent. In state government women in 1996 were 21 percent of the total. So change is occurring. But women's progress still encounters strong resistance especially from traditionalists. We must counteract those pressures if we want gender equality to grow. Progress cannot be made unless someone clears the path.

How do we help in this egalitarian movement of the Western world? Changing behavior is often a good way to start changing attitudes. We have seen in the history of our own civil rights movement that racial *behavior* often changed years before racial *attitudes* were altered. The 1954 Supreme Court ruling which ordered racial desegregation demanded only behavioral changes such as racially integrating the classrooms. The rulings that followed to promote easier access to voting and to public facilities also at first changed only behavior. But changes in attitudes did follow, and we have seen considerable progress even though we are certainly very far from full racial equality today.

There is also a body of research showing that people will change if they perceive the change to be in line with their moral values and feel it will enhance their sense of competence and self-esteem.[9] Most Americans support the idea of equal choice for people as a moral precept. As I've noted, Americans feel we all have the right to choose our lifestyles in religion and politics. This belief has also helped to support racial equality. It may well be easier than we think to persuade many people to support the idea of equal choice for women and men. If we make people aware of how such equality fits with their values and their self-image, I believe many of them will be willing to change.

We can help raise the likelihood of change by altering the behaviors we teach to young girls and boys. We can encourage further modifications in the segregated ways by which we prepare boys for positions of power and authority and girls for positions of nurturance and support. We can promote a full range of choices for both boys and girls and socialize girls and boys to combine a wide range of human abilities. We can raise human beings who are motivated to nurture and also knowledgeable about exercising power. What a wonderful generation that would be!

Of course, not everyone feels as I do. Specifically, some people will see the traditional female role as the only right way for women to live. These people feel the loss of the security that comes with believing that there is only one proper path to follow. To be sure, there is something lost as we move toward greater gender equality. As women have gained more economic and political power, they have placed less emphasis on the traditional roles of mother and wife and have increased their attention on occupational roles. Accordingly, we are losing some of the emphasis on nurturance and caring that women traditionally were taught to develop. And men have not been quick to take up the slack and expand their nurturing roles accordingly.

But there are significant gains for women. Women are losing their tendency toward feelings of depression and low self-esteem which are so often the product of the social straitjackets that go with the traditional female role. With pluralism, women can more easily choose the combination of home and employment that suits them best. That's a very important right to have if one is to feel worthwhile and equal. The pluralistic

philosophy offers increased opportunity for men as well to feel the satisfaction from greater involvement in their homes and families. Most
importantly, pluralism also encourages a man to express the softer and
more vulnerable parts of his personality, without fear of being viewed as
weak or unmanly.

University of California sociologist Arlie Hochschild's study of dual-
earner couples is of interest here.[10] Hochschild found what many of us
know from experience: those two-earner marriages where the husband
does an equal share of housework and childcare have much higher levels
of marital happiness than those households where the woman in effect
works a "second shift." In Hochschild's research sample, only about a
fifth of the wives had husbands who shared equally the "second shift"—
the work at home. Many of the other wives did not press their husbands
for more help for fear of increasing conflict in their marriage. Some wives
did not want to lose the prestige of being the "supermom" and the expert
on the home. The extra work that women did at home amounted to an
extra month of work done by women in every year! But husbands do not
get away scot-free. Over time, wives' resentments build up and so, one
way or another, these husbands will pay a price for their traditional attitudes toward "women's work."

There is so much that other countries do to make it easier for women
to be employed and thereby to gain equality with men. The Swedes have a
policy that allows either parent, after the birth of a child, to take twelve or
more months off from work and still receive their full base pay. Everything
doesn't work out perfectly even in Sweden. In spite of the official policies,
the wife is most often the one who takes time off to be with the children
because only about 20 percent of the husbands take advantage of this possibility. But the social attitudes there strongly encourage men to share this
time with the newborn and that does seem to be slowly happening.[11]

Swedes also have powerful local and national government support for
child-care facilities. The five Swedish political parties constantly vie with
each other as to which one will offer the best daycare programs. Since
men are not quickly assuming traditional homemaker roles even in
Sweden, there must be day care if women are to be able to choose to work
outside the home. In America we are just beginning to take the first steps
toward a government policy to help those millions of married couples in
which both husband and wife are employed and there are children at
home. There are bills before Congress now that would help dual-earner
couples cope with their needs for child care. During President Clinton's
first term Congress passed legislation allowing unpaid leave to care for a
child or other family member.

In many ways we are the foot draggers in the Western world's move toward more egalitarian family forms, even though the great majority of married couples in our country now live in dual-earner marriages. These millions of couples will increasingly pressure our politicians for change. Only with organized political help can we ease the burden on these dual-earner marriages. It will happen! The entire Western world is moving toward greater gender equality. As women gain political, economic, and other equalities, they will increasingly feel enfranchised to search for better sexual choices.

Poverty: The Fatalistic Inequality

There is no question about the growth of an underclass—a new, large, long-term poverty group living in our urban ghettos. As I have stressed throughout this book, all forms of extreme social inequality make free choices in sexuality much more difficult to achieve. William Julius Wilson, past president of the American Sociological Association, in a highly acclaimed book, has most succinctly and convincingly explained the problems of poverty in our country, particularly among blacks.[12]

Wilson notes that many of the good, well-paying, industrial blue-collar jobs that used to be present in our cities are now gone. Over the past few decades, our economy has increasingly shifted to a service economy and many of the new service jobs do not pay as well and require radically different skills. This situation has led to fewer jobs, especially for black men, and so the number of marriageable men has shrunk. With legitimate channels of education very difficult to pursue from the ghetto, we find more young black men under the criminal justice system's control than in college! Divorce, separation, and a disinterest in ever marrying have become much more common in these poverty groups. Women are still having children, but increasingly these children have been born out of wedlock. As Wilson notes, the majority of black births today are to unmarried women and one major cause of that is the poverty of black men.

Wilson and many others argue that it is in our economic interest to turn this situation around. Those in poverty have talents that are being wasted and their poverty requires many billions of dollars of support from the government. Wilson notes that the case of the black poor is not much different from that of other ethnic groups living in poverty. A government program that would include job training and child care would help reduce the hopelessness of all those living in our underclass. Such a program was promised as part of the 1996 new welfare bill, but it has not yet happened. Senator Paul Wellstone started his "poverty tour" of the country in May of 1997 to help move more of us to action. As I noted in chapter 3, it is the feeling of hopelessness that promotes a fatalistic approach to life and discourages any planning, whether it be about sex, drugs, or jobs.

Poverty has been found to be a major cause of unwanted sexual problems in all countries and we in America have a larger poverty group than most Western countries.[13] Carefully conducted studies report that the vast majority of the over thirty-six million Americans living in poverty—one out of every seven Americans—are not just looking for a handout; they would prefer to find a stable job and a way out of the ghetto. But one cannot expect people who see their lives as having no future to plan carefully to avoid things like unwanted pregnancy and disease. If we want this situation to change, we must change our economic policies to reduce poverty. Poverty leads to despair and erodes people's rights to free choice in their lives. It is a cancer growing on our democracy. The economic rewards of reducing poverty together with our concern for human suffering will make it politically possible to clean up the Third-World-style ghettos in our major cities. Our belief in political equality pressures us to create greater economic equality.[14] Can a country with our tradition of democracy and our great wealth do anything less?

Just How Much of a Pluralist Are You?

First, let me say that pluralism is not just a personal philosophy of mine. It is an increasingly influential way of looking at sexuality which has been rapidly growing in America. In 1960 I first predicted the growth of this pluralistic sexual philosophy.[15] Today, the vast majority of college-educated people give strong support to such a pluralistic sexual philosophy and in many ways they are living by that philosophy.

Nevertheless, many of these pluralists have not fully allowed this new philosophy to take root in their lives. When the AIDS scare grew in the mid-1980s, a few retreated back to become advocates of an "abstinence for everyone" position. Many other pluralists continue to move back and forth between their pluralism and much more restrictive beliefs, unsure of what is right. The serious conflict these people feel means that many Americans who have made an *intellectual* commitment to pluralism have not made the full *emotional* transition to that belief. One of the purposes of this book is to help those people complete that voyage to pluralism. I want to afford my readers a solid basis upon which to rethink their own sexual views and thereby to help promote the changes we need in the broader society. Where are the blocks that restrain the full *emotional* acceptance of sexual pluralism? Some people experience difficulty in accepting for others a sexual behavior that they cannot accept for themselves. For example, you may think that if *you* are turned off by the idea of people choosing to be tied up during sex, then such sadomasochistic sex must be wrong. What may be helpful here is to realize that *pluralism is about what you tolerate in others, not about what you personally prefer or accept for yourself.* A person can be a virgin and be a pluralist. Pluralism in religion means we tolerate lots of other religions that we would never want to join. Pluralism acknowledges that what any one person prefers and thinks is best for him- or herself may be quite inappropriate for someone else whose situation and personal values are different. George Bernard Shaw was a pluralist who made this point in his version of the Golden Rule: "Do not do unto others as you would have them do unto you. Their tastes may not be the same!"

Think about the consequences for the people who enjoy a sexual practice when that behavior is rejected as wrong. When we reject other people's sexual behavior, we are denying equal moral rights to anyone engaging in that behavior. The more we condemn other people's behavior as wrong, the more we restrict the right of other people to choose. For example, if we reject homosexual behavior, then we are not likely to accept fully the rights of people who practice that behavior. Not being treated equally is undemocratic and painful and we should think long and hard before we inflict that harm on anyone.

This inequality is particularly unjust when the opposition to a sexual act is based not on any demonstrable harm to HER values by such behavior but simply on personal distaste or because a church or some other group condemns that act. I see no evidence of serious harm done by *any* freely chosen sexual act that involves honesty, equality, and responsibility to others and oneself. Supporting pluralism is a way of affirming our belief in the rights of those who make choices different from our own. *The more people support that view, the safer are our own sexual rights.*

We in social science have a special obligation not just to sit by and report the tragic outcomes of our sexual crisis.[16] If we have spent our professional lives studying sexuality, we should be able to help America build a new sexual philosophy which will help us to resolve the sexual problems we face.[17] I have deliberately avoided promoting a narrow sexual code that would be unsuited for most Americans. I have also avoided any sexual code that would place unnecessary restrictions on people's choices. I have looked for a "minimalist" code that does not place unnecessary restrictions on our choices, and one that is best integrated with our values of democracy and individualism. I am convinced that HER pluralism is the philosophy that will permit each of us to choose more wisely and will make each of us feel more responsible for the sexual choices we make. There are pluralistic values dwelling within most all of us in America and they can easily be applied to our sexual lives.

Surely there are those who will object to sexual pluralism. They will say that even though sexual pluralism may greatly lessen our sexual crisis, it will take away top priority from abstinence, undermine traditional gender roles, and violate orthodox religious beliefs. Those people are right. I am making a choice. I do place higher value on resolving our sexual crisis than I do on genuflecting before the customs of our recent past.

Social customs always change. Many of our customs are different today than they were even a few generations ago. In my mind the fundamental values of honesty, equality, and responsibility that I have built into sexual pluralism are far more essential and lasting than the popular views of any one group at a particular point in history. Pluralistic values are not shared by every society in the world, but they are strongly endorsed by all Western societies and they are unlikely to change in the near future. These values are one part of our traditional past in America that I, and most of us, fully support and cherish. I find the choice of abiding by sexual pluralism and thereby creating a more humane society that is better able to handle its sexual problems a far more attractive choice than conforming to the latest version of sexual traditionalism.[18]

Ironically, sexual traditionalism bears within itself the seeds of its own demise. Once AIDS was publicized, it was precisely the morbid fear of sex promoted by traditionalism that encouraged the greater discussion of high-risk sexual behavior.[19] Today there is talk on the news not only of condom use but also of anal intercourse and oral sex—topics never discussed on broadcast television before. So traditional morality, by creating anxiety about the spread of HIV/AIDS, has unintentionally encouraged learning about how to have safer sex. That open dialogue about sex has made many people more knowledgeable and less naive and, as a result, more likely to reject a narrow traditional view of sexuality.

Organizing for Sexual Pluralism

Although we can make some changes in society by just accepting more pluralism for ourselves in our own lives, we cannot resolve our sexual crisis just by acting as millions of separate individuals. In this respect, the Religious Right can teach us how important national organization and planning are. We don't need a majority of the nation in order to make significant changes in our society. We need only a small percentage of the population who are dedicated to promoting all of our sexual rights. However, if we are to make progress, some national organizational structure is necessary.

The day after George Bush was elected president in 1988, Debra

Haffner, the executive director of the Sex Information and Education Council of the United States (SIECUS), prudently called for greater political activism in order to protect our rights to make our own free sexual choices:

> I am proud of the leadership of people like the SIECUS members who helped lead the fights for civil rights, women's rights, gay rights, the legalization of abortion, and sexuality education for our children. . . . All of us—sexuality educators, counselors, therapists, health professionals, religious leaders, and consumers—must become more political during the coming years in order to stop future assaults and to continue to press for a more progressive America for our children. We must seek new coalitions so that we can work together to protect our rights on a local, state, and national level. We must begin to know and communicate with our school boards, state legislators, and national representatives. I am committed to developing an advocacy program for SIECUS and to developing public policy education materials for members. We need to work together to assure that sexual rights are protected and that all people have access to quality sexuality information and education.[20]

SIECUS is one powerful organization, but there are many other organizations that have recently spoken out. Psychologist Donald Mosher from the University of Connecticut, a recent president of the Society for the Scientific Study of Sexuality (SSSS), summed up his feelings:

> Most Americans favor tolerance of sexual variations and lifestyles. Yet they remain confused about their moral grounds, cowed into a spiral of silence. Sexual freedom is justified by the universal ethical principle of concern and respect for persons.[21]

In organizations like the American Association for Sex Educators, Counselors and Therapists (AASECT) people (other than ex-president Theresa Crenshaw) have spoken out in this same vein. The Society for Sex Therapy and Research (SSTAR) and many other groups have added their support to protect our rights to sexual choices.

I believe that what we need now is for those organizations in the sex field to join together and form a *Sexual Science Association (SSA)*. There are a number of supporters of such a move and it would add much political strength to our field. All these organizations support the ideas of HER sexual pluralism that I have been promoting in this book. SSSS supports the research efforts the most, AASECT the counseling, and SSTAR supports both these efforts. SIECUS has focused principally on sexuality education. Under the leadership of Debra Haffner, that organization has obtained remarkable public support. Debra Haffner has been on scores of national TV shows and helped organize over a hundred organizations to support SIECUS's sexuality education programs.

In the first edition of this book I called for an organization of people throughout the country to support sexual pluralism, but I have since noted that SIECUS in particular and these other organizations were promoting my notions of HER sexual pluralism. So I now am calling for a federalist-type unification of sexuality organizations into a new Sexual Science Association. We need this organization to help us promote strong support for pluralism in our family, religious, economic, educational, and political institutions. Such institutional changes are needed for people to be free to choose wisely among the variety of honest, equal, and responsible sexual acts. With such institutional support HER sexual pluralism will continue to grow and we will be able to gain greater control over the myriad sexual problems that have plagued our society throughout this entire century.

One often hears that education is our only vaccine—that education alone will motivate people to change our society. I am a great believer in education. After all, I have been a college professor for many years and I am writing this book hoping to influence my readers. I fully favor a strong effort to insert greater sexual pluralism into our educational programs at all levels and for all groups. But I know from experience and from my sociology that to be successful, *we must also change the structure of power in our basic social institutions.*

For example, was education the basic cause of the advances feminists have made? I don't think so. Women have gained greater equality by the power of their votes, the organizational skill of their groups, and by the economic power gained from increased employment.[22] This has enabled them to change the laws and to exert pressure for increased gender equality. The same is true for racial inequality. Blacks gained greater equality in the 1960s and 1970s by organizing, registering voters, and exercising political clout. Certainly, educating the public on what they can do is helpful, but people usually require an easy path before they will venture forth. So our political institutions must change to incorporate into their leadership the ideas of sexual pluralism and thereby to encourage people to change. This has happened in the women's movement and the civil rights movement and it is happening now in this century's third sexual revolution.

There are many other professional groups that promote HER sexual pluralism. Those associated with family planning and abortion-rights groups like Planned Parenthood come to mind. The American Civil Liberties Union, which since 1920 has defended our constitutional rights, would be supportive. There are now several strong gay-rights organizations that would surely be sympathetic to promoting sexual pluralism. Also, since gender equality is a major part of any pluralistic philosophy, feminist organizations like the National Organization for Women would be sympathetic to our goals. Some of our churches and synagogues, particularly the more liberal ones like Unitarian-Universalist, United Church of Christ, and Reform Judaism would most likely support sexual pluralism. Some national Catholic groups would feel an affinity to sexual pluralism as well.

Social workers, particularly those who do family planning work, are called upon to patch up the extensive hurt and damage done by our current traditional system. This group deserves special mention because it plays a very influential role in shaping our sexuality. Carole Joffe, a professor of social work and social research at the University of California at Davis, has eloquently made this point:

> Family planning workers play a crucial role in the cultural shaping of sexuality . . . clinics offer many in this society an alternative view of sexual possibilities . . . societal ambivalence about these services has inhibited the development of consensus about what the character of these services should be . . . these workers are engaged not so much in subverting existing policy as in creating policy in a situation in which political impasse has created a void.[23]

Joffe's comments make us aware that when we don't deal with the sexual crises confronting our children and our country, others are forced to somehow fill in as best they can. We have seen this in the growth of rape crisis centers, numerous help lines, and many other groups that fill the gaps left by our unwillingness to realistically confront our sexual problems. How much better if as part of the functioning of a national organization like the Sexual Science Association and other affiliated organizations, we could encourage more open discussion of these problems and formulate strategies and recommendations for helping people. We Americans could then learn to *control the growth* of our sexual problems instead of being overwhelmed by them.

To learn to accept others who differ from ourselves and to protect the equal rights of minority groups is the essence of our democracy. If we work to make all this a reality, we can establish a true sexual democracy. In such a society all of us can achieve a much higher level of erotic well-being—an ability to satisfy one's sexual interests in honest, equal, and responsible relationships.

Our Present Pluralistic Sexual Revolution

Some readers may think that I am far too optimistic in expecting our society to change its sexual dogmas. That was the exact response I heard in 1960 when I wrote my first book predicting a sexual revolution that would radically change our society. I fully believe that the current sexual revolution will bring as many changes as did the 1960s. Many of them have already begun.

The leaders of today's sexual revolution are from the college-educated segment of our country. With these young people on our side we cannot lose. Half of our young people today continue education beyond high school. College-educated young people hold the strongest beliefs in equality and in individual rights, and that means they are pluralists at heart. I find today among my students the same sense of searching and of longing for a sexual philosophy they can live by that I sensed a generation ago among their parents. The older baby boomers, now in positions of power, led us into the sexual revolution of the 1960s. They and their children are now moving us further in the sexual revolution of the 1990s.

In the first edition of this book I predicted the third sexual revolution of the twentieth century. The changes I have discussed throughout this book document this event. This time the path is less tumultuous because the last few decades have given all of us an understanding and experience of sexuality that has prepared us for the changes that are now occurring. The sexual revolution of the 1960s and 1970s did not establish pluralism as an accepted belief. This is so because it liberated our sexual *behaviors* more than our sexual *beliefs*. The 1990s' sexual revolution is integrating pluralistic attitudes that add an ethical dimension to our more open sexual behaviors.

The pressures exerted by our present sexual crisis—pressures from HIV/AIDS, rape, teenage pregnancy, and child sexual abuse—are a major force speeding up our move toward sexual pluralism. It is becoming increasingly obvious to all that realism is an essential part of any treatment of our sexual problems. Realism demands the acceptance of the basic values inherent in sexual pluralism—that is, the values of honesty, equality, and responsibility. Instead of the government's chastity efforts, we need pluralistic values being promoted in new legislation on sexuality that will lay the foundation for laws that will enhance rather than restrict our sexual rights. The 1997 Supreme Court's overturning of the Communications Decency Act, which sought to restrict sex on the Internet, is a signpost of the increased pluralism toward which we are heading. Even this nonliberal Supreme Court is moving in a pluralistic direction. In addition, our government is increasingly aware that we cannot pay the bill for the sexual damage we are inflicting in the many sexual-crisis areas of our life. And economic pressures are always a powerful force for change.

We are discovering what most Western European countries already know—that teenagers can be sexually responsible. In the first edition of this book I predicted that our teenage unwanted pregnancy rates would be reduced in the next ten years. This has happened. We are becoming more tolerant of sexual choices and more careful and responsible regarding the risks and rewards in each choice we consider.

A major support of pluralism is the increasing equality of women with men in the economic and political spheres. I have documented this change earlier in this chapter and in many other places in this book. With such gender equality comes increased willingness to demand the important attributes of honesty, equality, and responsibility in sexual decisions. I predicted in this book's first edition that the risks that women take, such as being condemned for having sex, being forced to have sex, or being unprotected from pregnancy or disease, would significantly decline in the 1990s, and this is happening.

In 1990 I predicted that we would be able to see a reduction in the rates of HIV/AIDS, and that, too, has come about in just the last year or so. Also as predicted, the fear of AIDS has increased the likelihood that young people will use condoms. But since HIV infections are so widespread among the impoverished, our progress will be limited by how much empathy we develop for the poor. Any move we make toward alleviating poverty will help all of us in controlling HIV/AIDS. The long-range financial costs of taking care of impoverished AIDS patients are so immense that it will encourage politicians to enact legislation that will benefit all those who are living in poverty.

Our religious organizations are increasingly aware of the fact that they are in danger of losing their young people. Enlightened religious leaders like John Shelby Spong and James B. Nelson, who were mentioned in chapter 9, will increase their followings as sexual pluralism becomes more accepted. The pressures to change from the economic and political realm will make it easier for mainstream religions to more fully incorporate pluralistic beliefs into their ethical systems.

We are now increasingly blending the deep emotions of sexuality with the calm direction of reason. We are discovering how force and exploitation can be replaced by pleasure and empathy. But not even sexual pluralism can resolve all our private and public sexual problems.[24] Nevertheless, we are achieving a much higher level of sexual pluralism and a more cost-free enjoyment of erotic passion. We are putting our knowledge of social science to work in the service of building a far better way of life. Sexual pluralism is an important step toward realizing the great social democracy we have been building for over two hundred years.

I believe that the movement toward sexual pluralism will dominate the early twenty-first century and will unite the many social forces that are exerting pressure on society to adopt a pluralistic instead of a traditional approach to sexuality. We will have learned better how to treat sexuality as a valued human capacity. Instead of the gloomy ambivalence and somber dogmatism that has led us to our sexual crisis, we will in the new millennium decrease the pain and multiply the joy in our sexual lives. And we will have finally learned how to resolve our sexual crises.

Endnotes

Chapter 1: America's Rendezvous with Sexual Reality

1. Centers for Disease Control, *Morbidity and Mortality Weekly Report* 46, no. 8, "Update: Trends in AIDS Incidence, Deaths, and Prevalence—United States 1996," February 28, 1997: 165–73. For an early review of the social dimension of the epidemic see National Research Council, *AIDS: Sexual Behavior and Intravenous Drug Use* (Washington, D.C.: National Academy Press, 1989).

2. Alan Guttmacher Institute, *Sex and America's Teenagers* (New York: Alan Guttmacher Institute, 1994). See especially p. 41. See also Elise F. Jones, J. D. Forrest, N. Goldman, S. Henshaw, R. Lincoln, J. Rosoff, C. Westoff, and D. Wulf, *Teenage Pregnancy in Industrialized Countries* (New Haven: Yale University Press, 1986), ch. 2 and tables 2.1–2.5; Stanley K. Henshaw, A. M. Kenney, D. Somberg, and J. Van Vort, *Teenage Pregnancy in the United States: The Scope of the Problem and State Responses* (New York: The Alan Guttmacher Institute, 1989).

3. National Center for Health Statistics, "Fertility, Family Planning and Women's Health: New Data from the 1995 National Survey of Family Growth," *Vital and Health Statistics* 23, no. 19 (May 1997).

4. Richard J. Gelles and Glenn Wolfner, "Sexual Offending and Victimization: A Life Course Perspective," pp. 363–88 in Alice S. Rossi, ed., *Sexuality across the Life Course* (Chicago: University of Chicago Press, 1994); Diana E. H. Russell, *Sexual Exploitation: Rape, Child Sexual Abuse, and Workplace Harassment* (Beverly Hills: Sage Publications, 1984), ch. 1, and table 1.5; Ann W. Burgess, ed., *Rape and Sexual Assault*, vol. 2 (New York: Garland Publishing Inc., 1988).

5. David Finkelhor, "Current Information on the Scope and Nature of Child Sexual Abuse," *The Future of Children* 4, no. 2: 31–53 (Summer/Fall 1994); David Finkelhor, *A Sourcebook on Child Sexual Abuse* (Beverly Hills: Sage Publications, 1986), ch. 1, table 1.2; and Russell, *Sexual Exploitation*, ch. 10.

6. Ira L. Reiss, *Premarital Sexual Standards in America* (New York: The Free Press of Macmillan, 1960), ch. 10, esp. pp. 235–41.

7. *Minneapolis Star Tribune*, July 31, 1989.

8. *Minneapolis Star Tribune*, February 5, 1990. Quoted in an article by Marty Roth and Martha Roth.

9. *Minneapolis Star Tribune*, December 14, 1987.

10. Centers for Disease Control, "Guidelines for Effective School Health Education to Prevent the Spread of AIDS," *Morbidity and Mortality Weekly Report*, 1988: 37 (supp. no. S-2): 10.

11. For a brief overview of trends in premarital sexual intercourse see Ira L. Reiss, "Sexual Behavior," pp. 828–30 in George T. Kurian and Graham T. T. Molitor, eds., *The Encyclopedia of the Future* (New York: Macmillan, 1996), vol. 2. See also Sandra L. Hofferth, J. R. Kahn, and W. Baldwin, "Premarital Sexual Activity Among U.S. Teenage Women over the Past Three Decades," *Family Planning Perspectives* 19 (March/April 1987): 46–53; and National Research Council, *AIDS, Sexual Behavior and Intravenous Drug Use*, ch. 2.

12. William J. Bennett, *AIDS and the Education of Our Children: A Guide For Parents and Teachers* (U.S. Department of Education, 1987), p. 17.

13. *San Francisco Chronicle*, December 14, 1986.

14. Edward Laumann, Robert Michael, and John Gagnon, "A Political History of the National Sex Survey of Adults," *Family Planning Perspectives* 26 (January/February 1994): 34–38.

15. John Money, *The Destroying Angel: Sex, Fitness and Food in the Legacy of Degeneracy Theory, Graham Crackers, Kellogg's Corn Flakes and American Health History* (Amherst, N.Y.: Prometheus Books, 1985), pp. 109–10. For another discussion of Victorianism see Jeffrey Weeks, *Sex, Politics and Society: The Regulation of Sexuality Since 1800*, 2d ed. (London: Longman, 1989), ch. 2.

16. Money, *The Destroying Angel*, ch. 2.

17. *Newsweek*, February 16, 1987, p. 64.

18. Alan Guttmacher Institute, *Sex and American Teenagers*; Jones, et al., *Teen Age Pregnancy in Industrialized Countries*.

19. For evidence on the ineffective contraception of devoutly religious people, see William A. Fisher, L. A. White, D. Byrne, and K. Kelley, "Erotophobia-erotophilia as a Dimension of Personality," *Journal of Sex Research* 25 (February 1988): 123–51; Arland Thornton and Marlene Studor, "Adolescent Religiosity and Contraceptive Usage," *Journal of Marriage and the Family* (February 1987): 117–28; and John Delamater and Patricia Maccorquodale, *Premarital Sexuality: Attitudes, Relationships, Behavior* (Madison: University of Wisconsin Press, 1979).

20. C. Everett Koop, M.D., *Surgeon General's Report on Acquired Immune*

Deficiency Syndrome (U.S. Department of Health and Human Services, 1986), p. 17.

21. *Minneapolis Star Tribune*, September 8, 1987.

22. *Family Planning Perspectives* 21 (November/December 1989): 279–80. For more complete information on herpes see Stephen L. Sacks, *The Truth about Herpes*, 3d ed. (West Vancouver, Canada: Gordon Soules Book Publishers Ltd., 1988).

23. Centers for Disease Control, "Chlamydia Trachomatis Genital Infections—United States 1995," *Morbidity and Mortality Weekly Report* 46, no. 9 (March 7, 1997): 193–98. For complete coverage of all sexually transmitted diseases see King K. Holmes, P. Mardh, P. Sparling and P. Wiesner, eds., *Sexually Transmitted Diseases*, 2d ed. (New York: Mcgraw Hill, 1990).

24. Gayle Rubin, "Thinking Sex: Notes for a Radical Theory of the Politics of Sexuality," in Carole S. Vance, ed., *Pleasure and Danger: Exploring Female Sexuality* (Boston: Routledge & Kegan Paul, 1984): 267–319. The quotation is from p. 278.

25. Since the late 1970s, the majority of teenagers have had premarital intercourse by the time they turn eighteen. Sandra L. Hofferth and Cheryl D. Hayes, eds., *Risking the Future: Adolescent Sexuality, Pregnancy, and Childbearing*, vol. 2 (Washington, D.C.: National Academy Press, 1987), pp. 364–68.

26. The National Opinion Research Center (NORC) annual survey of Americans is the source for this statement. See *General Social Survey: 1972–1996: Cumulative Codebook* (Chicago: National Opinion Research Center, July 1996), p. 216. The average percent saying homosexuality is always wrong has been very close to 75 percent for the years 1973–1988 but dropped to 60 percent by 1996.

27. For a cross-cultural discussion of homosexuality and a list of further references see Ira L. Reiss, *Journey into Sexuality: An Exploratory Voyage* (New York: Prentice-Hall, Inc., 1986), ch. 6, "The Societal Linkages of Homosexuality."

28. Edward O. Laumann, John H. Gagnon, Robert T. Michael, and Stuart Michaels, *The Social Organization of Sexuality* (Chicago: University of Chicago, 1994): 294–96.

29. In everyday speech we often interchange the words "sex" and "gender." This can lead to confusion, for when we speak of "sexual" equality we can't be sure we are talking of equality in enjoying orgasms or equality of men and women in general. I use "sex" and "gender" as two different words in this book. "Gender" means the rights and duties that a society says goes with being male or female. For example, in a traditional society, men are expected to be macho and women to be weak and helpless. The term "sex" or "sexual" refers to all forms of erotic arousal that generally leads to genital response, such as oral sex, anal sex, and vaginal intercourse. These concepts are discussed at length in chapter 1 of my book, *Journey into Sexuality: An Exploratory Voyage*.

30. Many researchers have reported that there is an association between sexual conservatism and gender role conservatism. See Faye D. Ginsburg, *Con-*

tested Lives: The Abortion Debate in an American Community (Berkeley and Los Angeles: University of California Press, 1989). In addition see Barbara A. Finlay, "Sex Differences in Correlates of Abortion Attitudes among College Students," *Journal of Marriage and the Family* 43 (August 1981): 571–82; Donald Granberg and Beth Granberg, "Abortion Attitudes, 1965–1980," *Family Planning Perspectives* (September/October 1980): 250–61; Fisher et al., "Erotophobia-erotophilia as a Dimension of Personality"; Reiss, *Journey into Sexuality* and "Some Observations on Ideology and Sexuality in America," *Journal of Marriage and the Family* 43 (May 1981): 271–83.

31. You can divide respondents into anti-abortion rights and pro-abortion rights groups on the basis of any of seven different abortion questions that Norc asked its respondents. The basic differences I described between these two groups are quite similar no matter which one of these differently worded abortion questions one uses. For the full set of questions asked by Norc see *General Social Survey, 1972–1996*, pp. 207–209.

32. "The Controversial Dr. Koop," Public Broadcsting System (PBS), October 10, 1989.

33. Ginsburg, *Contested Lives*, p. 218.

34. *Minneapolis Star Tribune*, August 17, 1989, reprint of an article by Elizabeth Whelan in the *New York Times*.

Chapter Two: Alice in Wonderland: Sexual Upbringing in America

1. "Oprah Winfrey Show," January 6, 1988.

2. Steve Chapple and David Talbot, *Burning Desires: Sex in America* (New York: Doubleday, 1989), p. 53. For the full discussion of Tipper Gore see pp. 49–74.

3. On April 20, 1988, Congress banned pornographic telephone message services. Congress had earlier rejected this ban, originally proposed by Senator Jesse Helms of North Carolina, but analysts say the upcoming November 1988 election pressured the House to impose a complete ban. The vote was 397 to 1. The lopsidedness of the vote is good evidence that politics, not careful reasoning, was in control. See *Minneapolis Star Tribune*, April 21, 1988. In July 1989 the Supreme Court declared that ban unconstitutional, for the law did not clearly distinguish obscene materials from those that were simply sexually explicit.

4. Sigmund Freud, *Three Contributions to the Theory of Sex* (New York: Dutton, 1962), p. 1; originally published in 1905.

5. Alfred Kinsey, Wardell Pomeroy, Clyde Martin, and Paul Gebhard, *Sexual Behavior in the Human Female* (Philadelphia: W. B. Saunders, 1953), pp. 103–109.

6. Floyd Martinson, *The Sexual Life of Children* (Westport, Conn.: Bergen and Garvey, 1994); Larry L. Constantine and Floyd M. Martinson, *Children and Sex: New Findings, New Perspectives* (Boston: Little, Brown and Company, 1981).

7. Alfred Kinsey, Wardell Pomeroy, and Clyde Martin, *Sexual Behavior in the Human Male* (Philadelphia: W. B. Saunders, 1948), p. 167.

8. The Study Group of New York, *Children and Sex: The Parents Speak* (New York: Facts on File, 1983), p. 113.

9. Ibid., p. 114.

10. Ibid., p. 120.

11. Gary Fine, *With the Boys* (Chicago: University of Chicago Press, 1987), p. 105.

12. For a book that shares much of my view of parental resistance to recognizing child sexuality see Planned Parenthood, *How to Talk with Your Child about Sexuality* (Garden City, New York: Doubleday & Co., 1986). Another book that is helpful in talking to children about sex is: Lynn Leight, *Raising Sexually Healthy Children* (New York: Rawson Associates, 1988). For a list of recent books contact the Sex Information and Education Society of the United States (SIECUS) in New York City.

13. *Minneapolis Star Tribune*, February 12, 1988.

14. Bronislaw Malinowski, *The Sexual Life of Savages in N. W. Melanesia* (New York: Harvest Books, 1929).

15. Donald Marshall and Robert C. Suggs, *Human Sexual Behavior* (New York: Basic Books, 1971).

16. Gilbert Herdt, *Guardians of the Flutes: Idioms of Masculinity* (New York: McGraw-Hill, 1981), and Gilbert Herdt, *Ritualized Homosexuality in Melanesia* (Berkeley and Los Angeles: University of California Press, 1984).

17. In particular see the accounts given of Trobriand, East Bay, and Sambian cultures in Ira L. Reiss, *Journey into Sexuality: An Exploratory Voyage* (New York: Prentice-Hall, Inc., 1986).

18. Ronald Goldman and Juliette Goldman, *Children's Sexual Thinking: A Comparative Study of Children Aged 5 to 15 Years in Australia, North America, Britain and Sweden* (Boston: Routledge & Kegan Paul, 1982).

19. Ibid., p. 262.

20. Ibid., p. 323.

21. David Finkelhor, *A Sourcebook on Child Sexual Abuse* (Beverly Hills: Sage Publications, 1986), p. 242.

22. James J. Krivacska, "Child Sexual Abuse Prevention Programs: The Need for Childhood Sexuality Education," *SIECUS Reports* 19, no. 6 (August/September 1991): 1–7.

23. SIECUS, *Right from the Start: Guidelines for Sexuality Issues* (New York: SIECUS, 1995).

24. David Finkelhor, "Current Information on the Scope and Nature of Child Sexual Abuse," *The Future of Children* 4, no. 2 (Summer/Fall, 1994): 31–53.

25. Ibid., p. 42.

26. Diana E. H. Russell, *The Secret Trauma: Incest in the Lives of Girls and Women* (New York: Basic Books, 1986); and Diana E. H. Russell, *Sexual Exploitatation: Rape, Child Sexual Abuse, and Workplace Harassment* (Beverly Hills: Sage Publishing, 1984), ch. 9.

27. David Finkelhor, *Sexually Victimized Children* (New York: The Free Press, 1979), p. 88. Kinsey also had estimated about 1 percent of daughters had incest with their fathers. See the analysis of Kinsey's data in John H. Gagnon, "Female Child Victims of Sex Offenses," *Social Problems* 13 (Fall 1965): 176–92.

28. Sigmund Freud, *New Introductory Lectures of Psychoanalysis* (New York: Norton Library, 1933). For commentary on this see Florence Rush, "Freud and the Sexual Abuse of Children," *Chrysalis* 1 (1977): 31–45.

29. *Minneapolis Star Tribune*, November 15, 1987.

30. *Minneapolis Star Tribune*, January 31, 1988.

31. *Minneapolis Star Tribune*, November 15, 1987. See also "Sunday Magazine" section of the *Minneapolis Star Tribune*, September 6, 1987, pp. 6–12.

32. Other events in Minneapolis illustrate the points I am making here. See the stories in *Minneapolis Star Tribune*, October 21, 1989 by Donna Halvorsen and February 25, 1990 by Chuck Haga.

33. Several studies have reported that a sex-negative upbringing was common in sex offenders of various types. See Paul H. Gebhard, J. H. Gagnon, W. B. Pomeroy, and C. V. Christenson, *Sex Offenders: An Analysis of Types* (New York: Harper & Row, 1965); M. J. Goldstein, and Ron Langevin, *Sexual Strands: Understanding and Treating Sexual Anomalies in Men* (Hillsdale, N.J.: Lawrence Erlbaum Associates, 1983); Judith L. Herman, *Father-Daughter Incest* (Cambridge, Mass.: Harvard University Press, 1981); Gene G. Abel, Judith V. Becker, W. D. Murphy, and B. Flanagan, "Identifying Dangerous Child Molesters," in R. B. Stuart, ed., *Violent Behavior: Social Learning Approaches to Prediction, Management and Treatment* (New York: Brunner/Mazel, 1981), pp. 116–37; John Money and Margaret Lamacz, *Vandalized Lovemaps: Paraphilic Outcome of Seven Cases in Pediatric Sexology* (Amherst, N.Y.: Prometheus Books, 1989); and Finkelhor, *Sourcebook on Child Sexual Abuse*, ch. 3.

34. For evidence of the role of male dominance as a cause of sexual abuse see Letty Cottin Pogrebin, *Family Politics: Love and Power on An Intimate Frontier* (New York: Mcgraw Hill, 1983), ch. 5.; and Russell, *Sexual Exploitation: Rape, Child Sexual Abuse and Workplace Harassment*.

35. Herman, *Father-Daughter Incest*.

36. Ibid., p. 117.

37. Ibid., p. 202. See also Pogrebin, *Family Politics*, pp. 101–108.

38. Finkelhor, "Current Information on the Scope and Nature of Child sexual Abuse," and Robert Bauserman and Bruce Rind, "Psychological Correlates of Male Child and Adolescent Sexual Experiences with Adults: A Review of the Nonclinical Literature," *Archives of Sexual Behavior* 26, no. 2 (1997): 105–41.

Chapter Three: Teenage Sex: A Time for Acceptance

1. I summed up my comparisons of Sweden and the United States in Reiss, "Sexual Customs and Gender Roles in Sweden and America: An Analysis and

Interpretation," in H. Lopato, ed., *Research on the Interweave of Social Roles: Women and Men* (Greenwich, Conn.: Jai Press, 1980), pp. 191–220.

2. Alan Guttmacher Institute, *Sex and American Teenagers* (New York: Alan Guttmacher Institution, 1994); Elise F. Jones et al., *Teenage Pregnancy in Industrialized Countries: A Study Sponsored by the Alan Guttmacher Institute* (New Haven: Yale University Press, 1986), especially p. 181.

3. *Sexual Och Samlevnandsundervisning (Education for Sexuality and Living Together)* (Stockholm: Statens Offentilge Utredningar, 1974).

4. *Foster's Daily Democrat*, Dover, N. H., April 16, 1988.

5. Ibid., April 15, 1988.

6. Ibid., April 18, 1988.

7. Ibid., September 29, 1988.

8. The entire issue of *SIECUS Report* 25, no. 4 (April/May 1997), discusses recent legislation authorizing "abstinence only" sex education. SIECUS also did a study of sex education: Diane de Mauro, "Sexuality Education 1990: A Review of State Sexuality and AIDS Education Curricula," *SIECUS Report* 18, no. 2 (December 1989–January 1990): 1–9. See also Alan Gaubrell and Debra Haffner, "Unfinished Business," *SIECUS Report* 22, no. 2 (December 1993/January 1994): 27.

9. For an analysis of state programs see Stanley K. Henshaw, A. M. Kenney, D. Somberg, and J. Van Vort, *Teenage Pregnancy in the United States: The Scope of the Problem and State Responses* (New York: The Alan Guttmacher Institute, 1989). For an analysis of the effectiveness of abstinence programs see *SIECUS Report* 21, no. 2 (December 1992/January 1993) (the entire report is on this topic). See also F. Scott Christopher and Mark W. Roosa, "An Evaluation of an Adolescent Pregnancy Prevention Program: Is 'Just Say No' Enough?" *Family Relations: Journal of Applied Family and Child Studies* 39 (January 1990): 68–72.

10. National Opinion Research Center, *General Social Surveys, 1972–1996: Cumulative Codebook* (Chicago: NORC, 1996), p. 214. The very inadequate amount of contraceptive research in the United States and the reasons for it are explored in L. Mastroianni, P. J. Donaldson, and T. T. Kane, eds., *Developing New Contraceptives: Obstacles and Opportunities* (Washington, D.C.: National Academy Press, 1990).

11. Peggy Brick, "Toward a Positive Approach to Adolescent Sexuality," *SIECUS Report* 17, no. 5 (May/July 1989): 3. See also Peggy Brick and Colleagues, *The New Positive Images: Teaching Abstinence, Contraception and Sexual Health* (Hackensack, N.J.: Planned Parenthood of Greater Northern New Jersey, 1995).

12. Faye Wattleton, "The Case for National Action," *The Nation*, July 24/31, 1989, p. 140. See also the report of the National Commission on Adolescent Sexual Health: Debra W. Haffner, ed., *Facing Facts: Sexual Health for America's Adolescents* (New York: SIECUS, 1995).

13. National Opinion Research Center, *General Social Surveys*, p. 215.

14. I tested this idea and found strong support for it in a study of over two

hundred college students. Those who thought of people as basically "imitative" in their actions were much more sexually conservative than those who thought of people as basically "selective" in their actions. I have not published these data as of this writing.

15. Cheryl D. Hayes, ed., *Risking the Future: Adolescent Sexuality, Pregnancy, and Childbearing,* vol. 1 (Washington, D.C.: National Academy Press, 1987), p. 1. See also Alan Guttmacher Institute, *Sex and American Teenagers.*

16. National Center for Health Statistics, "Recent Declines in Teenage Birthrates in the United States." *Monthly Vital Statistics Report* 45, no. 5, Supplement (December 19, 1996), Public Health Service, Hyattsville, Md.

17. *Minneapolis Star Tribune,* Ann Lander's Column, October 20, 1987.

18. Personal communication from Catherine Chilman, April 9, 1988.

19. National Center for Health Statistics, "Recent Declines in Teenage Birthrates in the United States." See also a well-done project of a decade ago: The Panel on Adolescent Pregnancy and Childbearing consisted of fifteen nationally known experts working under a privately funded, two-year project. See Hayes, ed., *Risking the Future: Adolescent Sexuality, Pregnancy, and Childbearing*, vol. 1, and Sandra L. Hofferth and Cheryl D. Hayes, eds., *Risking the Future: Adolescent Sexuality, Pregnancy, and Childbearing*, vol. 2: Working Papers and Statistical Appendixes (Washington, D.C.: National Academy Press, 1987). The full data on teenage pregnancy rates are in vol. 2. For trends, see pp. 414–17 in vol. 2. Page 417 lists the pregnancy rates in 1960 and 1980. See also Maris A. Vinovskis, *An "Epidemic" of Adolescent Pregnancy?: Some Historical and Policy Considerations* (New York: Oxford University Press, 1988), ch. 2.

20. I will list alphabetically here what I consider *most* of the best sources for *nationally representative data* on sexuality in America since the Kinsey reports. These are national surveys done between 1963 and 1996. I will cite one representative publication for each survey. John Billy, Koray Tanfer, W. R. Grady, and D. H. Klepinger, "The Sexual Behavior of Men in the United States," *Family Planning Perspectives* 25 (1993): 52–60; Joseph A. Catania et al., "Prevalence of AIDS-Related Risk Factors and Condom Use in the United States," *Science* 258 (1992): 1101–1106; Centers for Disease Control, "Youth Risk Behavior Surveillance—United States, 1995," *Morbidity and Mortality Weekly Report* 45, no. SS-4 (September 27, 1996); Jacqueline Forrest and S. Singh, "The Sexual and Reproductive Behavior of American Women, 1982–1988," *Family Planning Perspectives* 22 (1990): 206–14; Al D. Klassen, C. J. Williams, and E. E. Levitt, *Sex and Morality in the United States* (Middletown, Conn.: Wesleyan University Press, 1989); Edward O. Laumann, John Gagnon, Robert Michael, and Stuart Michaels, *The Social Organization of Sexuality: Sexual Practices in the United States* (Chicago: University of Chicago Press, 1994); National Center for Health Statistics, "Fertility, Family Planning and Women's Health: New Data from the 1995 National Survey of Family Growth," *Vital and Health Statistics* 23, no. 19 (May 1997); National Opinion Research Center, *General Social Surveys, 1972–1996: Cumulative Codebook.* (Chicago: 1996); Ira L. Reiss, *The Social Context of Premarital Sexual Permissiveness* (New York: Holt, Rinehart and Winston,

1967); Freya L. Sonenstein, Joseph H. Pleck, and Leighton C. Ku, "Levels of Sexual Activity among Adolescent Males in the United States," *Family Planning Perspectives* 23, no. 4 (July/August 1991): 162–67; Melvin Zelnik and Joseph Kantner, "Sexual Activity, Contraceptive Use and Pregnancy among Metropolitan-Area Teenagers: 1971–79," *Family Planning Perspectives* 12: 230–37.

21. Hofferth and Hayes, *Risking the Future*, vol. 2, p. 376, gives the data on the increase in number of partners and p. 364 presents data on the drop in age at first coitus. On pp. 372–75 they report that in 1976 the percentage of teenage women who had intercourse only once was 15 percent and in the 1982 National Survey of Family Growth it was only 7 percent.

22. Ibid., table 2.1, p. 390, and table 3.4, p. 422.

23. Reiss, *An End to Shame: Shaping Our Next Sexual Revolution*, p. 235: "I predict that our teenage pregnancy rates will be dramatically reduced in the next ten years. We will become more tolerant of sexual choices but we will also become more careful and responsible regarding the risks and rewards in each choice we consider."

24. National Center for Health Statistics, "Fertility, Family Planning and Women's Health: New Data from the 1995 National Survey of Family Growth," *Vital and Health Statistics* 23, no. 19 (May 1997); National Center for Health Statistics, "Recent Declines in Teenage Birth Rates in the United States: Variations by State, 1990–1994," *Monthly Vital Statistics Report* 45, no. 5 Supplement (December 19, 1996): 1–16.

25. National Center for Health Statistics, "Fertility, Family Planning and Women's Health"; Zelnik and Kantner, "Sexual Activity, Contraceptive Use and Pregnancy."

26. National Center for Health Statistics, "Trends in Pregnancies and Pregnancy Rates: Estimates for the United States, 1980–1992," *Monthly Vital Statistics Report* 43, no. 11S (May 25, 1995).

27. This estimate came from Alan Guttmacher Institute, *Sex and American Teenagers* (New York: Alan Guttmacher Institute, 1994), p. 41.

28. Charles F. Westoff, "Unintended Pregnancy in America and Abroad," *Family Planning Perspectives* 20 (November/December 1988): 254–61. See especially Figure 1, p. 257.

29. I believe these rates have declined some in the 1990s, but the best sources for the 1980s support my estimate of 40 percent getting pregnant by the time they are twenty and half of those pregnant giving birth. This comes in part from a national study of unmarried twenty- to twenty-nine-year-old women: Koray Tanfer and Marjorie C. Horn, "Contraceptive Use, Pregnancy and Fertility Patterns among Single American Women in Their 20s," *Family Planning Perspectives* 17 (January/February 1985): 10–19. Compatible findings appear in other national studies. The 1982 National Survey of Family Growth (NSFG) found that among women twenty-five to twenty-nine who never married 39 percent had been pregnant and among that age group who had married, 40 percent had experienced a premarital pregnancy: National Center for Health Statistics, C. A. Bachrach and M. C. Horn, "Marriage and First Intercourse, Marital Dissolu-

tion, and Remarriage, United States, 1982," *Advance Data from Vital and Health Statistics* 107, Public Health Service (April 12, 1985). Koenig and Zelnik reported 36 percent of sexually active teenagers were pregnant after two years of sexual experience: M. Koenig and M. Zelnik, "The Risk of Premarital First Pregnancy among Metropolitan-area Teenagers: 1976 and 1979," *Family Planning Perspectives* 14 (September/October 1982): 239–47. Hofferth and Hayes, *Risking the Future*, p. 478, report 17 percent of sexually active teens having given birth by the time they are nineteen. Forrest reports 43.5 percent of the sexually experienced women experiencing a pregnancy by age twenty. J. D. Forrest, "Proportion of U.S. Women Ever Pregnant Before Age 20: A Research Note," Unpublished Paper, Alan Guttmacher Institute, New York, 1986.

30. Elise F. Jones et al., *Teenage Pregnancy in Industrialized Countries.*

31. Ibid., p. 87.

32. Ira L. Reiss, Al Banwart, and Harry Foreman, "Premarital Contraceptive Usage: A Study and Some Theoretical Explanations," *Journal of Marriage and the Family* 37 (August 1975): 619–30. Several other studies supported my view that uncertainty about your legitimate right to make sexual choices leads to poor contraceptive practices: Laraine Winter, "The Role of Sexual Self-Concept in the Use of Contraceptives," *Family Planning Perspectives* 20 (May/June 1988): 123–27; Ruth A. Levinson, "Contraceptive Self-Efficacy: A Perspective on Teenage Girls' Contraceptive Behavior," *Journal of Sex Research* 22 (August 1986): 347–69; John Delamater and Pat Maccorquodale, "Premarital Contraceptive Use: A Test of Two Models," *Journal of Marriage and the Family* 40 (May 1978): 235–47; Marlena Studer and Arland Thornton, "Adolescent Religiosity and Contraceptive Usage," *Journal of Marriage and the Family* 49 (February 1987): 117–28; and Hayes, *Risking the Future*, vol. 1, pp. 109–10.

33. William A. Fisher, Donn Byrne, and Leonard A. White, "Emotional Barriers to Contraception," in Donn Byrne and William A. Fisher, eds., *Adolescents, Sex and Contraception* (Hillsdale, N.J.: Lawrence Erlbaum Associates, 1983), ch. 9.

34. Paul R. Abramson, "Implications of the Sexual System," in Byrne and Fisher, *Adolescents, Sex, and Contraception*, p. 57.

35. See "Sweden: The Western Model," in Ira L. Reiss and Gary R. Lee, *Family Systems in America*, 4th ed. (New York: Holt, Rinehart and Winston, Inc., 1988), ch. 17.

36. Jones et al., *Teenage Pregnancy in Industrialized Countries*, p. 223.

37. Ibid., pp. 234–35.

38. Ibid., p. 230.

39. Ibid., p. 240.

40. Hayes, *Risking the Future*, vol. 1, pp. 3–4.

41. Catherine Chilman, *Adolescent Sexuality in a Changing American Society: Social and Psychological Perspectives For the Human Services Professions*, 2d ed. (New York: John Wiley, 1983), p. 298.

42. For an excellent summary of the role of poverty in teenage pregnancy see James Trussell, "Teenage Pregnancy in the United States," *Family Planning Perspectives* 20, no. 6 (November/December 1988): 262–72.

43. *Family Planning Perspectives* 20, no. 5 (September/October 1988): 241.

44. Cheryl D. Hayes, *Risking the Future,* vol. 1, p. 267. For a sensitively written, in-depth case study illustrating the same point see *Minneapolis Star Tribune,* May 22, 1988, pp. 1e–10e. For an excellent discussion on the terrible impact of poverty on people in our society and suggestions on what can be done, see William J. Wilson, *The Truly Disadvantaged: The Inner City, the Underclass, and Public Policy* (Chicago: University of Chicago Press, 1987).

45. For an excellent account of the public's views on inequality in America see James R. Kluegel and Eliot R. Smith, *Beliefs about Inequality: Americans' Views of What Is and What Ought to Be* (New York: Aldine De Gruyter, 1986).

46. Hyman Rodman, Susan H. Lewis, and Saralyn B. Griffith, *The Sexual Rights of Adolescents: Competence, Vulnerability, and Parental Control* (New York: Columbia University Press, 1984), pp. 132–58. Another book with important proposals of its own is Larry L. Constantine and Floyd M. Martinson, eds., *Children and Sex: New Findings, New Perspectives* (Boston: Little, Brown & Co., 1981). For an early overview of teenage pregnancy and a discussion of programs and policies see Susan Phipps-Yonas, "Teenage Pregnancy and Motherhood: A Review of the Literature," *American Journal of Orthopsychiatry* 50 (July 1980): 403–31.

47. Jacqueline Darroch Forrest, "The Delivery of Family Planning Services in the United States," *Family Planning Perspectives* 20 (March/April 1988): 88–98. The entire issue is devoted to contraception and family planning services in developed countries and points out the problems in our society. On the same topic see Elise F. Jones, Jacqueline D. Forrest, Stanley K. Henshaw, Jane Silverman, and Aida Torres, *Pregnancy, Contraception and Family Planning Services in Industrialized Countries* (New Haven: Yale University Press, 1989).

48. The 1995 National Survey of Family Growth did report increased condom use in the 1990s: National Center for Health Statistics, "Fertility, Family Planning and Women's Health." Other studies reported on changes prior to the 1990s: Jacqueline D. Forrest and R. R. Fordyce, "U.S. Women's Contraceptive Attitudes and Practice: How Have They Changed in the 1980s," *Family Planning Perspectives* 20, no. 3 (May/June 1988): 112–18; Freya L. Sonenstein, J. H. Pleck, and L. C. Ku, "Sexual Activity, Condom Use and AIDS Awareness among Adolescent Males," *Family Planning Perspectives,* 21, no. 4 (July/August 1989): 152–58.

49. For an analysis of trends in attitudes towards sex education and a wide variety of other sexual areas see National Opinion Research Center, *General Social Survey: 1972–1996* (Chicago: NORC, 1996).

Chapter Four: The Stalled Sexual Revolution of This Century

1. Edward Laumann, John Gagnon, Robert Michael, and Stuart Michaels, *The Social Organation of Sexuality* (Chicago: University of Chicago Press,

1994), p. 98. Married people reported having sex between 6.5 and 6.9 times a month.

2. Clelia Duel Mosher, *The Mosher Survey: Sexual Attitudes of 45 Victorian Women* (New York: Arno Press, 1980), p. xviii.

3. Kinsey's research was not based on a random sampling of the American population, but it does contain the most accurate data we have on sexual behavior for the first half of this century. Kinsey's respondents best represented people who were white, urban, college educated, Protestant, and who lived in the northeast quarter of the country. See Alfred C. Kinsey, W. Pomeroy, C. Martin, and P. Gebhard, *Sexual Behavior in the Human Female* (Philadelphia: Saunders, 1953), ch. 8, and Alfred C. Kinsey, W. Pomeroy, and C. Martin, *Sexual Behavior in the Human Male* (Philadelphia: Saunders, 1948), ch. 8.

4. Two of my early books comment upon the forces that produced these changes in our sexual customs: See Ira L. Reiss, *Premarital Sexual Standards in America* (New York: The Free Press of Macmillan, 1960), and *The Social Context of Premarital Sexual Permissiveness* (New York: Holt, Rinehart and Winston, Inc., 1967).

5. Paula Fass, *The Damned and the Beautiful: American Youth in the 1920's* (New York: Oxford University Press, 1977), p. 260.

6. Ibid., p. 326.

7. William A. Williams, T. McCormick, L. Gardner, and W. LaFeber, eds., *America in Vietnam: A Documentary History* (New York: Anchor Books, 1985): 288–89.

8. Cole Porter, "Let's Do It (Let's Fall in Love)," copyright 1928 by Harms, Inc. John Lennon and Paul McCartney, "Why Don't We Do It in the Road," by The Beatles, Apple Records, copyright 1968 Northern Songs, BMI.

9. Beatrice M. Hinkle, "Women and the New Morality," in Freda Kirchwey, ed., *Our Changing Morality: A Symposium* (New York: Albert and Charles Boni, 1924), p. 249. This is an early work by Kirchwey, who went on to become editor of *The Nation* from 1936 to 1955.

10. The key sources for these statistics are Arland Thornton, "Changing Attitudes toward Family Issues in the United States," *Journal of Marriage and the Family* 51 (November 1989): 873–93, table 1. The statistics on voting for a woman for president are from National Opinion Research Center, *General Social Surveys, 1972–1996* (Chicago: NORC, 1996), p. 204. The other statistics are from NORC surveys.

11. Ira L. Reiss and Gary R. Lee, *Family Systems in America*, 4th ed. (New York: Holt, Rinehart and Winston, Inc., 1988), chs. 7 and 12. Consult this text for information on any of the characteristics of the American family up to the late 1980s.

12. Lynda Lytle Holmstrom, *The Two-career Family* (Cambridge, Mass.: Schenkman Publishers, 1972), p. 147.

13. Lenore J. Weitzman, *The Divorce Revolution: The Unexpected Social and Economic Consequences For Women and Children in America* (New York: The Free Press of Macmillan, 1985), especially ch. 11. This book won an award in 1986 from the American Sociological Association.

14. Ibid., p. 209

15. Robert S. Weiss, *Marital Separation: Coping with the End of a Marriage and the Transition to Being Single Again* (New York: Basic Books, 1975), p. 288.

16. Thornton, "Changing Attitudes toward Family Issues in the United States," table 3, and Reiss and Lee, *Family Systems in America*, ch. 8.

17. The 1995 National Survey of Family Growth reported 89 percent of unmarried women aged twenty-five to twenty-nine had experienced intercourse.

18. The 76 percent figures comes from the National Opinion Research Center, *General Social Survey, 1972–1996*, p. 215.

19. On trends in premarital sexual attitudes and behavior see Ira L. Reiss, "Sexual Behavior," pp. 828–30, in George T. Kurian and Graham T. T. Molitor, eds., *Encyclopedia of the Future*, vol. 2 (New York: Macmillan Publishers, 1996). On extramarital sexual attitudes and behavior see Edward Laumann, John Gagnon, Robert Michael, and Stuart Michaels, *The Social Organization of Sexuality* (Chicago: University of Chicago Press, 1994), p. 216, who reported that 15 percent of the women and 25 percent of the men said they had extramarital sex. See also Philip Blumstein and Pepper Schwartz, *American Couples* (New York: William Morrow, 1983), who found that in a volunteer sample of 3,600 married couples from New York, Seattle, and San Francisco over 15 percent had an extramarital agreement that allowed affairs under special conditions. See pp. 289 and 585.

20. Steven D. McLaughlin et al., *The Changing Lives of American Women* (Chapel Hill: The University of North Carolina Press, 1988), ch. 6.

21. Bradley Smith, *The American Way of Sex: An Informal Illustrated History* (New York: Two Continents Publishing Company, 1978), p. 232.

22. Sally Wendkos Olds, *The Eternal Garden: Seasons of Our Sexuality* (New York: Times Books, 1985), p. 104. This view of the power of contraception is also held by some well-known researchers. See, for example, John Money, *Venuses Penuses: Sexology, Sexosophy and Exigency Theory* (Amherst, N.Y.: Prometheus Books, 1986), pp. 510–13. For a popular statement published during the sexual revolution see Robert Ostermann and Mark R. Arnold, *The Pill and Its Impact* (Silver Spring, Md.: Dow Jones & Company, Inc., 1967).

23. William H. Masters, Virginia E. Johnson, and Robert C. Kolodny, *Masters and Johnson on Sex and Human Loving* (Boston: Little, Brown and Company, 1986): 22–23. Sex therapist Helen Singer Kaplan was quoted in 1990 as saying: "The pill freed young men and women to have sex." In the *Minneapolis Star Tribune*, June 30, 1990.

24. The choices add to more than 100 percent because respondents were permitted to check more than one choice. See Kinsey et al., *Sexual Behavior in the Human Female*, p. 344. For similar evidence see Donn Byrne and William A. Fisher, *Adolescents, Sex, and Contraception* (Hillsdale, N.J.: Lawrence, Erlbaum Assoc., 1983), p. 181.

25. National Center for Health Statistics, "Fertility, Family Planning and Women's Health: New Data from the 1995 National Survey of Family Growth," *Vital Health Statistics* 23, no. 19 (May 1997).

26. Ira L. Reiss, "Premarital Sexual Standards," *SIECUS Study Guide* no. 5, rev. ed. (New York: Sex Information and Education Council of the United States, 1976). For a detailed history of contraceptive practices see Norman E. Himes, *Medical History of Contraception* (New York: Gamut Press, 1963).

27. The failure rate of condoms in preventing pregnancy during a one-year period varies tremendously by age, race, ethnic group, and income. Under conditions of perfect (consistent and effective) use of condoms the failure rate is 2 percent. When you look at all the groups together the rate can average as high as 14 percent. Clearly user failure is the reason for this great difference. Just for comparison, the failure rate of the pill averages 6 percent but fell to between 1 to 2 percent under conditions of perfect use. The diaphragm failure rate averaged 16 percent with a perfect use failure rate of 4 percent. Clearly "imperfect use" is a major factor in all methods of contraception. See Elise F. Jones and Jacqueline D. Forrest, "Contraceptive Failure in the United States: Revised Estimates from the 1982 National Survey of Family Growth," *Family Planning Perspectives* 21 (May/June 1989): 103–109. See also T. R. Eng and W. T. Butler, eds., *The Hidden Epidemic: Confronting Sexually Transmitted Diseases* (Washington, D.C., Institute of Medicine, 1996).

28. Carol Cassell, *Swept Away: Why Women Fear Their Own Sexuality* (New York: Simon and Schuster, 1984), pp. 20, 24.

29. In my book, *Journey into Sexuality: An Exploratory Voyage*, I examined the close relationship of power and sexuality not only in Western societies but in 186 non-Western cultures. Those interested in the development of a cross-cultural explanation of how society shapes our sexual makeup would find this book particularly interesting.

30. Lynn Atwater, *The Extramarital Connection: Sex, Intimacy, and Identity* (New York: Irvington Publishers, 1982), pp. 59 and 140. Kinsey found that among those born after 1900 30 percent of the wives and 50 percent of the husbands had an extramarital relationship by age forty. The percent today is probably somewhat higher if we include all affairs that happen before a final divorce decree.

31. Barbara Ehrenreich, Elizabeth Hess, and Gloria Jacobs, *Re-making Love: The Feminization of Sex* (Garden City, New York: Anchor Books, 1987), p. 9.

32. Ibid., p. 199.

33. Warren Farrell, *Why Men Are the Way They Are: The Male-female Dynamic* (New York: Mcgraw Hill, 1986), p. 249.

34. I found in my research on female contraception that one of the key determinants of contraceptive usage for female college students was whether they believed that they have the right to decide whether or not to have sexual relationships. The woman who feels she only has the right to say no is less likely to use contraception if she begins a sexual encounter. She is more likely to be a believer in the "swept away" mystique. See Ira L. Reiss, A. Banwart, and H. Foreman, "Premarital Contraceptive Usage: A Study and Some Theoretical Explorations," *Journal of Marriage and the Family* (August 1975): 619–30.

35. John D'Emilio, *Sexual Politics, Sexual Communities: The Making of a Homosexual Minority in the United States, 1940–1970* (Chicago: University of Chicago, 1983): 231–33.

36. Ibid., p. 247.

37. Frances FitzGerald, *Cities on A Hill: A Journey Through Contemporary American Cultures* (New York: Simon and Schuster, 1986), pp. 42, 47. This book contains an excellent account of the development of the homosexual community in San Francisco. For another insightful account of the ways in which we create our own sexuality, with special reference to homosexuality, see Jeffrey Weeks, *Invented Moralities: Sexual Values in an Age of Uncertainty* (New York: Columbia University Press, 1995). Also Jeffrey Weeks, *Sexuality and Its Discontents: Meanings, Myths, and Modern Sexualities* (London: Routledge and Kegan Paul, 1985).

38. For an excellent account of how our country responded to the AIDS epidemic from 1980 to 1985 see Randy Shilts, *And the Band Played On: Politics, People, and the AIDS Epidemic* (New York: St. Martin's Press, 1987).

39. Margaret Nichols, "Sex Therapy with Lesbains, Gay Men, and Bisexuals," in Sandra Leiblum and Raymond Rosen, *Principles and Practice of Sex Therapy*, 2d ed. (New York: The Guilford Press, 1989). The quote is from p. 276.

40. Lillian Faderman, *Surpassing the Love of Men: Romantic Friendship and Love Between Women from the Renaissance to the Present* (New York: William Morrow, 1981), p. 413. See also Lillian Faderman, *Odd Girls and Twilight Lovers: A History of Lesbian Life in 20th Century America* (New York: Penguin Books, 1991).

41. Our attitudes toward homosexuality have changed over the centuries. The late John Boswell's careful historical work shows that only in the latter part of the twelfth century did the Christian church become *intolerant* of homosexuality. John Boswell, *Christianity, Social Tolerance and Homosexuality: Gay People in Western Europe from the Beginning of the Christian Era to the Fourteenth Century* (Chicago: University of Chicago Press, 1980).

42. Weeks, *Sexuality and Its Discontents*, ch. 8. See also Jeffrey Weeks, *Sexuality* (London: Routledge, 1989) and *Invented Moralities*.

43. A Kinsey Institute-sponsored study documents the fact that many areas of sexuality remained rather conservative during the last sexual revolution. See Albert D. Klassen, Colin J. Williams, and Eugene E. Levitt, *Sex and Morality in the United States: An Empirical Enquiry Under the Auspices of the Kinsey Institute* (Middletown, Conn.: Wesleyan University Press, 1989).

44. John Modell, *Into One's Own: From Youth to Adulthood in the United States 1920–1975* (Berkeley and Los Angeles: University of California Press, 1989).

Chapter Five: AIDS, Condoms, and the Epidemic of Sexual Myths

1. It is confusing to use the term AIDS for both the virus and the disease caused by that virus. Hence it is now customary to use the name HIV (Human Immunodeficiency Virus) to define only the virus that can in time produce the disease called AIDS. Writers now often use HIV/AIDS as the referent unless speaking of only one of the two entities.

2. Randy Shilts, *And the Band Played On: Politics, People, and the AIDS Epidemic* (New York: St. Martin's Press, 1987).

3. Allan M. Brandt, *No Magic Bullet: A Social History of Venereal Disease in the United States Since 1880* (New York: Oxford University Press, 1987).

4. Ibid., p. 122.

5. *New York Post*, May 24, 1983.

6. Shilts, *And the Band Played On*, p. 347.

7. William F. Buckley, Jr., "Identify All the Carriers," *New York Times*, March 18, 1986. *Minneapolis Star Tribune*, June 15, 1987, quotes Senator Helms from the CBS "Face the Nation" show of the day before.

8. Even today, twelve years after the blood supply was cleansed, it is estimated that there is still a very small proportion of the blood that contains the HIV virus.

9. Brandt, *No Magic Bullet*, pp. 199, 202.

10. William H. Masters, Virgina E. Johnson, and Robert C. Kolodny, *Crisis: Heterosexual Behavior in the Age of AIDS* (New York: Grove Press, 1988), pp. 7, 93.

11. See, for example, William H. Masters and Virginia E. Johnson, *The Pleasure Bond: A New Look at Sexuality and Commitment* (New York: Little-Brown and Co., 1974).

12. In my first book I coined the term "permissiveness with affection" for the premarital standard that emphasized the importance of commitment for sexuality and which I predicted would grow in popularity. Ira L. Reiss, *Premarital Sexual Standards in America* (New York: The Free Press of Macmillan, 1960). See especially ch. 6. A 1983 nationally representative sample of single women aged twenty to twenty-nine reported that 80 percent felt love was essential to the acceptance of premarital coitus. See also Koray Tanfer and Jeannette J. Schoorl, *The Extent and Context of Sexual Promiscuity* (Philadelphia: Institute for Survey Research, Temple University, 1987); and Koray Tanfer and Lisa A. Cubbines, "Coital Frequency Among Single Women: Normative Constraints and Situational Opportunities," *Journal of Sex Research* 29, no. 2 (May 1992): 221–50.

13. In his 1983 national study of single women twenty to twenty-nine years old Tanfer found that half of the sexually active women had some "short-term" partners and that one quarter of those with short-term partners had six or more such partners. For most of these women such short-term sexual relations were not in accord with their standards. Some of these did develop into lasting relations. Tanfer and Schoorl, *The Extent and Content of Sexual Promiscuity*, table 3.

14. Masters, Johnson, and Kolodny, *Crisis: Heterosexual Behavior in the Age of AIDS*, pp. 7, 93.

15. The prevalence estimate of 1 in 5,000 (precisely .021 percent) was largely based on prevalence rates for the HIV virus in low-risk heterosexual blood donors and military applicants. Of course these estimates will be revised as time goes on. Centers for Disease Control, "Human Immunodeficiency Virus Infection in the United States: A Review of Current Knowledge," *Morbidity and Mortality Weekly Report* 36, Supplement no. S-6 (December 19, 1987), especially pp. 14 and 40.

16. National Center for Health Statistics, "Fertility, Family Planning and Women's Health: New Data from the 1995 National Survey of family Growth," *Vital and Health Statistics* 23, no. 19 (May 1997).

17. Helen Singer Kaplan, *The Real Truth about Women and AIDS: How to Eliminate the Risks without Giving Up Love and Sex* (New York: Simon and Schuster, 1987), p. 111–13. I should note that we now know that the virus can be in the body for *over three years* before being detectable by current antibody tests. All this makes Kaplan's suggestions even more unrealistic.

18. William W. Darrow, "Behaviors Associated with HIV Infection and the Development of AIDS," paper presented at the American Association for the Advancement of Science annual meeting in Boston, February 14, 1988.

19. Spermicides are an additional protection against a variety of diseases, as well as pregnancy.

20. *San Francisco Chronicle*, February 24, 1987.

21. *General Social Surveys, 1972–1996: Cumulative Codebook* (Chicago: National Opinion Research Center, July 1996), p. 214.

22. "Medical News and Perspectives," *Journal of the American Medical Association* 257 (May 1, 1987): 2263.

23. "Twin Cities Live," Channel 5, Minneapolis, Minnesota, June 3, 1988.

24. Kaplan, *The Real Truth about Women and AIDS*, p. 134.

25. Masters, Johnson, and Kolodny, *Crisis: Heterosexual Behavior in the Age of AIDS,* p. 119.

26. Centers for Disease Control, "Condoms For Prevention of Sexually Transmitted Diseases," *Morbidity and Mortality Weekly Report* 37, no. 9 (March 11, 1988): 134.

27. Centers for Disease Control, "Update: Barrier Protection against HIV Infection and Other Sexually Transmitted Diseases," *Morbidity and Mortality Weekly Reports* 42, no. 30 (August 6, 1993): 587–89, 597. Also "Consistent Condom Use Greatly Lessens Heterosexual Transmission of HIV," *Family Planning Perspectives* (Digests) 26, no. 6 (November/December 1994): 278–79.

28. Margaret A. Fischl, G. M. Dickinson, G. B. Scott, N. Klimas, M. A. Fletcher, and W. Parks, "Evaluation of Heterosexual Partners, Children and Household Contacts of Adults with AIDS," *Journal of the American Medical Association* 257 (February 6, 1987): 640–44. See also her manuscript: "Heterosexual Transmission of Human Immunodeficiency Virus (HIV): Relationship of Sexual Practices to Seroconversion."

29. Centers for Disease Control, "Update: Barrier Protection against HIV Infection and Other Sexually Transmitted Diseases."

30. William W. Darrow, "Condom Use and Use-Effectiveness in High Risk Populations," *Sexually Transmitted Diseases* 16 (September 1989): 157–60. Padian's comments on condom use were made in her presentation as part of a roundtable titled "Heterosexual Transmission" on June 7, 1989, at the Fifth International Conference on AIDS in Montreal, Canada.

31. Masters, Johnson, and Kolodny, *Crisis: Heterosexual Behavior in the Age of AIDS*, pp. 115–16; Kaplan, *The Real Truth about Women and AIDS*, pp. 84–85. Crenshaw's views are in her statements at the meeting on condom effectiveness as well as in statements made on the two "Donahue" shows in April 1987 covering the American Association of Sex Educators, Counselors and Therapists' annual meeting in New York City.

32. Masters, Johnson, and Kolodny, *Crisis: Heterosexual Behavior in the Age of AIDS*, pp. 113–14. See also M. Conant, D. Hardy, J. Snatinger, D. Spicer, and J. A. Levy, "Condoms Prevent Transmission of AIDS Associated Retrovirus," *Journal of the American Medical Association* 256 (1986): 1706.

33. Jacqueline D. Forrest and Richard R. Fordyce, "U.S. Women's Contraceptive Attitudes and Practice: How Have They Changed in the 1980s," *Family Planning Perspective* 20 (May/June 1988): 112–18.

34. Freya L. Sonenstein, Joseph H. Pleck, and Leighton C. Ku, "Sexual Activity, Condom Use and AIDS awareness," pp. 152–58. See also William F. Pratt, "Premarital Sexual Behavior, Multiple Partners, and Marital Experience," paper presented at the Population Association of America meeting, May 3–5, 1990, Toronto, Canada.

35. This statement was part of Professor Anderson's presentation at the Fifth International Conference on AIDS in Montreal, June 8, 1989, in the "Mathematical Modeling" section over which he presided.

36. Ira L. Reiss and Robert K. Leik, "Evaluating Strategies to Avoid AIDS: Number of Partners vs. Use of Condoms," *Journal of Sex Research* 26 (November 1989): 411–33. If one was using condoms with 90 percent effectiveness there was only a slight increase in risk of infection with the addition of partners above twenty.

37. Centers for Disease Control, "AIDS and Human Immunodeficiency Virus Infection in the United States: 1988 Update," *Morbidity and Mortality Weekly Report* 38, no. S-4 (May 12, 1989): 9. See also *Minneapolis Star Tribune*, May 23, 1989. The prevalence at that time of the HIV virus in military recruits was about 1 in 700 and in hospital admissions it was about 1 in 350.

38. Public Health Service, *The National Adolescent Student Health Survey: A Report on the Health of American Youth* (Oakland, Calif.: Third Party Publishing Company, 1989), table 2–20, p. 53. See also Centers for Disease Control, "Results from National Adolescent Student Health Survey," *Morbidity and Mortality Weekly Report* 38, no. 9 (March 10, 1989): 147–50.

39. The 1988 study is reported in National Research Council, *AIDS: Sexual Behavior and Intravenous Drug Use* (Washington, D.C.: National Academy

Press, 1989), p. 105. The 1983 national study is reported in Koray Tanfer and Jeannette J. Schoorl, "The Extent and Context of Sexual Promiscuity," draft of an unpublished paper sent to me in 1988 by Tanfer.

40. Centers for Disease Control, "Youth Risk Behavior Surveillance—United States 1995," *Morbidity and Mortality Report*, 45, no. ss4 (September 27, 1996): 17.

41. Michael A. Fumento, "AIDS: Are Heterosexuals at Risk?" *Commentary*, November 1987, pp. 21–27. The quote is from p. 26. See also Michael Fumento, *The Myth of Heterosexual AIDS: How a Tragedy Has Been Distorted by the Media and Partisan Politics* (New York: Basic Books, 1990).

42. Norman Hearst and Stephen B. Hulley, "Preventing the Heterosexual Spread of AIDS: Are We Giving Our Patients the Best Advice?" *Journal of the American Medical Association* 259, no. 16 (April 22/29, 1988): 2428–32. Quote on p. 2431.

43. Institute of Medicine, National Academy of Sciences, *Confronting AIDS: Update 1988* (Washington, D.C.: National Academy Press, 1988), pp. 176–77.

44. These estimates are based on examination of blood from homosexuals taken in the late 1970s as part of a study of hepatitis. Results indicate that half of those who were HIV positive in the late 1970s developed AIDS within ten years and most of the others are showing serious health problems and have what was called AIDS Related Complex (ARC). Centers for Disease Control, "First 100,000 Cases of Acquired Immunodeficiency Syndrome—United States," *Morbidity and Mortality Weekly Report* 38, no. 32 (August 18, 1989): 561–63.

45. Donahue, April 18, 1987.

46. Hearst and Hulley, "Preventing the Heterosexual Spread of AIDS."

47. For a discussion of risk-taking in general see John D. McGervey, *Probabilities in Everday Life* (New York: Ivy Books, 1986). For risk of sexually transmitted diseases see Thomas A. Peterman, R. L. Stoneburner, J. R. Allen, H. W. Jaffe, and J. W. Curran, "Risk of Human Immunodeficiency Virus Transmission from Heterosexual Adults with Transfusion-associated Infections," *Journal of the American Medical Association* 259, no. 1 (January 1, 1988): 55–58. The risks vary by gender. The risk of transmission of gonorrhea infection from male to female is higher (50 percent) than female to male (25 percent).

48. Centers for Disease Control, *Morbidity and Mortality Weekly Report* 37 no. 9. Safe sex has also led to "Jack and Jill Off" clubs.

49. Hearst and Hulley estimate that five hundred unprotected acts of coitus with an infected partner produces a 67 percent chance of infection. Those same five hundred acts would only have a 9 percent chance of infection if condoms were used. The estimates of a 1 in 500 chance of infection is based upon studies of couples in which one person is infected. Such studies are described in Peterman et al., "Risk of Human Immunodeficiency Virus Transmission from Heterosexual Adults"; Padian et al., "Ethnic Differences in the Heterosexual Transmission of HIV"; and Fischl et al., "Evaluation of Heterosexual Partners." The final estimates are summed up in Hearst and Hulley, "Preventing the Het-

erosexual Spread of AIDS." For other comments on estimates of infection see Centers for Disease Control, "Human Immunodeficiency Virus Infection in the United States: A Review of Current Knowledge," *Morbidity and Mortality Weekly Report*. Others have estimated that the risk of infection from one unprotected act of heterosexual coitus is 1 in 1,000 rather than 1 in 500. See Warren Winkelstein, N. S. Padian, and J. A. Wiley, "Observations on the Potential for Sexual Transmission of Human Immunodeficiency Virus Infection among Heterosexuals in San Francisco," *American Journal of Epidemiology* (1990); Harvey V. Fineberg, "Education to Prevent AIDS: Prospects and Obstacles," *Science* 239 (February 5, 1988): 592–96.

50. Centers for Disease Control and Prevention, *HIV/AIDS Surveillance Report* 8, no. 2 (1997). See also T. R. Eng and W. T. Butler, eds., *The Hidden Epidemic: Confronting Sexually Transmitted Diseases* (Washington, D.C.: Institute of Medicine, 1996).

51. Sevgi Aral and King Holmes, "Sexually Transmitted Diseases in the AIDS Era," *Scientific American* 264, no. 3 (February 1991): 62–69; Division of STD Prevention, *Sexually Transmitted Disease Surveillance, 1995* (Atlanta: CDC, September 1996).

52. Warren Winkelstein, D. Lyman, N. Padian, R. Grant, M. Samuel, J. Wiley, R. Anderson, W. Lan, J. Riggs, and J. Levy, "Sexual Practices and Risk of Infection by the Human Immunodeficiency Virus: The San Francisco Men's Health Study," *Journal of the American Medical Association* 257, no. 3 (January 16, 1987): 321–25; R. M. Grant, J. A. Wiley, and W. Winkelstein, "Infectivity of the Human Immunodeficiency Virus: Estimates from a Prospective Study of Homosexual Men," *Journal of Infectious Diseases* 156, no. 1 (July 1987): 189–93; Padian et al., "Ethnic Differences in the Heterosexual Transmission of HIV."

53. Edward Laumann et al., *The Social Organization of Sexuality*, p. 107. Similar estimates were made earlier. See Bruce Voeller, "Heterosexual Anal Intercourse," *Mariposa Occasional Paper* #B (April 1983): 1–8; Bruce Voeller, "Heterosexual Anorectal Intercourse: An AIDS Risk Factor," *Mariposa Occasional Paper* #10 (December 1988): 1–19; David R. Bolling and Bruce Voeller, "AIDS and Heterosexual Anal Intercourse," *Journal of the American Medical Association* 258, no. 4 (July 24/31, 1987): 474.

54. L. Wigersma and R. Oud, "Safety and Acceptability of Condoms for Use by Homosexual Men as a Prophylactic against Transmission of HIV during Anogenital Sexual Intercourse," *British Medical Journal* 295 (1987): 94; Richard Gordon, "A Critical Review of the Physics and Statistics of Condoms."

55. There has been a large decrease in the number of hepatitis B cases among homosexual men. The CDC feels that this is most likely a result of condom use in high-risk sexual behaviors—like anal intercourse—in the attempt to avoid HIV infection. The percentage of all AIDS cases that occur in homosexuals has been dropping significantly and the share of all cases by IV drug users has been rising. This is further indication of changes taking place in homosexual behavior.

56. Patti Breitman, Kin Knutson, and Paul Reed, *How to Persuade Your*

Lover to Use A Condom . . . And Why You Should (Rocklin, Calif.: Prima Publishing and Communications, 1987), p. 22. See also Myron H. Redford, Gordon W. Duncan, and Denis J. Prager, eds., *The Condom: Increasing Utilization in the United States* (San Francisco: San Francisco Press Inc., 1974).

57. Personal interview by Harriet Reiss with Ceci Ogden in February 1987, in San Francisco, California.

58. Lennart Ajax, "How to Market a Nonmedical Contraceptive: A Case Study from Sweden," ch. 2 in Redford, Duncan, and Prager, *The Condom: Increasing Utilization in the United States.*

Chapter Six: Clarifying Our Fantasies about Pornography

1. For a very similar definition see Alan Soble, *Pornography: Marxism, Feminism, and the Future of Sexuality* (New Haven, Conn.: Yale University Press, 1986), pp. 8–9.

2. Ellen Willis, "Feminism, Moralism, and Pornography," in Ann Snitow, Christine Stansell, and Sharon Thompson, eds., *Powers of Desire: The Politics of Sexuality* (New York: Monthly Review Press, 1983), p. 463.

3. Deirdre English, Amber Hollibaugh, and Gayle Rubin, "Talking Sex: A Conversation on Sexuality and Feminism," *Socialist Review* 11, no. 4 (1981): 50.

4. Willis, "Feminism, Moralism, and Pornography," p. 462.

5. Other authors have also proposed using the term erotica as the general term for *all* sexual turn-on materials. See William Fisher, "Gender, Gender Role Identification and Response to Erotica," ch. 12 in E. Allgeier and N. McCormick, eds., *Changing Boundaries: Gender Roles and Sexual Behavior* (Palo Alto, Calif.: Mayfield, 1983).

6. *Minneapolis Star Tribune*, December 16, 1983.

7. Andrea Dworkin, *Pornography: Men Possessing Women* (New York: Perigee, 1981), p. 200.

8. Steve Chapple and David Talbot, *Burning Desires: Sex in America* (New York: Doubleday, 1989), p. 221.

9. *Minneapolis Star Tribune*, May 23, 1989.

10. Willis, "Feminism, Moralism, and Pornography," p. 464.

11. Sobel, *Pornography*, pp. 167–68. The difficulty resulting from uniting feminists with conservatives in the battle against pornography is also brought out in Charles E. Cottle, P. Searles, R. J. Berger, and B. A. Pierce, "Conflicting Ideologies and the Politics of Pornography," *Gender and Society* 3 (September 1989): 303–33.

12. Betty Friedan, "How to Get the Women's Movement Moving Again," *New York Times Magazine*, November 3, 1985, p. 98.

13. For a detailed discussion of this evidence see Ira L. Reiss, *Journey into Sexuality: An Exploratory Voyage* (New York: Prentice-Hall, Inc., 1986), ch. 7. I submitted an affidavit with my views to the American Civil Liberties Union for use in their appeal of an antipornography statute passed in Indianapolis.

14. Nadine Strossen, *Defending Pornography: Free Speech, Sex, and the Fight for Women's Rights* (New York: Scribner, 1995), p. 220.

15. Ibid., p. 237.

16. Ellen Willis, "An Unholy Alliance," *New York Newsday*, February 25, 1992.

17. Majorie Heins, *Sex, Sin and Blasphemy* (New York: The New Press, 1993), p. 142. See also Robert H. Rimmer and Patrick Riley, *The X-rated Videotape Guide IV* (Amherst, N.Y: Prometheus Books, 1994).

18. Thomas Radecki, *Film Comment* 20, no. 6 (November/December 1984): 43–45.

19. Chapple and Talbot, *Burning Desires*, pp. 252–53.

20. Ibid., p. 252.

21. Donahue, 1987 show, transcript no. 01243, p. 10.

22. Chapple and Talbot, *Burning Desires*, p. 285.

23. Claire Coles and M. Johanna Shamp, "Some Sexual, Personality, and Demographic Characteristics of Women Readers of Erotic Romances," *Archives of Sexual Behavior* 13 (June 1984): 187–209.

24. Ann Barr Snitow, "Mass Market Romance: Pornography for Women Is Different," in A. B. Snitow, C. Shappel, and S. Thompson, eds., *The Politics of Sexuality* (New York: Monthly Preview Press, 1983), p. 261.

25. For a full account of my findings on this point see Ira L. Reiss, *Journey into Sexuality*, pp. 182–86.

26. Philip Nobile and Eric Nadler, *United States of America vs. Sex: How the Meese Commission Lied about Pornography* (New York: Minotaur Press, Ltd., 1986), p. 59. Also Strossen, *Defending Pornography*.

27. Susan Brownmiller, *Against Our Will: Men, Women and Rape* (New York: Simon and Schuster, 1975), p. 395.

28. Robin Morgan, "Theory and Practice: Pornography and Rape," in L. Lederer, ed., *Take Back the Night: Women on Pornography* (New York: William Morrow, 1980), p. 139.

29. For a discussion of sexual fantasies see Albert R. Allgeier and Elizabeth R. Allgeier, *Sexual Interactions*, 2d ed. (Lexington, Mass.: D.C. Heath and Company, 1988), pp. 221–28; and William H. Masters, Virginia E. Johnson, and Robert C. Kolodny, *Human Sexuality*, 3d ed. (Glenview, Ill.: Scott, Foresman and Company, 1988), ch. 13.

30. English, Hollibaugh, and Rubin, "Talking Sex," p. 57. See also Soble, *Pornography*, p. 19, n. 32, for a supportive report on his own survey of an adult book store.

31. *Report of the Commission on Obscenity and Pornography* (Washington, D.C.: Government Printing Office, 1971), p. 139.

32. Carol Vance, "The Meese Commission on the Road," *The Nation*, August 2/9, 1986, pp. 1, 76–82. By far the best detailed discussion of the Meese Commission can be found in Barry Lynn, *Polluting the Censorship Debate: A Summary and Critique of the Final Report of the Attorney General's Commission on Pornography* (New York: American Civil Liberties Union Public Policy Report, July 1986).

33. Vance, "The Meese Commission on the Road," p. 79.

34. There are many studies with similar findings on sex offenders. Some of the key pieces: Paul H. Gebhard, John H. Gagnon, Wardell B. Pomeroy, and Cornelia V. Christenson, *Sex Offenders: An Analysis of Types* (New York: Harper and Row, 1965); Gene Abel, David Barlow, Edward Blanchard, and Donald Guild, "The Components of Rapists' Sexual Arousal," *Archives of General Psychiatry* 34 (August, 1977): 895–903; Berl Kutchinsky, "The Effect of Easy Availability of Pornography on the Incidence of Sex Crimes: The Danish Experience," *Journal of Social Issues* 29, no. 3 (1973): 163–81; and Mary Kearns Condron and David E. Nutter, "A Preliminary Examination of the Pornography Experience of Sex Offenders, Paraphiliacs, Sexual Dysfunction Patients, and Controls Based on Meese Commission Recommendations," *Journal of Sex and Marital Therapy* 14 (Winter 1988): 285–98.

35. Strossen, *Defending Pornography*, pp. 255–56.

36. Testimony given in Minneapolis, Minnesota, on March 6, 1984. See also Edward Donnerstein, "Pornography: Its Effect on Violence against Women," ch. 2 in Neil M. Malamuth and Edward Donnerstein, eds., *Pornography and Sexual Aggression*, p. 79. For a more recent statement of the same point see Edward Donnerstein, Daniel Linz, and Steven Penrod, *The Question of Pornography: Research Findings and Policy Implications* (New York: The Free Press, 1987).

37. Edward I. Donnerstein and Daniel G. Linz, "The Question of Pornography: It Is Not Sex but Violence That Is an Obscenity in Our Society," in Ollie Pocs, ed., *Human Sexuality: 88/89* (Guilford, Conn.: The Dushkin Publishing Group, 1989), p. 210.

38. *Minneapolis Star Tribune*, June 24, 1989.

39. National Opinion Research Center, *General Social Surveys, 1972–1996: Cumulative Codebook* (Chicago: National Opinion Research Center, 1996), p. 218. In 1996 58 percent of the public said there should be no laws restricting pornography for those eighteen and older, and 4 percent said no laws for any age. Only 38 percent said there should be laws against pornography for all age groups.

40. Milton Diamond and James E. Dannemiller, "Pornography and Community Standards in Hawaii: Comparisons with Other States," *Archives of Sexual Behavior* 18 (December 1989): 475–95.

Chapter Seven: Rape: The Ultimage Inequality

1. Susan Brownmiller, *Against Our Will* (New York: Simon and Schuster, 1975), pp. 5–8.

2. W. Kay Martin and Barbara Voorhies, *Female of the Species* (New York: Columbia University Press, 1975); and Janet Saltzman Chafetz, *Sex and Advantage: A Comparative, Macro-structural Theory of Sex Stratification* (Totowa, N.J.: Rowman and Allenheld, 1984). I analyzed the development of male-female

power differences in Ira L. Reiss, *Journey into Sexuality: An Exploratory Voyage* (New York: Prentice-Hall, Inc., 1986), ch. 4.

3. A. Nicholas Groth, *Men Who Rape: The Psychology of the Offender* (New York: Plenum Press, 1979).

4. These two studies of rape in nonindustrial societies by Gwen Broude and Peggy Sanday do not always agree with each other. For example, Broude found 41 percent of her societies to be rape prone and 24 percent to be rape free, whereas the respective percentages for Sanday are 18 and 47. The remaining societies fell in between these two extremes. Peggy Reeves Sanday, "The Socio-cultural Context of Rape: A Cross-Cultural Study," *Journal of Social Issues* 37, no. 4 (1981): 5–27; Gwen J. Broude and Sarah J. Greene, "Cross-Cultural Codes on Twenty Sexual Attitudes and Practices," *Ethnology* 15 (October 1976): 409–29.

5. Julia R. Schwendinger and Herman Schwendinger, *Rape and Inequality* (Beverly Hills, Calif.: Sage Publications, 1983).

6. Eleanor Burke Leacock, *Myths of Male Dominance: Collected Articles on Women Cross-Culturally* (New York: Monthly Review Press, 1981); Ruby Rohrlich-Leavitt, Barbara Sykes, and Elizabeth Weatherford, "Aboriginal Woman: Male and Female Anthropological Perspectives," in Rayna R. Reiter, ed., *Toward An Anthropology of Women* (New York: Monthly Review Press, 1975); Janet Saltzmann Chafetz, *Sex and Advantage: A Comparative, Macrostructural Theory of Sex Stratification* (Totowa, N.J.: Rowman and Allanheld Publishers, 1984); Janet Saltzman Chafetz, *Gender Equity: An Integrated Theory of Stability and Change* (Newbury Park, Calif.: Sage Publications, 1990).

7. Minnesota Security Hospital, *Description of Intensive Treatment Program for Sexual Aggressives*, 1980, p. 1. This treatment program was modeled after the program at Western State Hospital in Ft. Steilacoom, Washington. That facility boasts only a 9 percent recidivism rate after ten years.

8. For a detailed description of this sample of societies and the findings on rape see Ira L. Reiss, *Journey into Sexuality*, pp. 190–93.

9. Psychologists Donald Mosher and Mark Sirkin have developed a thirty-item measure of a macho personality. See Donald L. Mosher and Mark Sirkin, "Measuring a Macho Personality Constellation," *Journal of Research in Personality* 18 (1984): 150–63.

10. *Minneapolis Star Tribune*, July 25, 1988.

11. A study by the National Victim Center in 1991 estimated that almost 700,000 rapes occurred in 1990. This is a much higher figure than the about 100,000 rapes that the FBI reports. I use a figure of 1,000,000 as the likely maximum number of rapes in any one year in the 1990s. The FBI reported that rapes did drop to 97,000 in 1995, but it is too early to know if this is due to fewer young people or to a real change.

12. This estimate comes from Diana Russell's study, but similar estimates have been reported elsewhere. See Diana E. H. Russell, *Sexual Exploitation: Rape, Child Sexual Abuse, and Workplace Harassment* (Beverly Hills, Calif.: Sage Library, 1984), ch. 3; Ann Wolbert Burgess, ed., *Rape and Sexual Assault*, vol. 2 (New York: Garland Publishing, 1988), ch. 1.

13. Mary P. Koss, "Hidden Rape: Sexual Aggression and Victimization in a National Sample of Students in Higher Education," ch. 1 in A. W. Burgess, *Rape and Sexual Assault*. For a popular account of Koss's study see Robin Warshaw, *I Never Called It Rape: The Ms. Report on Recognizing, Fighting and Surviving Date and Acquaintance Rape* (New York: Harper and Row, 1988).

14. Most of the states have revised their laws to include under rape, oral, anal, and other forced penetrations in addition to vaginal intercourse. However, the FBI still retains the old male-oriented definition of rape being only forced vaginal intercourse. Thus, FBI estimates will be lower in part because of this difference in definition. In addition, any police estimates will miss most rapes for they are not reported to the police.

15. Sarah K. Murnen, Annette Perot, and Donn Byrne, "Coping with Unwanted Sexual Activity: Normative Responses, Situational Determinants, and Individual Differences," *Journal of Sex Research* 26 (February 1989): 85–106.

16. Warshaw, *I Never Called It Rape*, p. 42.

17. Charlene Muelenhard's work on rape is ongoing and has been reported at several professional meetings. See Charlene L. Muehlenhard and Lisa C. Hollabaugh, "Do Women Sometimes Say No When They Mean Yes? The Prevalence and Correlates of Women's Token Resistance to Sex," *Journal of Personality and Social Psychology*, 54, no. 5 (1988): 872–79. Other studies supporting the traditional male role involvement in rape can be found in Ilsa L. Lottes, "Sexual Socialization and Attitudes toward Rape," ch. 12 in Ann Wolbert Burgess, ed., *Rape and Sexual Assault*; and Diana E. H. Russell, *Sexual Exploitation: Rape, Child Sexual Abuse, and Workplace Harassment*, ch. 7.

18. Susan Sprecher et al., "Token Resistance to Sexual Intercourse and Consent to Unwanted Sexual Intercourse in College Students' Dating Experiences in Three Countries," *Journal of Sex Research* 31, no. 2 (1994): 125–32.

19. There is more willingness to report rape today and part of the rise in rape rates may be due to this factor. For evidence on this see J. D. Orcutt and R. Faison, "Sex Role Attitude Change and Reporting of Rape Victimization: 1973–1985," *Sociological Quarterly* 29, no. 4: 589–604.

20. Allan Griswold Johnson, "On the Prevalence of Rape in the United States," *Signs: Journal of Women in Culture and Society* 6, no. 1 (1980): 136–46. The quote is from p. 146.

21. Catherine MacKinnon, *Only Words* (Cambridge, Mass.: Harvard University Press, 1993), p. 12.

22. Katie Roiphe, *The Morning After: Sex, Fear and Feminism on Campus* (New York: Little Brown, 1993).

23. Sociologist Judith Howard has elaborated on this point and noted how women in a secure relationship feel it is safe to pursue sexual pleasures that they resisted in less secure settings because of their low social status. See Judith A. Howard, "Gender Differences in Sexual Attitudes: Conservatism or Powerlessness?" *Gender and Society* 2 (March 1988): 103–14. Another study trained students to approach other students they did not know and proposition them for sex or a date. The results showed our traditional roles among college students and

indicated that men were very willing to have a sex with a stranger—even more willing than to date an unknown woman; conversely, women were unwilling to accept the casual sexual proposition but more willing to accept dating a stranger: Russell D. Clark III and Elaine Hatfield, "Gender Differences in Receptivity to Sexual Offers," *Journal of Psychology and Human Sexuality* 2, no. 1 (1989): 39–55.

24. The First International Conference on the Treatment of Sex Offenders was held in Minneapolis, Minnesota, in May 1989. It was sponsored by the Program in Human Sexuality at the University of Minnesota. An account of some of the papers at the conference can be found in *Minneapolis Star Tribune*, May 23, 1989.

25. Paul R. Abramson and Haruo Hayashi, "Pornography in Japan: Cross-cultural and Theoretical Considerations," in Neil M. Malamuth and Edward Donnerstein, eds., *Pornography and Sexual Aggression* (Orlando, Fla.: Academic Press, 1984), pp. 180–81; and Gilbert Geis, "Forcible Rape: An Introduction," in Duncan Chappell, Robley Geis and Gilbert Geis, eds., *Forcible Rape: The Crime, the Victim and the Offender* (New York: Columbia University Press, 1977), pp. 30–34.

26. For a popular statement of how men and women misunderstand each other and what we can do about it, see Warren Farrell, *Why Men Are the Way They Are* (New York: McGraw Hill, 1986). In chapter 8 of this book Farrell also makes some of the same points as I have made concerning causes of rape.

27. Steven D. McLaughlin, B. D. Melber, J. O. Billy, D. M. Zimmerle, L. D. Winges, and T. R. Johnson, *The Changing Lives of American Women* (Chapel Hill: The University of North Carolina Press, 1988). Also relevant to understanding changes in female roles, particularly in the 1950s, is Elaine Tyler May, *Homeward Bound: American Families in the Cold War Era* (New York: Basic Books, 1988).

28. David Finkelhor and Kersti Yllo, *License to Rape: Sexual Abuse of Wives* (New York: The Free Press, 1985), p. 7; and Diana E. H. Russell, *Rape in Marriage* (New York: Macmillan Publishing Company, 1982), p. 57.

29. Finkelhor and Yllo, *License to Rape,* pp. 186–87.

Chapter Eight: Sex Therapy: Conforming to a Troubled Society

1. Helen Singer Kaplan, *The Illustrated Manual of Sex Therapy* (New York: Brunner/Mazel Publishers, 1987), pp. 82–87.

2. William H. Masters, Virginia E. Johnson, and Robert C. Kolodny, *Human Sexuality*, 3d ed. (Glenview, Ill.: Scott, Foresman and Co., 1988), p. 507. See pp. 587–88 in the fifth edition of this book (1995) for a similar but somewhat softened viewpoint. The book that introduced the country to Masters and Johnson's sex therapy program was: William H. Masters and Virginia E. Johnson, *Human Sexual Inadequacy* (Boston: Little, Brown, and Co., 1970).

3. Carl N. Degler, "What Ought to Be and What Was: Women's Sexuality

in the Nineteenth Century," *American Historical Review* 79 (December 1974): 1467–90. The quote is from p. 1467.

4. Masters, Johnson, and Kolodny, *Human Sexuality*, p. 506.

5. Ibid., p. 499.

6. Alice Kahn Ladas, B. Whipple, and J. D. Perry, *The G Spot: And Other Recent Discoveries about Human Sexuality* (New York: Holt, Rinehart and Winston, Inc., 1982).

7. J. E. Burt and J. C. Burt, *The Surgery of Love* (New York: Carlton Press, 1975).

8. On May 15, 1989, Oprah Winfrey devoted her program to this operation and interviewed many women upon whom Dr. Burt had operated and who were suing him.

9. Helen Singer Kaplan, *How to Overcome Premature Ejaculation* (New York: Brunner/Mazel Publishers, 1989).

10. Michael Metz et al., "Premature Ejaculation: A Psychophysiological Review," *Journal of Sex and Marital Therapy* 23, no. 1 (Spring 1997): 3–23.

11. Kaplan, *The Illustrated Manual of Sex Therapy*, p. 166.

12. American Psychiatric Association, *Diagnostic and Statistical Manual of Mental Disorders* (DSM-III), 3d ed. (Washington, D.C.: APA, 1980), p. 280.

13. American Psychiatric Association, *Diagnostic and Statistical Manual of Mental Disorders* (DSM-IV) (Washington, D.C.: APA, 1994), pp. 509–11.

14. William Davenport, "Sexual Patterns and Their Regulation in a Society of the Southwest Pacific," pp. 164–207 in Frank A. Beach, ed., *Sex and Behavior* (New York: John Wiley, 1965).

15. Lawrence K. Hong, "Survival of the Fastest: On the Origin of Premature Ejaculation," *Journal of Sex Research* 20 (May 1984): 109–22.

16. John Mirowsky and Catherine E. Ross, *Social Causes of Psychological Distress* (New York: Aldine de Gruyter, 1989).

17. Partrick Carnes, *Out of the Shadow: Understanding Sexual Addiction* (Minneapolis, Minn.: Compcare Pub., 1983), p. 135.

18. Ibid., p. 17.

19. Ibid., p. 137.

20. Stanton Peele, *Diseasing of America: Addiction Treatment out of Control* (Lexington, Mass.: Lexington Books, 1989).

21. For a critique of the "recovery movement" see Wendy Kaminer, *I'm Dysfunctional, You're Dysfunctional* (New York: Vintage Books, 1993). For a popularly written account of the growth of addiction groups, see *Newsweek*, February 5, 1990, pp. 50–55.

22. See in particular James Christopher, *How to Stay Sober: Recovery without Religion* (Amherst, N.Y.: Prometheus Books, 1986).

23. Carnes, *Out of the Shadows*, p. 159.

24. For a criticism of the Alcoholics Anonymous approach see Peele, *Diseasing of America*, and Herbert Fingarette, *Heavy Drinking: The Myth of Alcoholism as a Disease* (Berkeley and Los Angeles: University of California Press, 1988).

25. Marty Klein, "Why There's No Such Thing as Sexual Addiction—and Why It Really Matters," a paper presented at the annual meeting of the Society for the Scientific Study of Sex in Toronto, Canada, in November 1989, p. 5.

26. I believe the sensate focus approach developed by Virginia Johnson is the most useful part of their sex therapy program. Basically it involves setting up an anxiety-free atmosphere for physical contact that allows each person to discover what they enjoy and what their partner enjoys without any performance pressures. See Masters, Johnson, and Kolodny, *Human Sexuality*, pp. 520–21.

27. In the 1960s Thomas Szasz, professor of psychiatry at the State University of New York, challenged the use of medical concepts for all mental illnesses. Szasz, himself a medical doctor, has also questioned the use of medical concepts like dysfunction in sex therapy. See Thomas Szasz, *The Myth of Mental Illness* (New York: Hoeber-Harper and Row, 1964), and *Sex by Prescription* (New York: Penguin Books, 1980). More recently these same issues have been raised in John Mirowsky and Catherine Ross, "Psychiatric Diagnosis as Reified Measurement," *Journal of Health and Social Behavior* 30 (March 1989): 11–25. See also Ross Morrow, "A Critique of Master's and Johnson's Concept and Classification of Sexual Dysfunction," *Revue Sexologique* 4, no. 2 (1996): 159–80.

28. For a discussion and explanation of sexuality in a wide variety of societies see Ira L. Reiss, *Journey into Sexuality: An Exploratory Voyage* (New York: Prentice-Hall Inc., 1986).

29. For a discussion of how medicine took over the Church's control of sexuality in the nineteenth century, see Michel Foucault, *The History of Sexuality*: Vol. 1: *An Introduction* (New York: Vintage Books, 1980); and Jeffrey Weeks, *Sexuality* (London: Routledge, 1989).

30. Phyllis Grosskurth, *Havelock Ellis: A Biography* (New York: Knopf, 1980).

31. For an approach to sex therapy in this direction see David M. Schnarch, *Constructing the Sexual Crucible: An Integration of Sexual and Marital Therapy* (New York: W. W. Norton, 1991).

32. World Health Organization, "Education and Treatment in Human Sexuality: The Training of Health Professionals," Technical Report no. 572 (Geneva: WHO, 1975), p. 6.

33. British sociologist Jeffrey Weeks, in *Sexuality*, also promotes a pluralistic sexual philosophy that is supportive of my own ideas.

34. See the *Diagnostic Statistical Manual* for the various years. For a discussion of this issue see Martin P. Levine and Richard R. Troiden, "The Myth of Sexual Compulsivity," *Journal of Sex Research* 25 (August, 1988): 347–63.

35. Harry F. Harlow, "The Heterosexual Affection System in Monkeys," *American Psychologist* 17 (January 1962): 1–9.

36. Masters, Johnson, and Kolodny, *Human Sexuality*, pp. 511–12.

37. Kaplan, *Premature Ejaculation*, pp. 34–35.

38. For a discussion of these issues see Ira L. Reiss, *Journey into Sexuality: An Exploratory Voyage* (New York: Prentice-Hall, 1986); Paul R. Abramson and Steven D. Pinkerton, eds., *Sexual Nature: Sexual Culture* (Chicago: University

of Chicago Press, 1995); Paul R. Abramson and Steven D. Pinkerton, *With Pleasure: Thoughts on the Nature of Human Sexuality* (New York: Oxford University Press, 1995).

39. An interesting criticism of the medicalization of sex therapy can be found in Jerome Wakefield, "Female Primary Orgasmic Dysfunction: Masters and Johnson versus DSM-III on Diagnosis and Incidence," *Journal of Sex Research* 24 (1988): 363–77.

Chapter Nine: The Role of Religion in Our Sexual Crises

1. Elaine Pagels, *Adam, Eve, and the Serpent* (New York: Random House, 1988), pp. xxiii–xxv.

2. John Boswell, *Christianity, Social Tolerance, and Homosexuality: Gay People in Western Europe from the Beginning of the Christian Era to the Fourteenth Century* (Chicago: University of Chicago Press, 1980), p. 165.

3. Ibid., p. 164.

4. St. Augustine, *The Confessions of St. Augustine: Books I to X*, trans. F. J. Sheed (New York: Sheed and Ward, 1942), p. 139 (italics added). For another fine scholarly coverage of early Christianity see Vern Bullough, *Sexual Variance in Society and History* (New York: John Wiley and Sons, 1976).

5. Pagels, *Adam, Eve, and the Serpent*, p. 141.

6. Ibid., p. 145.

7. Ibid., p. 150.

8. Boswell, *Christianity, Social Tolerance, and Homosexuality*, p. 334.

9. Jeffrey Weeks, *Sexuality* (London: Routeledge, 1986), p. 82. See also Vern Bullough, *Sexual Variance*, p. 380, and Boswell, *Christianity, Social Tolerance, and Homosexuality*, pp. 318–32.

10. George Gallup and Jim Castelli, *The People's Religion: American Faith in the 90s* (New York: Macmillan Publishing Company, 1989), p. 90.

11. George H. Gallup Jr., *Religion in America, 1996* (Princeton, N.J.: Princeton Religion Research Center, 1996).

12. The Gallup Report, *Religion in America: 50 Years: 1935–1985*, Report no. 236 (May 1985): 24–25.

13. Elaine Tyler May, *Homeward Bound: American Families in the Cold War Era* (New York: Basic Books, Inc., 1988), p. 207.

14. The Gallup Report, *Religion in America: 50 Years: 1935–1985*, pp. 4–5.

15. Ibid., p. 42.

16. For national data on attitudes toward birth control and abortion in different religious groups see *General Social Surveys, 1972–1996: Cumulative Codebook* (National Opinion Research Center, University of Chicago, 1996); William F. Pratt, W. D. Mosher, C. A. Bachrach, and M. C. Horn, "Understanding U.S. Fertility: Findings from the National Survey of Family Growth, Cycle 111," *Population Bulletin* 39, no. 5 (1984).

17. Stanley K. Henshaw and Jane Silverman, "The Characteristics and Prior

Contraceptive Use of U.S. Abortion Patients," *Family Planning Perspectives* 20 (July/August 1988): 158–68.

18. For a few introductory comments on some of these controversies see Kendell Cronstrom, ed., *Tradition and Transition: Religion in the Twin Cities* (Minneapolis, Minn.: March, 1987); Daniel C. Maguire, "Catholic Sexual and Reproductive Ethics: A Historical Perspective," *SIECUS Report,* 15 (May/June 1987); Wilson Yates, "The Church and Its Holistic Paradigm of Sexuality," *SIECUS Report* 16 (May/June 1988); Ruth A. Wallace, "Catholic Women and the Creation of a New Social Reality," *Gender and Society* 2 (March 1988): 24–38; Pagels, *Adam, Eve and the Serpent*; and Lawrence Lader, *Politics, Power and the Church: The Catholic Crisis and Its Challenge to American Pluralism* (New York: Macmillan Publishing, 1987).

19. Gallup, *Religion in America, 1996,* pp. 39–44.

20. *Minneapolis Star Tribune,* December 11, 1987.

21. *Minneapolis Star Tribune,* March 1, 1989. See also Charles E. Curran, "Roman Catholic Sexual Ethics: A Dissenting View," pp. 49–56 in James B. Nelson, ed., *Sexual Ethics and the Church: A Christian Century Symposium* (Chicago: The Christian Century Foundation, 1989); and James Davison Hunter, *Evangelicalism: The Coming Generation* (Chicago: University of Chicago Press, 1987), p. 219.

22. Wade Clark Roof and William McKinney, *American Mainline Religion: Its Changing Shape and Future* (New Brunswick, N.J.: Rutgers University Press, 1988), pp. 211–12.

23. The Princeton Religion Research Center, *The Unchurched American: 10 Years Later* (Princeton, N.J.: Princeton University Press, 1989), p. 7.

24. Roof and McKinney, *American Mainline Religion,* p. 165.

25. Robert Wuthnow, *The Restructuring of American Religion: Society and Faith Since World War II* (Princeton, N.J.: Princeton University Press, 1988), p. 132.

26. Tom W. Smith, "America's Religious Mosaic," *American Demographics* 12 (June 1984): 18–23.

27. A simple but interesting account of the Bakkers can be found in Joe E. Barnhart, *Jim and Tammy: Charismatic Intrigue inside PTL* (Amherst, N.Y.: Prometheus Books, 1988). See also parts of Jeffrey K. Hadden and Anson Shupe, *Televangelism: Power and Politics on God's Frontier* (New York: Henry Holt and Co., 1988).

28. Barnhart, *Jim and Tammy,* p. 140.

29. Frances FitzGerald, *Cities on A Hill: A Journey through Contemporary American Cultures* (New York: Simon and Schuster, 1986), pp. 121–201 ("Liberty Baptist"). See also Lader, *Politics, Power and the Church,* and Hadden and Shupe, *Televangelism.*

30. Arthur Schlesinger Jr., the noted Harvard historian, has commented on the long-standing clash in American society between a view of America as an experiment with risks that requires a realistic approach to succeed, and a messianic view of America as a country of destiny, a redeemer nation that can save the world. See Arthur Schlesinger Jr., *The Cycles of American History* (Boston: Houghton Mifflin, 1986).

31. *Minneapolis Star Tribune*, March 15, 1989.

32. *Newsweek*, December 18, 1989, p. 28.

33. *Minneapolis Star Tribune*, February 11, 1990, column by Colman McCarthy. For an excellent account of authoritarianism and its relation to religion see Bob Altemeyer, *Enemies of Freedom: Understanding Right-wing Authoritarianism* (San Francisco: Jossey-Bass, 1988). Altemeyer found that fundamentalist religious training tends to foster authoritarianism.

34. Genesis 35:22–26.

35. Ephesians 5:22–28.

36. For an excellent brief summary of historical changes in the family see David Popenoe, *Disturbing the Nest: Family Change and Decline in Modern Societies* (New York: Aldine D. Gruyter, 1988), ch. 4.

37. Bert Adams, *The Family: A Sociological Interpretation*, 5th ed. (New York: Hartcourt Brace, 1995); and Arlene Skolnick, *The Intimate Environment: Explaining Marriage and the Family* (New York: Harper Collins, 1996).

38. Hadden and Shupe, *Televangelism*, p. 297.

39. Hunter, *Evangelicalism: the Coming Generation*.

40. Ibid., p. 24.

41. Ibid., p. 77.

42. Ibid., p. 100.

43. Ibid., pp. 111–12.

44. Ibid., p. 176.

45. Lionel S. Lewis and Dennis D. Brissett, "Sex as God's Work," *Society* 23 (March/April 1986): 67–75.

46. Ibid., p. 70.

47. The Princeton Religion Research Center, *The Unchurched American*, p. 3; also Gallup, *Religion in America*, 1996.

48. John Shelby Spong, *Living in Sin: A Bishop Rethinks Human Sexuality* (New York: Harper and Row, 1988), p. 147.

49. Ibid., p. 226.

50. James B. Nelson, *Between Two Gardens: Reflections on Sexuality and Religious Experience* (New York: Pilgrim Press, 1983), pp. 81–85.

51. Quoted from a personal conversation in Ruth Westheimer and Louis Lieberman, *Sex and Morality: Who Is Teaching Our Sex Standards?* (Boston: Harcourt, Brace, Jovanovich, 1988), p. 192.

52. Nelson, *Sexual Ethics and the Church: A Christian Century Symposium*, p. 69.

53. Rodney Stark and William Sims Bainbridge, *The Future of Religion: Secularization, Revival, and Cult Formation* (Berkeley and Los Angeles: University of California Press, 1985). For a short, updated, one-chapter presentation of this perspective see Rodney Stark, *Sociology*, 6th ed. (Belmont, Calif.: Wadsworth Publishers, 1996), ch. 14.

Chapter Ten: Shaping Today's Sexual Revolution

1. George Will, "The Reign of the Accusers," *Newsweek*, March 13, 1989, p. 76.

2. *New York Times*, June 9, 1997. Polls show most Americans do not want a law against adultery.

3. For an excellent overview of ethics and free will see the relevant sections of: Paul Edwards (editor in chief), *The Encyclopedia of Philosophy*, vols. 1–8 (New York: Macmillan Publishing Co., 1967).

4. Jeffrey K. Hadden and Anson Shupe, *Televangelism: Power and Politics on God's Frontier* (New York: Henry Holt and Co., 1988), ch. 6.

5. For a cross-cultural overview on gender equality see United Nations, *The Worlds' Women 1970–1990: Trends and Statistics* (New York: United Nations, 1991); and Joni Seager, *The State of Women in the World Atlas* (New York: Penguin Reference, 1997). See also Janet Saltzman Chafetz, *Gender Equity: An Integrated Theory of Stability and Change* (Newbury Park, Calif.: Sage Publications, 1990).

6. Figures based on 1996 government estimates. For a discussion of some key problems in dual-earner marriages see Arlie Hochschild, *Second Shift: Working Parents and the Revolution at Home* (New York: Viking-Penguin Inc., 1989).

7. Karen Oppenheim Mason and Yu-Hsia Lu, "Attitudes toward Women's Familial Roles: Changes in the United States, 1977–1985," *Gender and Society* 2 (March 1988): 39–57.

8. Arland Thornton, "Changing Attitudes toward Family Issues in the United States," *Journal of Marriage and the Family* 51 (November 1989): 873–93. For a popularly written summary of gender equality studies in America today see Steven D. McLaughlin, B. D. Melber, J. O. Billy, D. M. Zimmerle, L. D. Winges, and T. R. Johnson, *The Changing Lives of American Women* (Chapel Hill: University of North Carolina Press, 1988). See also Duane F. Alwin, "From Obedience to Autonomy: Changes in Traits Desired in Children 1924–1978," *Public Opinion Quarterly* 52 (1988): 33–52.

9. Sandra J. Ball-Rokeach, Milton Rokeach, and Joel W. Grube, *The Great American Values Test: Influencing Behavior and Belief Through Television* (New York: The Free Press, 1984), chs. 8 and 9. A related but distinct method of change is discussed in Bob Altememey, *Enemies of Freedom: Understanding Right-Wing Authoritarianism* (San Francisco: Jossey-Bass Publishers, 1988), ch. 8.

10. Arlie Hochschild, *Second Shift*.

11. An insightful study of how this parental leave program is working out can be found in Phyllis Moen, *Working Parents: Transformations in Gender roles and Public Politicies in Sweden* (Madison: University of Wisconsin Press, 1989). See also Margaret Jean Intons-Peterson, *Gender Concepts of Swedish and American Youth* (Hillsdale, N.J.: Lawrence Erlbaum Associates Publishers, 1988). For a short popular discussion of problems of gender equality in Sweden see *Inside Sweden*, November 1989, Stockholm, Sweden. This magazine is published by the Swedish Labor Movement (AIC).

12. William Julius Wilson, *The Truly Disadvantaged: The Inner City and the Underclass and Public Policy* (Chicago: University of Chicago Press, 1987).

13. I discussed the connection of poverty with teenage pregnancy in chapter 3. For other books that discuss the impact of inequality on our sexual customs see Edwin M. Schur, *The Americanization of Sex* (Philadelphia: Temple University Press, 1988); and John D'Emilio and Estelle B. Freedman, *Intimate Matters: A History of Sexuality in America* (New York: Harper and Row, 1988).

14. An interesting and informative comparison of equality in the United States, Sweden, and Japan can be found in Sidney Verba, *Elites and the Idea of Equality* (Cambridge, Mass.: Harvard University Press, 1987).

15. My prediction of the sexual revolution of the late 1960s was put forth in Ira L. Reiss, *Premarital Sexual Standards in America* (New York: The Free Press of Macmillan, 1960), pp. 235–41. In 1967 I spoke of autonomy as the key to understanding sexuality. Autonomy, or self-rule, is directly related to pluralism. See Ira L. Reiss, *The Social Context of Premarital Sexual Permissiveness* (New York: Holt, Rinehart and Winston, Inc., 1967). For a more recent and brief overview of trends in sexual standards see Ira L. Reiss, "Sexual Behavior," in George T. Kurian and Graham T. T. Molitor, eds., *The Encyclopedia of the Future*, vol. 2 (New York: Macmillan Publishers, 1996), pp. 828–30.

16. For an explanation of the new meaning of science see Ira L. Reiss, "The Future of Sex Research and the Meaning of Science," *Journal of Sex Research* 30, no. 1 (February 1993): 3–11.

17. A variety of books elaborate on this activist position. Bernard Barber, *Effective Social Science: Eight Cases in Economics, Political Science and Sociology* (New York: Russell Sage, 1987); Robert N. Bellah, Richard Madsen, William M. Sullivan, Ann Swidler, and Steven M. Tipton, *Habits of the Heart: Individualism and Commitment in American Life* (New York: Harper and Row, 1985); Peter DeLeon, *Advice and Consent: The Development of the Policy Sciences* (New York: Russell Sage, 1988); Alan Wolfe, *Whose Keeper? Social Science and Moral Obligation* (Berkeley and Los Angeles: University of California Press, 1989); Douglas Kellner, *Critical Theory, Marxism and Modernity* (Baltimore: Johns Hopkins University Press, 1989); and Robert C. Bannister, *Sociology and Scientism: The American Quest For Objectivity, 1880–1940* (Chapel Hill: University of North Carolina Press, 1987).

18. Several books discuss pluralism as one way to help resolve sexual and gender problems. Jeffrey Weeks, *Sexuality* (London: Routledge, 1986); Ronald Bayer, *Private Acts, Social Consequences: AIDS and the Politics of Public Health* (New York: The Free Press, 1989); and Carole Joffe, *The Regulation of Sexuality: Experiences of Family Planning Workers* (Philadelphia: Temple University Press, 1986).

19. Michael Fumento, *The Myth of Heterosexual AIDS: How a Tragedy Has Been Distorted by the Media and Partisan Politics* (New York: Basic Books, 1990).

20. Debra W. Haffner, "The Day After—November 9, 1988," *SIECUS Report* 17 (November/December 1988): 19.

21. Donald L. Mosher, "Threat to Sexual Freedom: Moralistic Intolerance Instills a Spiral of Silence," *Journal of Sex Research* 26 (November 1989): 492–509. The quote is from p. 492. Mosher also encourages interrelations among sexual science organizations in Donald L. Mosher, "Advancing Sexual Science: Strategic Analysis and Planning," *Journal of Sex Research* 26 (February 1989): 1–14.

22. For a good overview on issues concerning feminism and change see Gail Hawkes, *A Sociology of Sex and Sexuality* (Philadelphia: Open University Press, 1996); Joyce Mccarl Nielsen, *Sex and Gender in Society: Perspectives on Stratification* (Prospect Heights, Ill.: Waveland Press Inc., 1990); and Janet Saltzman Chafetz, *Gender Equity: An Integrated Theory of Stability and Change* (Newbury Park, Calif.: Sage Publications, 1990).

23. Carole Joffe, *The Regulation of Sexuality: Experiences of Family Planning Workers* (Philadelphia: Temple University Press, 1986), pp. 4–6.

24. I am not able to cover all sexual issues in one book. The issue of sexual harassment did not get sufficient attention. A good early book on the topic is Barbara A. Gutek, *Sex and the Workplace* (San Francisco: Jossey-Bass, 1985). Prostitution is another very important issue that I have not dealt with adequately. I do believe that a decriminalized prostitution for both men and women of legal age would be quite different than the current criminalized form of prostitution. I believe that much of the force and fraud in prostitution today relates to its illegal status. See Vern Bullough and Bonnie Bullough, *Women and Prostitution: A Social History* (Amherst, N.Y.: Prometheus Books, 1987). I did discuss homosexuality in a number of places in this book but clearly the book focused on sexual issues heavily related to heterosexuality. However, the HER sexual pluralism ethic applies equally to both homosexuality and heterosexuality and that is an important point. Finally, extramarital sexuality needs to be dealt with at length. See Ira L. Reiss, Ron E. Anderson, and G. C. Sponaugle, "A Multivariate Model of the Determinants of Extramarital Sexual Permissiveness," *Journal of Marriage and the Family* 42 (May 1980): 395–411. I encourage others to develop the relevance of my HER sexual pluralism for these and other areas that I have not been able to cover fully in this book.

Name Index

273

Subject Index